Abandoned
WOMEN

BY THE SAME AUTHOR

No Place for a Nervous Lady

A Face in the Glass

Wilde Eve

The Journal of Annie Baxter Dawbin 1858–68 (ed.)

Those Women Who Go to Hotels (with Marion Halligan)

Chain Letters (ed. with Hamish Maxwell-Stewart)

Scottish Convicts
Exiled Beyond the Seas

Abandoned
WOMEN

LUCY FROST

ALLEN&UNWIN
SYDNEY·MELBOURNE·AUCKLAND·LONDON

Australian Government

This project has been assisted by the Commonwealth Government through the Australian Council, its arts funding and advisory body.

Allen & Unwin
Sydney, Melbourne, Auckland, London

83 Alexander Street
Crows Nest NSW 2065
Australia
Phone: (61 2) 8425 0100
Fax: (61 2) 9906 2218
Email: info@allenandunwin.com
Web: www.allenandunwin.com

Cataloguing-in-Publication details are available from the National Library of Australia
www.trove.nla.gov.au

ISBN 978 174237 7 605

Index by Geraldine Suter
Text design by Melissa Keogh
Set in 12/16.5 pt Garamond by Midland Typesetters, Australia

10 9 8 7 6 5

Printed and bound in Australia by the SOS Print + Media Group.

MIX
Paper from responsible sources
FSC® C011217

The paper in this book is FSC® certified. FSC® promotes environmentally responsible, socially beneficial and economically viable management of the world's forests.

For my sisters far away
RUTH *and* ELAINE

CONTENTS

I
'FULLY RIPE FOR TRANSPORTATION'

'Abandoned' women, the Scottish convicts were called by an eminent twentieth-century Australian historian—worse than the English, even worse than the Irish. And the worst of the worst were shipped to the island of Van Diemen's Land, later re-named Tasmania to cover its convict stain. The fulminating historian quoted a judge in Edinburgh who pronounced 'utterly irreclaimable' a 64-year-old domestic servant found guilty of theft, and of being 'habite and repute a thief'. Into a weighty Minutebook of Scotland's High Court of Justiciary, a clerk duly inscribed her sentence in the ritual phrasing, 'to be transported beyond Seas'.

But who were these 'abandoned' women? What were their lives like in Scotland? And what happened to them in Australia? Sentenced to transportation, they became travellers who left behind the life they knew in industrial cities, villages, and the countryside. Sailing to the other side of the world, they entered the peculiar society of a penal colony where they would serve their sentences not in prison, but as the unfree domestic servants of settlers scrambling to make their fortunes. Though some convicts were alert to the similarity between their circumstances and those of slaves, there was an important difference. While slavery was for life, most convicts were serving defined sentences of seven or fourteen years, and their lives would continue after they were 'free by servitude'. What then? What did freedom mean to women without money to pay for a passage Home? What kinds of lives could they lead when they were stranded on an island 'beyond Seas'?

These are questions I have been asking as I follow the lives of women convicted in Scotland and transported to Van Diemen's Land on a ship called the *Atwick*. To my surprise, I found that more than half the women on this ship were Scottish convicts, 78 of the 151 who started down the Thames on 30 September 1837. Little attention has been paid to convicts tried in Scotland because within the total scheme of transportation to eastern Australia between 1788 and 1853 their numbers are few, less than 10,000 of the 150,000 transportees, about five per cent of the men and nine per cent of the women. But statistics are levellers, blotting out the people they count.

Legal language does something similar. A Glasgow prosecutor added a note about one of the *Atwick* convicts, Catherine Chisholm, when he submitted a file of evidence to the authorities in Edinburgh who would decide whether her case was to be heard by the High Court of Justiciary. 'Fully ripe for transportation', he wrote, and the collection of evidence—the 'precognition' file as it is called—supported his claim that she was 'an incorrigible trafficker' in counterfeit coin. But the precognition file is more than legal evidence. Its witness statements are miniature stories, and from their details, 'the incorrigible trafficker' takes shape as a 40-year-old itinerant hawker who travelled the country with her children peddling caps and lace, and passing homemade counterfeit coins. 'Highland Kate' knew the roads of Scotland from Inverness where she was born, to the cities of the south where she lived with her husband before he abandoned her and disappeared abroad. As a counterfeiter, Catherine was more determined than clever, and in the past five years she had been imprisoned five times in four different places. The month before her Glasgow arrest in April 1836 she emerged from prison in Stirling, where she and her children had spent the winter freezing in a medieval gaol on a street below the famous castle.

Penniless, they left the ancient and royal town behind to try their luck in Glasgow, the booming industrial city of 270,000, its population more than doubled within three decades. It was a cosmopolitan place, with ships from foreign ports tied up along the docks of the Broomielaw on the River Clyde, but the real lure for people like Catherine was the influx of workers drawn to the cotton factories and textile mills. As families squeezed into the ever more densely packed tenements of the old town, the moneyed classes turned their backs on the medieval centre and moved west, rarely venturing into the dirty narrow streets where Catherine was headed, carrying her small son Alexander, with nine-year-old Agnes stumbling behind. They made their way through the filth and mud into one of the narrow lanes known as closes or wynds, and up the stair to the lodging 'house' (just a room or two) where Agnes could be left to look after her little brother while their counterfeiting mother headed off to do some business. She needed a place where she could work, and she cut a deal with Betty Scott, another counterfeiter who lived in an attic in the Old Wynd. There Catherine set out her tools of trade, the pewter spoons she used for metal, and her mould for turning the melted pewter into sixpences.

That night Catherine Chisholm and Betty Scott were arrested for passing 'base coin'. Glasgow's chief prosecutor, the Procurator Fiscal, was determined to see the women tried at the High Court of Justiciary, the only Scottish court imposing sentences of transportation. The police set to work tracking down 26 witnesses to give statements, and the Lord Advocate's Office agreed that the case should be tried when the Court sat in Glasgow for the autumn Circuit. Before their trial on 16 September 1836, Betty Scott decided to plead guilty, perhaps after doing a deal with the Procurator Fiscal because she was apparently allowed to serve her time in Scotland in spite of her sentence to transportation. Catherine Chisholm, according to the *Glasgow Herald*, pleaded not guilty but 'after a short trial' was found guilty, and her sentence was carried out a year later when she boarded the *Atwick* as it waited in the Thames for its cargo of convict women. Agnes and Alexander sailed with their mother. When Catherine arrived in Van Diemen's Land, she said she was a widow with four children, but who looked after the other two or what became of them remains unknown. Unless they made their own way to Australia—which seems unlikely—they never saw their mother again.

ABANDONED TO THEIR FATE

Whether or not the Scottish convicts destined for the *Atwick* were the morally depraved women the judgmental historian had in mind when he called them 'abandoned', they were about to be abandoned by the justice system which handed them over to the control of foreigners, the English. Proud though the Scots were of retaining their own independent legal system after the Acts of Union joined the kingdoms of Scotland and England, the sentences to transportation pronounced by their supreme criminal court, the High Court of Justiciary, were implemented by the English. While 'banishment' had long been a sentence imposed by Scottish courts, and the person so banished might well end up in England, the English had not been involved in inflicting that punishment. A sentence to transportation, however, allowed the English to take charge.

Sometime during the late summer of 1837 the Home Office in London sent instructions north to Edinburgh, specifying the number of female prisoners to be conveyed to the Thames for embarkation on the *Atwick*. Before the coming of railways, the most efficient and least expensive way to move 92 people (fourteen children were coming with the 78 prisoners) from Scotland to the south of England would be to send them by sea from Leith, the port of Edinburgh. They could sail down along the English coast and up the Thames, and be transferred directly onto the *Atwick* without their feet touching English soil. Gathering the women for this departure from Scotland took time, coming as they did from the gaols and tollbooths of Aberdeen, Dumfries, Dundee, Edinburgh, Glasgow, Paisley, Perth, Stirling, and Stonehaven.

Prisoners, after their trials in centres where the High Court of Justiciary met, had been returned to their places of arrest so that the cost of keeping them housed and fed would fall to the local authorities. Mary Harper, a homeless thief sent back to the town of Stonehaven after her trial in Aberdeen, would have to be returned to the city so that she and another five Aberdeen prisoners, one bringing five children, could travel by sea the 150 kilometres down to Leith. Prisoners sent shorter distances from Dumfries, Dundee and Perth could have gone by ordinary coaches, shackled in chains and guarded by turnkeys. Special coaches may have been hired to move the 29 women originating from Glasgow and its surrounds. Women confined in Edinburgh were fortunate because the port was nearby, and their families and friends could come down to the dock to wave a final farewell. Whether transferred to Leith by sea or land, the women destined for the *Atwick* experienced no doubt a taste of the discomfort of travels to come.

At least they had left the stark prisons behind. Most had been locked up for no more than a year, but not all. Forty-year-old Catherine Gates, who had spent almost three years in the tollbooth of Dundee since her arrest, may have been astonished and outraged to find herself actually slated for transportation at this stage of her seven-year sentence—and of her life. Described by the local Procurator Fiscal as 'a poor deseased Wretch but a most incorrigible Thief', Catherine does not seem to have been all that bright. On an October night in 1834 she stole wet shirts from a laundry basket in a kitchen. As she was wandering around Dundee's narrow streets near the harbour, she saw a woman come out of a tenement, and whispered to her that she had men's shirts to sell, pushing a striped cotton shirt into the woman's hand. Come into the house so that I can have a good look at it, said the woman, and Catherine followed after a moment's hesitation. The woman saw that the shirt was mended at the shoulder, and told Catherine she didn't need old shirts. I have a better one, said Catherine, and took a new shirt from her apron, saying that the shirts belonged to her husband, and they had quarrelled and she was going to leave him. The woman turned around to examine the shirt under the light, and when she turned back again, she saw Catherine hastily stuffing into her clothes a shawl, a bag, and the shoe brushes lying on a table. Catherine ran out the door, pursued by the woman yelling 'thief', and with the help of a little girl who rushed into a shop to get a man, they cornered Catherine and found a policeman to take her away.

Yes, Catherine Gates admitted to the magistrate, I did steal the laundry, but I really didn't know what I was doing at the time, being 'the worse of drink'. She said that she was married to a labourer, 'but she has not seen him for some years, & does not know where he now is, tho' she has heard that he is somewhere in Aberdeenshire'. Catherine was taken from Dundee to Perth for her trial on 5 May 1835, and after she pleaded guilty, police witnesses testified that she had been 'habite & repute a Thief for the last 3 or 4 years', giving details of her prior convictions under various names in the courts of Aberdeen, Perth, and Dundee. She was duly sentenced, and then returned 'to the Tolbooth of Dundee there to remain till removed for Transportation'.

As the months passed without her name appearing on the list for any ship, she may have grown hopeful that she would be among the prisoners who served their time in gaol, although sentenced to transportation. Her 'deseased' state may have offered some protection. If she had been sent down to a transport in the Thames and then rejected as infectious or dangerously unfit to travel, the local authorities would have been charged for her return to Scotland. However, the Admiralty specified 'that old age or bodily infirmity alone, if not such as to make the Voyage dangerous to the Life of the Prisoner, is not to prevent his being embarked', and when prisoners were collected for the *Atwick* Catherine was deemed fit to make the voyage to Van Diemen's Land, where she survived less than three years.

In contrast to Catherine Gates with her extended incarceration in Dundee, Mary Ann Webster was exiled from Scotland little more than a month after her trial. She was a 33-year-old Edinburgh prostitute, and while women were not transported for prostitution, prostitutes like Mary Ann who stole from their clients were transported as thieves. About eleven o'clock one Saturday night, she saw a man she knew coming out of a public house. He 'was a little tipsy', she later said, and Alexander Duff agreed that 'he had been drinking'. They also agreed that they went into another public house together, drank two gills of whisky, and left around midnight. At that point their stories diverged. According to Mary Ann, Duff wanted her to go home with him but she refused and they parted company. No, said Duff, she did not refuse, and she must have stolen 15 shillings from his pocket while they were climbing the tenement stair to his mother's house, because the moment his mother opened the door and asked him for money 'to buy next day's provisions', he found he had nothing but coppers. He said that he went into the house without his mother seeing Mary Ann, though how that could be if the prostitute was close enough to wriggle her hands into his pockets, he did not explain.

He admitted sneaking the 'woman of bad fame' into his mother's house on other occasions, and justified this behaviour by saying that he had known Mary Ann 'when she was more respectable than she is now, and at one time [she] lived with him and his wife about 5 years ago, and they were paid 4/ [shillings] a week for her board by a society for reclaiming girls in her situation'. Ignoring any moral responsibility for someone who had been in his paid care, he concentrated on his own victimhood. His trump card was an accurate description to the arresting officer of a distinctive coin later prised from Mary Ann's clenched fist by the female searcher at the police station. The coin, said Duff, bore a 'black mark upon the brow or side of the head of the King' as if burnt with gunpowder. Mary Ann was trapped. Her fate was sealed by this theft combined with four previous convictions recorded before the 'society for reclaiming girls' had turned her over to the Duffs (and how did they treat the prostitute they were supposedly helping to reform? was there payback in her theft?). After Mary Ann pleaded guilty at her trial, she was automatically sentenced to seven years' transportation. Almost exactly a year after she arrived in Van Diemen's Land, she died in the Cascades Female Factory on 29 January 1839.

LAST-DITCH EFFORTS TO STAY AT HOME

Not all the women sentenced by the High Court of Justiciary in Edinburgh or on Circuit accepted the inevitability of exile. Seven petitioned the Home Office in London, and their files survive today. How these prisoners learned that they could beg the English authorities for clemency is unclear. A few years later, women sent from Scotland to wait in London's Millbank Penitentiary learned about petitions from benevolent 'Lady visitors', who often filled out printed forms on behalf of those who could not write, but there were no such forms in 1837 when the *Atwick* sailed, and no helpful Ladies visited Scottish gaols. The process was more haphazard, the petitions more varied.

Some petitioners formulated precise requests. Margaret McNiven, described by the Governor of the Edinburgh Gaol as 'of a mild & inoffensive disposition', begged that she 'be removed to the General

Penitentiary, Millbank, there to remain for whatever period of her sentence your Lordship may appoint', and then be reunited with her Scottish relatives who 'are in such circumstances as will enable them to establish her in a reputable way, when she again returns to Society'. Other petitioners had only a vague inkling of what to do. Elizabeth Forbes wrote a simple letter 'from my own hand' explaining to a member of parliament whom she had seen 'often in the country' that she was 38 years old, came from good farming people in Perthshire, and had been 'making an endustress livelihood in an honest way' until she left the countryside for Edinburgh where she forgot her God and fell 'into a Disgracefull Snare'.

Some semi-literate person, perhaps a turnkey at the gaol, was paid to write the laboriously worded 'humble potiton of Andrew Lees and his wife' as a tale of family sorrow. 'Misfournens unforssen' forced the family to leave their 'rural life' near the Midlothian village of Newbattle, and come into Edinburgh to run a pub. This was the time of the Clearances, best remembered as the brutal removal of crofters by landlords in the Highlands, though the practice of turning farmland into sheep runs extended into the Lowlands as well. Whether or not Andrew Lees lost his living specifically because of the Clearances, rural poverty more generally was pushing people from the countryside into cities, and the Lees family were poor, too poor to give their daughter Agnes an education. She may have been able to read a little, but she could not write and did not sign her name for the 'panel statement' she made as the accused person at the time of her precognition. Writing, as the demographer R.V. Jackson reminds us, 'because it took so much longer to learn, was not an expectation among the children of the poor. Writing was a privilege.' Only fifteen of the 78 Scottish convicts on the *Atwick,* just over 19 per cent, could sign their names. 'Cannot write' is a refrain throughout the precognitions.

Agnes Lees was about twenty years old on the winter's night when she was one of five young women arrested for assault and robbery. A man named Thomas Hope had brought his cattle to the market in Edinburgh, and after selling all but one, put his profit of £25 in small notes into a black leather pocketbook. As he walked along the High Street with another man, three women came up and persuaded them to go into the public house of Andrew Lees in North Foulis Close. Agnes Lees showed them into a private room and served them gills of whisky. After his companion went into another room with one of the women, Hope proposed to 'have connexion with' Elizabeth Goldie on a bed in the room where they were drinking. The third woman left, and seventeen-year-old Goldie—also destined for the *Atwick*—began feeling his breast pocket. Hope jumped up, saying 'I see what you want', and tried to leave, but Goldie gave a signal and the women, including Agnes, rushed into the room, forced him against the bed, held their hands over his mouth, and robbed him.

Andrew Lees in his 'humble potiton' tried to wring pity from the far-away decision-makers, stressing his old age and broken heart. How could he and his elderly wife raise the child Agnes would be leaving behind? If only his daughter were restored to her distraught parents, they would 'endeavour to teach her that path which leadeth to virtue'. To this petition there was no reply, and learning that Agnes would soon be moved south, her desperate father tried again. This time at great expense he commissioned a professional document to be presented through a member of parliament to the Secretary of State, for the consideration of 'Her Gracious Majesty Victoria the First, Queen of Great Britain and Ireland', who had acceded to the throne just that summer and was a little younger than Agnes. Unlike the earlier petition with its appeal to sentiment, this plea for 'the royal clemency' rehearsed 'the facts of the case' to argue wrongful conviction, claiming that Agnes was merely serving in the family pub when 'girls of the Town' stole money from the drunken cattle dealer. She had nothing to do with the theft. The petition ends by saying that for some time Agnes had 'laboured under a decease in the head, which there is reason to fear will soon terminate fatally'. No one in Whitehall was moved. The petition was folded up for filing and tied with a pink ribbon. On the outside of the file was written: 'Result: Nil'. The prediction that Agnes was mortally ill proved true, and although she survived the voyage to Van Diemen's Land, within a few months she was dead.

No heartstrings at Whitehall were tugged by the petition from Jess Mitchell, either, though at her trial the jury had been moved by the plight of this impoverished 23-year-old widow of a ropemaker. Jess's story was that she had set off from her Highland home in Dingwall, northwest of Inverness, on a long journey to visit her godparents on the other side of the country in Dundee, taking along one of her two children, a 'lassie of three years of age'. When they reached Edinburgh they had to turn back because the little girl became seriously ill. Jess was now 'so short of money that she had to sell in Edinburgh her mantle and petticoat (for which she got five shillings and six pence) to bear her expences to Glasgow'. Somehow the mother and child travelled on another 40 kilometres west from Glasgow to Greenock, where they waited for the *Rob Roy* steamer to take them back north to Inverness. Greenock was a noisy, dirty port, its population of 40,000 noted for the unsanitary living conditions which explained a disturbingly high mortality rate. The town was always filled with itinerants, and Jess claimed to have met one, a fiddler who played in the band of 'Cook the Equestrian'. Instantly, he was besotted, 'pressed her to go with him to Glasgow to live', and offered his watch as a token of serious intent. She took the watch, said neither yes nor no to the proposal, and slipped aboard the *Rob Roy*. As the steamer pulled away, she saw the man 'walking on the pier, and she has no doubt looking for her'. On board, she gave the watch to a boy she knew, an uncle's son, as surety for a loan of money to pay her passage.

Jess Mitchell was fond of story-telling. The besotted fiddler was a figment of her imagination conjured up for the magistrate at the time of her first interrogation. The story she told the Greenock lodging-house keeper from whom she rented a bed was of a husband recently lost at sea, 'drowned from a whale ship belonging to Kirkaldy'. She had gone there to arrange for his chest and things to be sent up to Dingwall, she said, and was following the chest home with her fatherless child. The experienced lodging-house keeper must have been furious at being taken in by the 'youngish woman carrying a child who had six toes on one of its feet', and presumably at her insistence a sheriff's officer was sent all the way north to pursue Jess when she left the lodgings with the cherished finery of the deaf old woman and her almost totally blind niece. From a locked chest of drawers, Jess stole a worsted black-and-white shawl and a red silk shawl, a gauze ruff and a fur ruff, four linen caps, four linen shirts, and two petticoats. She stole a small looking-glass, some grey worsted yarn, and even a bible. From the lodging-house keeper's own bed she took a silver watch belonging to the woman's nephew, one of the crew of the *Canada* sailing towards Montreal.

The sheriff's officer who brought Jess down from the Highlands to be charged at Greenock asked what had induced her to take the things 'and put people to so much trouble sending so far for her, and in answer the woman said the Devil had prompted her and that it was a pity, for she had ruined both herself and her children as she was going to be banished beyond seas'. She was right. At her trial in Glasgow on 6 January 1837 she was found guilty of theft and sentenced to seven years' transportation, but even though the court protocols offered the accused no opportunity to tell their stories on the witness stand, something about Jess stirred the jury, who according to the *Glasgow Herald* 'recommended her to the mercy of the Court'. All fifteen jurymen then signed a petition asking for royal clemency on the grounds that 'the crime committed by the Petitioner arose from the pressure of poverty and starvation being in a distant part of the country with an infant child far from her home & without friends or money, & without the means of paying for her passage home'. The petition was sent down to London. Result: Nil. Jess sailed into banishment without her two young children.

Christian Myles also left behind a child. She wrote her own petition, explaining that she was 'the wife of a soldier in the 55th Regiment, at present in India, and might urge the necessitous circumstances to which she was reduced by the absence of her husband, to commit the offence of which she was found guilty'. She enclosed an affectionate letter from her husband, couched in the stilted language of a man unaccustomed to expressing the sentiments of intimacy, a man probably dictating his letter to someone who could write, 'I have the Happiness to Inform you that I am well and hope you and my Boy are the same'. Please take pity on the situation of your petitioner, Christian pleaded with the far-distant Secretary of State, who 'now feels the deepest sorrow at the prospect of being for ever separated from her husband'. Please order her instead 'to be sent to the General Penitentiary so that she may yet have a prospect, however distant, of again meeting her husband and passing the remainder of her days as a useful member of the Community in her humble sphere of life'. Result of petition: Nil. Christian probably saw neither her husband nor her young son again.

ELIZA DAVIDSON LIGHTS A FIRE

One petition came from a married couple. Eliza Davidson, the only *Atwick* convict who could be called middle-class, and her husband John Julius McDonald requested 'that they may not be separated, and that they may, together, end their days in preparation for a future state'. They stressed their respectable connections and the previously 'unblemished reputation' of McDonald, who had been a teacher in Edinburgh for 28 years, and was 'well known to the most respectable Divines in the City', several of whom signed the petition. Their lawyer forwarded the petition to the Secretary of State, and added a covering letter to say that he had not prepared the document and did 'not participate in the doubt there expressed of the justice or propriety of the sentence of the court'.

Few in Edinburgh would have felt much sympathy for the McDonalds. If their neighbours had been less suspicious, the self-centred couple might have burned down the neighbourhood. Edinburgh's old town is crowded onto Castle Rock, with Edinburgh Castle perched dramatically at its highest point. A thoroughfare, known to visitors today as the Royal Mile, ran down the spine of the rock from the castle, and vertical stacks of tenements lined closes and wynds branching off on either side. Through the valley below the castle escarpment ran another thoroughfare, the Cowgate, down which farmers drove their livestock to the weekly horse and cattle markets held in the Grassmarket, a busy commercial space throughout the week, surrounded by public houses and frequented by prostitutes and thieves, an area well known to women of the *Atwick* convicted in Edinburgh.

A winding street called the West Bow connected these upper and lower parts of the medieval town, and it was here that the McDonalds had their shop. Edinburgh, like Glasgow, had grown rapidly over recent decades, and the prosperous classes were moving to the north side of Castle Rock where the elegant enclave of New Town beckoned those who could afford gracious living. As in Glasgow, the originally mixed-class tenements in the old town were being subdivided and packed with transients and criminals as well as respectable labourers and remnants of the middle class like John Julius McDonald, who planned to fund his retirement by turning book-seller. This might have been a good idea if he were an affable man who could chat amiably to potential customers. Unfortunately, he was a cantan-kerous old snob of 64, with a wife half his age who simply did his bidding, as she had no doubt been trained to do throughout a marriage which began when she was in her mid-teens and he in his late forties. It was Eliza who arranged to rent the shop the year before, and it was her name over the door. Most of the space in the shop was taken up by furniture belonging to the second-hand business for which she was responsible.

Until a month before the fire, the McDonalds actually lived in their shop, sleeping in a bed hidden during the day behind a screen. Recently they had rented a room nearby. Neighbours, from whom they kept them-selves aloof, noticed books and furniture being carried off, and 'suspected they were going to flit'. The local night patrol had been alerted, and that was why two men were already keeping an eye on the shop when Eliza Davidson emerged about twenty minutes past midnight on a Saturday, locked the door, crossed to the dark side of the street, and hurried away. The watchman who went over to have a look at the shop heard a crack-ing noise as if sticks were burning. 'There's something wrong here,' he called to his partner, 'I think the place is on fire'. Immediately they sum-moned the firemen, and just as well, testified the Master of Fire Engines, because 'the shop is part of a large tenement occupied by a great many families and had the fire made farther progress before it was checked, the whole tenement must have been consumed and the houses on each side of it would most likely have shared the same fate, as they are all old tene-ments, with much wood about them'. Eliza was arrested next morning when she showed up as if to open the shop for the day's business.

It had been Eliza's job to light the fire, and now it was up to her to lie about it. She was also supposed to stop the police from bothering her husband, and she tried to send them off on a false scent, saying she lived 'a wee bit out of the Town', though she would not say where. When asked her husband's name and whether he lived with her, she told the policeman 'that was no business of his'. The police located porters who on the afternoon of the fire had been hired by the McDonalds to carry a chest of drawers and a wooden chest from the shop to a room nearby. They led the police to the rented room, and there was McDonald, claiming to have neither wife nor shop—it was his niece, he said, who kept a Broker's shop in the West Bow. The room where they found McDonald was so full of furniture that it looked 'just like a Broker's shop', while the shop in the West Bow was almost empty. Its contents, damaged rather than destroyed, were valued at a mere £2 10 shillings, though insured for £100. Eliza, an incompetent arsonist, had spread straw around the place, and turned the books with their backs to the shelves and their pages open in the hope that the paper would quickly catch fire. As evidence that this strategy had failed, the police retained 'a book without a title page being part of Caesar's Commentaries in Latin, commencing at the 53rd page and ending at the 382nd—which book was upon the shelves near the south window and is burned in the centre'.

In spite of an 'able and ingenious defence' mounted by the lawyer at their trial, the jury consulted for just ten minutes before finding the couple guilty. Instructed to stand for sentencing, Eliza Davidson 'who had been sobbing bitterly from the time the Jury retired, was unable for the exertion', and her husband kept muttering that the witnesses had 'all sworn false', the jury had brought in 'a false verdict', and 'they have all been conspiring against me'. Over the sobs and mutterings, Lord Mackenzie commented that if the wife 'has a spark of conscience', which he thought her husband had not, 'she must feel that she has committed a crime and a sin of the deepest dye'. Admonishing the prisoners directly, the presiding Judge continued: 'In the centre of the most populous district of Edinburgh, for the sordid love of money, you raised a fire by which much property might have been destroyed and many lives lost. For this you are to suffer a punishment which leaves you only your life.'

It was not a life that John Julius McDonald wanted anymore. Teaching had bestowed status in a city priding itself on culture and education. Now, late in life, he had become a criminal and was treated as such, first when confined to a hulk in the Thames and afterwards on the male transport *Minerva*. One morning while the prison ship was sailing through tropical waters, McDonald refused an order to bathe before breakfast. The surgeon superintendent, who was responsible for the health and well-being of all convicts during the voyage, considered the elderly prisoner 'a man of most ungovernable and unhappy Temper', and he personally intervened to order McDonald below. 'The prisoner,' wrote the surgeon superintendent in his later account of the incident, 'replied he would do whatever I ordered, but he would not obey the orders of a Boatswains Mate. On account of his advanced years he was only put in handcuffs and solitary Confinement for two hours, when he seemed very penitent and expressed to me his sorrow for what had taken place, I advised him to curb his violent temper.' Later that day while the officers were at dinner and the convicts were on deck, the Edinburgh schoolmaster climbed a few rungs up the rigging, 'took off his Hat and looking at the Prisoners on deck laughed and threw it amongst them, and the next moment threw himself into the Sea'. The alarm was raised, a boat was lowered, and sailors 'found the Body laying on the belly, the face wholly under water; the arms extended and spread out, the legs also extended and nearly close together, without exhibiting the slightest motion'. They hauled the unconscious McDonald up on deck, and, amazingly, resuscitated him. 'Oh! He said in a feeble voice it is cruel in you to bring me to, and shortly after said he preferred to have been at the bottom of the Sea.' For the rest of the voyage he slept in the ship's hospital, 'his wrists being tied in the night', and upon arrival in Hobart Town was transferred first to the Colonial Hospital, and then to the hospital at New Norfolk where he died a year later. It seems unlikely that the unhappy husband and wife saw each other again in Van Diemen's Land.

EXILE AS A SECOND CHANCE

Not all *Atwick* convicts were as miserable as the McDonalds when they thought about leaving Scotland for a land on the other side of the world about which they knew virtually nothing. At least it was some place new.

Mary Ann McAllister might have agreed that she was 'fully ripe for trans-portation', though her reasons would have been different from those the Procurator Fiscal had in mind when describing Catherine Chisholm. Mary Ann was ready to leave because she had no reason to stay. She had been caught red-handed stealing gingham pieces and handkerchiefs from a warehouse in the merchants' district of Glasgow. A clerk looked up from his desk in the counting room on one side of the lobby and saw a black-haired stranger go into the warehouse. He went into the lobby to investigate just as Mary Ann was coming out with her arms full of gingham. Seeing the clerk, she dropped the cloth, and dashed out the door and down the stair, with the man in hot pursuit calling 'thief' as he went and alerting others in the building. Mary Ann didn't stand a chance, and when she was cornered, she just kept repeating that it was another girl who took the things and ran away.

By the time she was brought before a magistrate to make her panel statement, she had changed her mind and admitted the theft, saying that 'she would rather be transported for this crime, than be sent into confine-ment, as she can get nothing to do, and has no person to look after her'. She described herself as 'a native of Glasgow in the fifteenth or sixteenth year of her age', and the police who gave evidence at her trial said they had known her since she was about twelve, and considered 'her to have been habite & repute a thief during the greater part of that period'. This was her fourth arrest for theft in less than a year. Each time she came out of the Bridewell, a city prison, she went back to stealing again. Alone in the world, illiterate and unskilled, Mary Ann had decided that life in Australia could be no worse than a bleak future in her homeland.

2

'TRANSPORTED BEYOND SEAS'

Wherever the Scottish convicts were tried, and whatever the length of their sentences, all faced the same punishment, 'to be transported beyond Seas'. The vague geography seems appropriate. Few of these mostly illiterate women could have known much about maps, though they would have heard stories about prisoners shipped to places from which they never returned. In September 1837, the *Atwick* convicts began that journey themselves. What did they feel when they stepped for the final time from the soil of Scotland, and boarded a vessel of banishment? They knew what it meant to be a prisoner in a Scottish gaol, but what would it mean to be a convict in Van Diemen's Land? For some, the sea itself was frightening, and their stomachs churned as the voyage south unsettled bodies accustomed to the solidity of city streets. When they made it to the River Thames and climbed the rope ladder up the side of the *Atwick*, the world they found was strange. Prisoners already on deck spoke to the newcomers in accents at first as incomprehensible as gobbledygook.

English prisoners had been boarding the *Atwick* in dribs and drabs, coming from up and down the country, from Devon and Dorset in the south, from Windsor, Bath and Oxford, from Chester on the Welsh border and from the eastern port of Hull, from Liverpool, Lincoln, Leicester, Northampton, Nottingham. These women, wrote the daughters of Elizabeth Fry in a memoir of their mother the famous prison reformer, 'arrived from the country in small parties, at irregular intervals, having been conveyed on the outside of stage coaches, by smacks, or hoys, or any conveyance that offered'. They climbed aboard the ship 'wayworn, and ill; or perhaps a solitary outcast brought upon deck, lamenting her misfortunes in the broad dialect of some far distant county; a small bundle of insufficient clothing being frequently the only preparation for the long voyage before her'.

The women coming from London were equally ill-clothed, but their transfer from prison to ship was a matter of hours rather than days. Since their trials at the Old Bailey they had been held in Newgate Prison, and from the prison they travelled along city streets to the River Thames in closed coaches. The departure of the *Atwick* convicts from Newgate created none of the hullabaloo which greeted a similar contingent setting out three months earlier when a reporter from the London *Times* joined unruly crowds gathered at the gates to see women off 'to New South Wales for the periods for which they are so banished—some of them for ever'. Spectators jostled 'to get a glimpse of Sarah Gale, the paramour of James Greenacre, of notorious memory'. Greenacre, the so-called Edgware Road Murderer, had killed a widowed washerwoman after she handed over her savings to fund his mythical invention of a washing machine. He cut her into pieces, which Sarah Gale helped distribute around London. Twenty thousand people watched as Greenacre was hanged in front of Newgate that May, and the curious were back again in June to farewell the more fortunate Sarah. No one on the *Atwick* carried such a sensational tale.

Just the same, they had plenty of stories to tell each other as they whiled away the hours. Edinburgh and Glasgow were not London (or Liverpool) of course, but city women had much in common—and everyone could talk about prisons and trials and the tough lives they had led. Left to their own devices, they might have lounged around on deck or retreated below to lie on the berths in gloom. But this was a prison ship, and their days were not their own. From the moment they stepped on deck they were under the control of Dr Peter Leonard who as surgeon superintendent had complete charge of the prisoners and their children. He had been appointed by the Admiralty, which was responsible for the convict transports, and he was answerable to the officials of Whitehall. Before their salaries were paid, the surgeons superintendent were required

to submit a journal including a sick list with case notes of significant illnesses, and a section of 'General Remarks' about the voyage.

While the ship was still anchored in the Thames, Dr Leonard received
help (whether he wanted it or not) from members of the Ladies' British
Society. Elizabeth Fry and her similarly well-connected friends had persuaded the Admiralty to let them come on board each female transport
before it left the Thames. During their visits, they helped divide the convicts into messes; organised a school and often appointed the teacher;
distributed uplifting literature; and offered moral encouragement and
advice. The Scottish prisoners, from what I know of them, were unlikely
to respond well to messages delivered in middle-class English accents by
well-dressed and well-fed visitors—but their gift packages to make the
voyage more bearable were another matter. The Ladies for all their lofty
benevolence were practical women, and the gift packages were personal
and homely. The Ladies gave each convict things the provisioning officers from the Admiralty would not think of—a bag for her clothes, two
aprons, a comb, black cotton cambric to make a cap, spectacles for those
who needed them, a work bag with scissors, thimbles, pins, needles and
thread (but no cloths to cope with menstruation, a subject perhaps too
intimate for the comfort of Ladies). The Ladies handed out packages
for each mess as well: a knife and fork, a ball of string, two coarse tidy
aprons for cooks, and two large bags to hold the most surprising gift,
2 pounds (almost a kilogram) of patchwork pieces for each woman so
that during the voyage she could make a quilt. Quilting would break the
monotony, and upon arrival in the colonial port, the woman could sell
her quilt and keep the profit. I can imagine some of the Scottish convicts
taking to patchwork, though whether they finished quilts, or how they
would sell them when they reached Hobart Town, I don't know.

Eventually the last convict name was ticked off the list of transportees, and the final supplies were loaded for the long voyage directly to
Van Diemen's Land without stopping at any port along the way. On
30 September 1837 the *Atwick* sailed down the Thames. For the Scottish
convicts who had already experienced the jolt of leaving the world they
knew, the journey down the river may have been less distressing than it

was for the English passengers, but the English Channel and the Bay of Biscay probably sent almost everyone down below in an agony of seasickness. Though most would recover fairly quickly, the illness which felled Jane Keith before the *Atwick* left the Thames would prove fatal.

The dying Scottish patient was young, just 24 years old. Her crime, as usual, was theft. Her victim had been a country horse dealer who came into the Edinburgh market during the summer of 1836, sold his horses for about £50, and spent several hours wandering from pub to pub with friends. About 9 pm he met a woman at the entrance to one of the closes in the Grassmarket, and went home with her for the night. Next morning about six he woke to find Jane Keith in the room, sitting beside his bed companion. Immediately suspicious, he felt his pocket and 'found that all his silver money had been stolen' but the notes in his vest were still there. As the women watched, he put the notes into a pocket of his breeches. After chatting for a few minutes, the woman with whom he had slept went out to get them all some whisky (at six in the morning!). Hardly had she gone before Jane 'started up, cried out "she has forgotten something", and ran out of the house, as fast as she could'. The man felt his breeches, and found the pocket empty.

For a brief moment, Jane Keith enjoyed her ill-gotten gains, spending the windfall on setting up house with William McConnochie, described by the police as 'her Fancy man'. First, she and McConnochie visited a pawnbroker, where he picked out a silver watch, and then off they went to the Canongate, where she rented a room from a painter. By evening, they had acquired a tent bedstead with curtains, a grate, chairs, and a table, and to show off their stylish quarters, they invited friends around for whisky. Jane also sent a pound note to the woman who was caring for her child. Unfortunately, even at this moment of triumph, not everything was perfect. The porter paid by Jane to set up the complicated bed remembered a quarrel, 'Keith saying to McConnochie what was his business with what the bed cost—it cost him nothing—to which McConnochie replied,—it cost her as little'.

The theft was on a Wednesday night. By the weekend, Jane and her lover were both in custody, and a year later she was dying on the *Atwick*.

'Patient has all the appearance of having been a dissipated person', wrote Dr Leonard, 'and confessed to having drunk hard and led a very irregular life—that she was long ill in jail at Edinburgh from whence she was sent to this ship and took much medicine: seems melancholy and despondent'. Over the next fortnight Jane appeared to improve, and on 9 October 'went out of Hospital to her mess saying she felt much better but was ordered back again and the medicines continued'. During the night of 14 October Dr Leonard wrote in his journal that she was moaning, and at midnight 'a change has taken place for the worse—the pulse is now scarcely perceptible'. By six o'clock the next morning, she was 'gradually sinking—very quiet—pupils fixed—pulse scarcely perceptible—rapid— no convulsions'. Four hours later, 'Lower extremities cold—Body covered with the profuse clammy perspiration preceding dissolution', and at 1.45 in the afternoon, she 'Expired with a struggle'. Summarising the case in his 'General Remarks', Dr Leonard wrote that 'after repeated attacks of intermittent fever [Jane Keith] ultimately fell a victim to that species of apoplexy dependent upon nervous and vascular debility, which occurs in Individuals whose constitutions have been weakened by intemperance'.

Jane Keith was the only person who died on the voyage, and if she had not come all the way down from Edinburgh, Dr Leonard might well have rejected her as unfit to travel, and sent her back. Like most of the surgeons superintendent on convict transports during this period, he was very serious about the health of his charges and keen to make a report to the Admiralty which would reflect well on his professional competence. At the heart of his programme was cleanliness. Women accustomed to the filthy tenements of Glasgow and Edinburgh (or indeed to life in any Scottish town or village) must have been astonished by the amount of time and energy spent on keeping the ship and its passengers clean. Every morning they had to get up at sunrise, and drag their bedding from the communal dormitory up the ladder to the deck. They had to shake out the blankets and put them into nettings to air. Then they had to wash themselves—every day! If the weather was warm, they bathed in a tub behind a screen on the Quarter Deck. Grumbling, no doubt. They even had to wash the clothes they were given to wear during the voyage (their own clothes were packed away and stowed). Each day some of the prisoners were detailed to go back down into the dormitory to scrub out the whole place with stones and sand. Three times a week the deck, water closets, and hospital were fumigated by sprinkling chloride of lime.

Unless the weather was stormy, anyone who was not in the hospital spent the day on deck in the open air. After all the washing was over, they ate breakfast at 8 am, and then went to school or did needlework, using their gifts from the Ladies. Although few of the Scottish prisoners could read or write, it's difficult to imagine them turning up diligently for school each morning (maybe they sent the children). Needlework looks like the better option. At least while you were playing around with patch-work pieces, you could chat, tell stories, speculate on the future. A little before noon, the prisoners were mustered and given a drink made from wine, lime juice, sugar, and water. Dr Leonard watched to make sure each woman drank her ration, determined to keep scurvy at bay—and to stop those alcoholically inclined from scrounging extra wine from the others. After the muster came the main meal of the day, dinner. In the afternoon, it was back to school or needlework until tea at four o'clock. Then the bedding was taken out of the nettings and down to the berths, before everyone gathered on deck for the most light-hearted part of the day, two hours described by Dr Leonard as 'devoted to dancing and various innocent amusements for the sake of exercise'—and for the sake of morale, he might have added if he were writing in a less medical mode. Once the sun had set, the prisoners and the children were sent below and locked in for the night.

It was a boring routine day after day, week after week, and yet to women who had been locked up in prisons for months before, it may have seemed a benign confinement. The food was regular and not too bad, the beds were clean and the air fresh. Most of the Scottish con-victs stayed healthy and off the sick list, but not all. Margaret Gillon was brooding, and three times during the voyage her misery escalated into hysteria of sufficient intensity for Dr Leonard to record her illness in his journal, though he does not write up the case with notes to say how he treated her. Margaret was in her early twenties, and had only recently emerged from a fifteen-month sentence in the Glasgow Bridewell when she stole from a five-year-old whose mother had sent her and her three-year-old sister with a message for their aunt. Margaret stopped them and asked whether they'd like some jam berries? Yes, they would. Come with me, she said, and I'll get you some.

They walked for a few minutes until Margaret Gillon stopped at the foot of a stair leading to the flats in a tenement. I'll need your silk hand-kerchief to hold the berries, she told the child as she untied the shawl wrapped round the little girl's shoulders. Away went Margaret, and did not come back. The children, who fortunately knew where they were in the maze of old town streets, made their way home. The girl told her mother what had happened. Keep a look-out for that thieving woman, said the mother, and the little girl did. A few times the five-year-old caught sight of Margaret scurrying along the street, but the thief had disappeared before the child could fetch her mother. At last they were lucky. One day the mother was along when the girl cried out—there she is, she stole my silk handkerchief! Cornered, Margaret 'appeared confused and exclaimed, "Good God I know nothing of the Handkerchief".' A crowd gathered, and someone 'said she ought to be sent to the Police office'. Yes, said the mother, and started off with a seemingly compliant Margaret.

As they walked along, Margaret Gillon tried to strike a bargain, offer-ing to 'take her to the place where the handkerchief was', and the mother, who just wanted her property back, 'was disposed to agree'. The two women changed direction and were heading off toward a pawnbroker's, when a man from the crowd objected, saying he 'thought it a pity that the girl should be allowed to get off so easily for such a crime, and he accord-ingly interfered to prevent it'. Insisting that they first inform the police, he took hold of Margaret and marched her to the station. There she immediately 'confessed she had stolen the handkerchief and expressed regret for having done so, adding that it was poverty had made her do it'. She told the arresting officer that 'it was a pity she had done it, as she had just come out' of the Bridewell. She mentioned no family, only that she 'is a native of Ireland . . . follows no lawful employment and resides in the High Street'. Since most prisoners named a specific place or the people they lived with, Margaret may have been one of the homeless who slept on tenement stairs in the wynds opening off the High Street. If she had been living rough, that would explain why a witness asked to identify Margaret after she had spent a few days in the Glasgow gaol commented that she was 'differently dressed and cleaner and healthier looking'.

Looking better does not mean feeling better. Margaret had no one to care for her or, seemingly, about her. She was illiterate and unskilled. I can imagine her on the deck of the *Atwick*, feeling abandoned and hopeless about herself and her future as she stared out to the horizon. No wonder she grew hysterical. Eliza Davidson, the Edinburgh arsonist, was also in bad shape. She was suffering from rheumatism and, wrote Dr Leonard, 'is of delicate habit and enfeebled constitution'. He knew she was too weak to go out to work, and when the *Atwick* reached its destination, he sent her to the Colonial Hospital.

Even women who were not ill must have been relieved when the four-month voyage came to an end on 23 January 1838. As the ship entered Storm Bay and sailed up the River Derwent, they crowded the railings, eager to see what their new home might look like. Fifty years earlier, on another January day in 1788, the very first fleet of convict ships disembarked its human cargo at Botany Bay in New South Wales, beginning the British colonisation of Australia. Little more than 34 years had passed since the British set up their tents in Van Diemen's Land. The new colony had grown slowly as an outpost dependent on New South Wales, until in 1825 it became a separate colony with its lieutenant governor no longer subservient to Sydney, though he could make no important decision or even issue a conditional pardon without consulting London. Numbering over 40,000, the European population of Van Diemen's Land in 1838 was already nearly half that of New South Wales—and growing with the arrival of every convict transport, for this was still a penal colony in spite of the influx of free settlers dreaming of fortunes made in a new land.

If the women and children on the *Atwick* hoped to stretch their sea-tossed legs on solid land by nightfall, they were disappointed. Nothing happened quickly when groups of convicts were being moved, and the handover of transportees from the metropolitan centre to colonial authorities on the periphery of Empire was an occasion for extensive paperwork. As soon as the anchor dropped, Dr Leonard wrote officially to the Colonial Secretary 'to acquaint you for the information of His Excellency the Lieutenant Governor that this Ship sailed from Woolwich on the 29th September and arrived here today'. The efficient surgeon superintendent had ensured that his paperwork was ready:

> *Enclosed are the following lists—of the convicts specifying the behaviour of each during the Voyage—of their Children—of the Free Women & Children Passengers—of the Sick at present on board—a Return of Casualties—and the usual list sent from the Home Office of the Convicts embarked. Until local officials rowed out to the ship in reply, there was nothing to do except wait and watch from the deck.*

Luckily, there was always plenty of action in the small harbour. Whalers were stopping to re-supply before they headed home with their season's take from the Great Southern Ocean. The *Colonial Times* was revelling that week in the cosmopolitan atmosphere: 'The streets of Hobart Town have, for the last ten days, been enlivened by the presence of scores and scores of Frenchmen; so much so indeed, that this little antepodian [sic] metropolis now closely resembles a small sea port town of the old world.' Nothing could better please the merchants of this thriving port, and these entrepreneurs were the sort of men who had already sent in their applications to the Assignment Board for women to be 'assigned' to them as servants working in their homes and shops. The sooner the prisoners on the *Atwick* were disembarked, the sooner they could get to work, but first came the bureaucratic processing.

The ship and its passengers had to be checked for infection. The colony's Principal Medical Officer, Dr John Arthur, came on board, pronounced the ship uncontaminated by any disease requiring quarantine, and declared the voyage properly managed from a medical point of view. Bedding and clothing were 'sufficient', as were provisions for water and food, although oatmeal was missing from the diet. The 'medical comforts' had been hot chocolate 'for breakfast and tea in the evening'. The women in general 'appeared remarkably healthy and free from Scurvy'.

Next came the Principal Superintendent of Convicts, Josiah Spode, whose duty was to ascertain 'what has been the previous line of life of each woman'. Under Spode's questioning, their answers were translated into a skill-set matching the needs of settlers. Here was an opportunity for the prisoners to exert some influence over their fates. Sarah Stevenson said she was a 'farm servant' who could milk, make butter, wash and iron. Apparently she wanted a life completely different from the Edinburgh streets where she had been two years 'on the town', which generally meant working as a prostitute. Catherine McBrayne said she was a 'dressmaker and flouncer', although at the time she was arrested in Glasgow she said she occasionally 'gets employment' from a warehouse. Mary Harper, petty thief and wandering hawker of trim and lace, was translated into 'plain cook and house servant, wash and iron'. None of the Scottish convicts who had worked in the mills were described as having industrial experience. Those skills were not relevant in a colony which shipped its wool back to Britain for processing.

Principal Superintendent Spode, self-assured grandson of the founder of the Staffordshire pottery renowned for its fine bone china, may have seemed an imposing and indeed intimidating figure to women when he demanded 'their characters from their own mouths which I compare with the Gaol & Ship reports'. This information, transcribed on the deck of the *Atwick* by a clerk who was usually himself a convict, would later be copied as an individual entry in one of the massive volumes of the alphabetical convict conduct registers. Here future offences would be duly recorded, as well as the hierarchy of 'indulgences' enabling a convict to move slowly or quickly through her sentence and out of the system. Spode had before him the list sent from the Home Office in London, stating the crime for which the woman was transported, together with a report from the gaol where she had been held, including information about marital status and children. As each woman gave her own version of the same information, he could check her account against the official record. No point in trying to deceive him.

Sarah Stevenson, 'transported for theft and previous conviction', was described in her gaol report as 'Irregular for some time but industrious in prison and of quiet disposition', convicted before, single. Instructed to state her offence, she said, 'Stealing articles, prosecuted by my father'. Catherine McBrayne, transported for theft, was described in her gaol report as a woman 'of dissipated habits, in prison before, connexions very bad. Married'. 'Stealing money from the person', she said, 'tried with my Husband', and she went on to talk about her family: 'Married, 5 children, Husband John transported to VDL [Van Diemen's Land], 2 Children on Board, James 13 years, George 5 years'. She may have said more, may have named the three children left behind, but the clerk recorded only what might be relevant while she served her sentence. Mary Harper 'transported for theft, Bad Character, in Gaol Before', said she had been transported for 'Stealing clothes, prosecutor at Stonehaven', convicted twice before of the same offence. And then she spoke of a fractured family, mentioned a child and a husband, 'Patrick Short at Glasgow', saying her 'real name' was Short. The clerk recorded as aliases other names she went under: Short, Stewart, McMullen. Hours and hours must have passed as each of the 150 women stood in turn to answer questions, hours and hours while the others milled about the deck with nothing to do except wait.

Or stand to be measured. Another examination, another list, a printed form with details to be filled in: name, trade, height, age, complexion, head, hair, visage, forehead, eyebrows, eyes, nose, mouth, chin, remarks. 'Native place', unasked-for by the form, was entered on the right-hand side of the page. While some of the categories seem useless descriptors— every woman's head is described as either 'round' or 'oval', whatever that means—the measurement of height offers a window which allows us, says the demographer R.V. Jackson, 'to see deep into the life they are leaving behind. Their heights bear witness to when and where they were born, to the food they ate as children, the clothes they wore, the houses they grew up in, the illnesses they endured, the water they drank, the very air they breathed.' The average height, calculated Jackson, was 155.3 centimetres— just over 5 foot 1 inch in the measurement scale used on the records.

All this measuring and listing was slow and laborious, and the *Atwick* had been in the harbour for six days when Principal Superintendent Spode finally told the Colonial Secretary that he expected to 'have finished the exams' by early afternoon and would be 'ready to land the women in the morning', so if the colonial chaplain, Reverend William Bedford, wished to conduct a religious service, 3 pm would be a good time. And then, before dawn on 30 January, the convict women and their children walked down the gangplank and stood at last on dry land. Coming on shore while most of the town still slept, they made their way uphill to Macquarie Street, past the fine two-storey brick houses of merchants, past modest cottages and mere shacks, until after an hour or so of what may have been a pleasant walk as the sun rose on a summer's morning, they left the town behind and entered a valley at the foot of the mountain which dominated the landscape for miles around. From some vantage points Mount Wellington seemed benign, shading into a figure called the Sleeping Beauty, but from the valley towards which they walked its face was riven by sheer dolomite precipices, reminder that wilderness lay just beyond the walled compound of their destination, the Female House of Correction, or 'Female Factory' as it was commonly known, a rather confusing term inherited from New South Wales to indicate that places for incarcerating female convicts were more than prisons. They were supposed to be institutions where women learned to be industrious workers who would become useful members of society, not burdens upon it. To distinguish this Factory on the edge of Hobart Town from others in the colony, it was unofficially given the name of the area and called the Female Factory at Cascades, or simply the Cascades Female Factory— 'the Cascades' being the name of the area alongside the Hobart Rivulet where the factory was located.

The high windowless walls of the compound left the women and children in no doubt that they were entering a prison. Once the great iron gates had closed, they found themselves shut into a small and crowded space where they milled around until sorted out by Superintendent John Hutchinson and his wife Mary, the matron, who took charge of any bundles of clothes and belongings they may have retrieved briefly before they left the ship, recorded the women's admission into the establishment, and sent them to their allocated space in this compound of walls within walls. Five women were breastfeeding infants, including Sarah Ferguson, whose daughter born on the *Atwick* would shortly be baptised as 'Hose-annah', though she would be buried the following year as 'Oceana'. Nursing mothers and their babies went through a door on the left into the nursery yard, where the older children went as well. This may have been the last time two of the Scottish convicts ever saw their children. Jean Smith and Elizabeth Brown were unmarried mothers who left their children con-fined by the state even after they themselves were freed. Jean Smith's son, Joseph Douglas, was four years old when he arrived in Van Diemen's Land; Elizabeth Brown's daughter, Margaret Callaghan, was six. Neither of these children would grow up with any experience of family.

With the *Atwick* children shut away in the nursery yard, their mothers could join the other convicts ready to go out on assignment. One of the first women to leave was probably Sarah Stewart, selected by Josiah Spode for his own household during the days he spent on board inter-rogating the prisoners. Sarah told Superintendent Spode that she was a widow with two children (neither of whom came with her) whose sailor husband 'has been dead 7 years'. When arrested in Glasgow for stealing rope, she told the magistrate 'that she is a native of Belfast, 27 years of age, earns a livelihood by shoe binding', but on the deck of the *Atwick* in the harbour of Hobart Town she revised her skills to those of 'Dress-maker, house maid, Ladies' maid', all of which would be useful in the Spode household where the mistress was an heiress, and there were many children. It may have been stressful to live under the constant surveil-lance of the Principal Superintendent of Convicts, a man described in the *Australian Dictionary of Biography* as taking pride in 'the accuracy of the extensive records he had to keep' but lacking in personal generosity, 'a humourless, slightly arrogant and colourless civil servant'.

The more than 'slight' arrogance of Josiah Spode's wife Maria is apparent from the complaint lodged by another convict servant ten years after Sarah lived in the Spode household. Jane Miller, who like Sarah was handy with her needle, was educated, and had books of her own to lend a Spode daughter. She also had the confidence and skill to compose an articulate and detailed account of how badly she had been treated when Mrs Spode, refusing to believe she was ill, vowed to 'humble [her] pride' by implicating her in a theft of which she knew nothing. 'I said O Mrs Spode take care what you say for your conscience will not always sleep. She told me to [give] her none of my cant. The constable came up and I was given into charge.' How Sarah Stewart managed in this household we do not know, though the fact that she spent almost three years in the colony before being charged with any offence suggests that she was adroit in negotiating her way through its arrogance and egos. It looks as if Josiah Spode, with his practised eye, chose well.

He used the same expertise to handpick other servants for the colony's elite. 'I always select the most respectable among them for the most respectable situations', he told the 1841 committee of inquiry into female convict discipline. The appropriation record listing each *Atwick* convict, her skills, and the master or mistress to whom she was assigned shows evidence of Spode's interventions. Eight women were assigned to masters of sufficient importance in colonial Australia to merit entries in the *Australian Dictionary of Biography*. Elizabeth Honour, who could 'cook jellies, fish, soups, pastry', went to the Colonial Treasurer. Ann Crawley, convicted at the Old Bailey of housebreaking, was assigned to Rev. Philip Palmer, the Anglican clergyman at Trinity Church, Hobart, who had until recently held a seat in the Legislative Council, and was known as an evangelical with a strong interest in education. Sarah Thompson, convicted at the Old Bailey of stealing money, a watch, and a gold ring from an elderly pensioner of the Greenwich Hospital, was assigned to Rev. William Bedford, the combative clergyman of St David's Church. 'Holy Willie', as the prisoners derisively called him, preached to the inmates at the Cascades Female Factory, and conducted burial services for the convicts and children who died there. The nurse and needlewoman Grace Heinbury, convicted in Leicester of theft, was sent across the Derwent to the estate of Algernon Sidney Montagu, the Supreme Court judge whose father was the natural son of the fourth Earl of Sandwich, and who had spent much of his own childhood in the Lake District under the care of the poet William Wordsworth and his sister Dorothy. Elizabeth Archer, convicted in Nottingham of shoplifting, was assigned to George Hull who had retired as assistant commissary general and was living in style on the 2560-acre property near Hobart Town named 'Tolosa' in homage to the Spanish town where he had served during the Peninsular War. Seventeen-year-old Mary Lynch, who had stolen money from the Liverpool dressmaker to whom she was apprenticed, may have been horrified to learn that her skills with the needle were going to send her more than a hundred kilometres from town to the farming property of George Meredith on the east coast, but at least when she arrived at 'Cambria', she found a 27-roomed Georgian mansion with spectacular views across Great Oyster Bay to the Freycinet Peninsula. Mary King, a 24-year-old widow who left her child behind when she was convicted at the Norfolk Quarter Sessions of stealing ribbon, had claimed much-needed country skills: 'farm servant', she said, 'milk, butter, wash', and yet for some inexplicable reason she was sent to the town house of Simeon Lord, son of the controversial entrepreneur of the same name who was one of the few convict emancipists to make a fortune in Australia.

These women were being assigned to families confident of their own social standing, to households large enough to have several servants who could share the work, and hopefully some companionship as well. All women assigned to these prosperous settlers were English. National bias influenced Superintendent Spode's program for sending the most 'respectable' convicts to the colonial elite. The servant he selected for his own household, Sarah Stewart, had been born in northern Ireland, though convicted in Scotland, and his general prejudice against the Scots informs a message he asked the *Colonial Times* to pass along to its readers on the day the women left the *Atwick* for the Female Factory:

> We are requested by the Principal Superintendent of Convicts, to say, that so numerous are the applications for female servants, ex the last vessel [the Atwick], that it is impossible that he can comply with one half the demand. The greater portion of the women are Scotch, and hence another difficulty— the generality of Scotch prisoner women not being admired in this Colony.

Admired or not, 'the generality of Scotch prisoner women' were among the 99 *Atwick* convicts assigned within a week of their arrival at the Female Factory. They were probably matched to their new employers by the Factory's superintendent and matron, John and Mary Hutchinson, since it seems unlikely that Josiah Spode was interested in masters without social or political clout.

Most people approved by the Assignment Board were socially unimportant, small shopkeepers in Hobart or in villages dotted across the island, struggling farmers on bush blocks, minor officials in the government or lower-ranking officers in the army. For masters far from town, it took time to make the arrangements for a new servant to be collected, which may explain why 40 women remained on the Factory list for two weeks, and 28 for three. Some women were apparently difficult to place, in spite of the 'numerous' applications for female servants, and the twelve who remained unassigned a month after the *Atwick* dropped anchor must have been worrying about what dregs of jobs they would eventually face.

3

DEATHS IN THE FEMALE FACTORY

The Scottish children must have been stunned when the door closed behind them and they found themselves locked into the nursery yard. They stood in a small courtyard paved with flagstones, without a tree or a bush or even a blade of grass in sight. In front of them ran the double-storeyed wards, built onto the Cascades Female Factory's perimeter wall. The nursery yard was a prison for babies and children. Those who did not arrive on the convict transports were born to mothers who became pregnant while working as assigned servants. Pregnant convicts were returned to the Factory to give birth, and then went into the nursery to breastfeed until their babies were weaned at the age of nine months. At that moment mother and child were separated. The mother went back into the crime class to serve her punishment for becoming pregnant, and then out she went to work again. The babies stayed in the nursery until aged two before leaving the Female Factory (for the first time in their lives) to be admitted into the Male and Female Orphan Schools.

Prison was nothing new to the Scottish children, but the prison spaces of their experience were places for grown-ups, and the noises they associated with prison were the sounds of adults chatting and shouting, not the whimpering cries of babies. Some of the Scottish children were too young to register the strangeness. Two were about a year old, and came into the Yard with their mothers because they were still breastfeeding. The other twelve were more than four years old, five of them ten years or older, the oldest three in their early teens. These twelve children were old enough to be sent immediately to the Orphan Schools. Instead, they remained incarcerated in the Female Factory for six weeks. Why add to the crowded conditions in the nursery over summer? What was to be gained by confining older children to the ward with weaned infants? Like so much about the Cascades Female Factory, the underlying rationale remains mysterious. This was an institution governed by expediency and chance rather than policy. Or misgoverned, perhaps.

The children of the *Atwick* entered the nursery at a moment when the Female Factory itself had come to the attention of the local press, and by following the newspaper campaign we can see into spaces usually hidden from the public. Over a four-week period between 6 March and 3 April 1838, seventeen editorials, news stories and snippets of comment about the Factory were published in three weekly newspapers, *Murray's Review*, the *Colonial Times*, and the *True Colonist*. All decried the 'mismanagement and bad state of the Female Factory'. The opening salvos in their campaign were occasioned by inquests. An editorial in *Murray's Review* on 6 March lamented 'distressing disclosures made at the inquest held last week upon the remains of the miserable woman who died in the female factory, (having a child at the breast,) of diseases originating in syphilis'. The editor went on to bemoan the Factory's location 'in a morass at the foot of surrounding mountains', and its 'system' of 'heartlessness' 'carrying vengeance even to infants'.

The next week the *Colonial Times* took up the story, attacking the secrecy of the Factory's 'internal arrangements': 'With the exception of the medical attendant, and the Principal Superintendant [sic] of Convicts, no persons, that we are aware of, except the resident officers, are admitted within its gloomy walls'. Even death was kept suspiciously secret, said the editor, who reminded his readers that 'Every person who dies in a place of confinement requires, by Act of Parliament, an Inquest, in order to ascertain whether any neglect has been used or not, towards the deceased'. 'Ascertaining' meant investigating, meant a coroner going with a jury inside the Factory and asking questions. An inquest could serve as a people's court passing judgement on institutions. This might be a penal colony, but it was not a prison colony, and its free citizens had a right and obligation to know what was happening to those incarcerated in their midst.

Inquests had been carried out inside the Cascades Female Factory before the newspaper campaign, though they were not the sort of 'people's court' the newspapers were demanding. In the first place, they were not held systematically, and even when the Coroner *was* called, and *did* hold an inquest, his inquiry was perfunctory, as is evident from papers filed in the Colonial Secretary's correspondence not as a matter of routine reporting, but because the dead woman was found to have died from what the Coroner called 'constitutional debility incurred by a "venereal affection"', and this triggered panic all the way up the line to Lieutenant Governor Franklin, who did not want to be accused of sending out infected women as assigned servants. The dead woman was Elizabeth Johns, and the nurse responsible for her care was Sarah Rafferty, a Scottish convict from the *Atwick*.

Sarah was one of the older women on board, giving her age as 'forty five years or thereby' when she was arrested in 1836 while trying to persuade the wife of a Dundee pawnbroker to buy 'a wooden tub which was wet at the time and very dirty'. The tub had been stolen from outside the shop of a meal-seller in the Overgate where it had been placed to catch rain running off the shingled roof on a wet summer's day. The policeman who interrupted Sarah in the pawnshop was already after her for the theft of clothes from a drying green. The description of the laundry thief fitted the woman he had seen convicted three times in the police court during the past year.

Sarah seems to have been a woman on her own with no regular means of support, a community nuisance rather than a canny thief. She described herself as a widow with five children, though where they were she did not say, nor did she say how long ago she had left her native home near Dublin. Upon arrival in Van Diemen's Land, she called herself a 'sick nurse'. Maybe she had helped Dr Leonard on the voyage out? Whatever her actual nursing experience (or lack thereof), Sarah was assigned to the hospital in the Female Factory and put in charge of a ward. At least she had some skills in literacy. As one of the few Scottish convicts who signed her precognition, she could probably read a little, and reading the labels on medicine bottles was useful in nursing. 'I positively swear', she told the Coroner at the inquest on 26 February, that 'I gave [Elizabeth Johns] every due attention and administered to her every thing that the Doctor ordered'.

No one at the inquest cross-examined Sarah Rafferty, and the case was of no apparent interest to the Coroner until he heard testimony from a wardswoman in the Nursery Yard where Elizabeth Johns lived for two months with her newborn son before going into the hospital. Because Elizabeth hid her disease, the wardswoman did not 'suspect that any thing ailed her' until one day she saw something to make her believe Elizabeth 'was not well and I taxed her with it. She confessed the nature of her complaint and I reported accordingly and she was removed immediately to the Hospital.' Within a colonial world of incessant and petty intrigue, the Coroner decided to use this case to fire off a pompously worded missive informing the Principal Superintendent of Convicts that 'during [his] stay at the Female House of Correction' he had heard 'that there are very many female persons now in the institution labouring under a venereal disease', and concealing their infection.

Spode passed the problem on to the Colonial Secretary for the Lieutenant Governor to deal with as a medical matter outside the responsibility of the Convict Department. Lieutenant Governor Franklin directed the Principal Medical Officer to investigate, and he in turn sent an assistant colonial surgeon to examine the women. The visit was a fiasco. Retreating quickly to town, the doctor reported that the 'outrageous and insubordinate' women of the crime class met his 'calm' request with 'general shouts and uproarious laughter'. Examining their private parts, he told Dr Arthur, the Principal Medical Officer, 'could not be carried into effect but by force'. The next day Dr Arthur went off to the Factory himself, with his unsuccessful subordinate in tow. This time he intended to ask Mrs Cato, the midwife, to do the actual examinations while the doctors just watched, but once again, female voices stymied his efforts, 'my presence being speedily announced to the Prisoners in the different Yards, clamour and tumult commenced & prevailed to an extreme degree during the entire time I remained'. Eventually two doctors 'inspected' the women in some unspecified and probably quite general way, and reported their findings as an official board of inquiry: two women 'affected with Gonorrhoea' were already 'under medical Treatment'; the remainder of the prisoners were 'singularly exempted from diseases of that character'. Case closed.

Neither the Elizabeth Johns inquest nor the farcical attempts to investigate the prevalence of venereal disease came to the attention of the press, but during the week the doctors were struggling with the inmates of the Factory, the crusading newspapers turned the spotlight on an inquest held across town at the Rose and Crown Hotel. Although the same coroner was involved, this inquest was not of his choosing. In fact, as the *True Colonist* told its readers on Friday 16 March, this was an inquest 'some of the neighbours, much to their credit, *had demanded* to be held on the body of the little victim', a 'poor little helpless, innocent child' named Thomas Vowles who had entered the Female Factory with his mother as a healthy infant, had sickened there, and was retrieved by his father in time to die at home.

On the following Tuesday the *Colonial Times* gave readers a blow-by-blow account of the inquest in a lengthy article of small print covering four and a half columns. The star witness, reported the newspaper, was the child's mother, Mary Vowles. She told the Coroner 'and a highly intelligent jury of fifteen' that she had come free on the *Princess Royal*. Her criminal conviction was local. When Mary was 'ordered into the Factory', her husband 'applied to Mr Spode for special leave to suckle my baby'. The Principal Superintendent of Convicts granted this request, and Mary carried 'the child in my arms when I went in'. Once inside the gates, 'I was undressed, as is customary, and clothed in the prison dress'. Then a woman came and 'took the child away from me, by Mr Hutchinson's orders . . . I told Mr Hutchinson that I was suckling the baby, when he said, if I made any noise, and did not go into the yard, he would put me in a [solitary] cell'. In spite of her loud and fervent protestations, Mary was sent to the crime class to serve her term of hard labour, while Thomas was sent to the nursery to be abruptly weaned.

Less than a week before Thomas was brought into the weaning ward, two Scottish convicts had come into the nursery from the *Atwick*, Janet

Bonar and Grace Logan. Both were breastfeeding daughters more than a year old, and they were probably ordered to start weaning them immediately. At least these convict mothers could comfort the little girls who suddenly found themselves in a strange and forbidding place. Thomas, not quite a year old, was on his own. No one at the inquest was named as responsible for ensuring that he ate even the nutritionally inadequate diet of milk, bread, and sugar prescribed for children while they were being weaned. He may have eaten nothing during the five days before his mother saw him. When Mary joined the other mothers for their visit to the nursery yard on the one day of the month when Superintendent Hutchinson permitted them to see their children, 'I did not know my own child, it was looking so sickly, and altered so much for the worse; the baby, after being with me a few minutes, recognised me'. It may have been after Mary's visit and her evident distress that the convict mother appointed as overseer for the weaning ward put Thomas on another diet: 'the children that were sick had sago and wine; the deceased child got sago and wine; I gave it to him myself, because it was ill', she said, adding defensively, 'not *very* ill'. His mother, locked behind walls not far away, knew better. Frantic, Mary 'could not rest day or night, for thinking about my baby', and tried unsuccessfully to trade her ration of bread for a piece of paper to send a message to her husband. Eventually, she contacted him 'by word of mouth', and on 21 February, Job Vowles successfully petitioned Josiah Spode for an order releasing Thomas.

After a fortnight and three days in the Cascade Female Factory, 'the baby was all but dead', testified his father, 'it could scarcely move itself; I carried it home . . . I fed it with a little chicken and mutton broth; I took the child to Rowe and Maclachlan's Dispensary; Mr Rowe said it was teething, and gave it some powders'. The distraught father asked his neighbour Judith Panton for help, and the mother of six children testified that at her suggestion, Vowles fed 'the child on arrow-root and sago'. Each day Job brought Thomas 'to my place . . . I used to wash and dress the child every morning . . . the evacuations of the child were green, with peas in them. The father said "Is it not surprising, Mrs Panton, how this poor child is passing green peas through it?" I saw the peas in the cloth—they were round and hard; for two or three mornings, I noticed the child to be evacuating peas; the evacuations were generally of a green liquid matter.' Five weeks after mother and child first entered the Female Factory, Josiah Spode agreed to Mary's early release: 'my husband was anxious that I should go home, and see my baby before it died; it was my only child'.

The risk-averse Coroner couched the inquest's findings in abstract language laying no blame: 'the said Thomas Vowles came to his death in a natural way by Diarrhoea, induced by teething and weaning'. The *Colonial Times* reported the bland verdict, and then in an editorial seethed with righteous indignation: the 'infant came by its death—we state the facts, without any technical circumlocution—in consequence of being separated from its mother, and afterwards neglected'. If the Coroner's case was closed, the newspaper's was not: 'As we have now fairly commenced with the Female Factory, we shall not stop till some reformation is effected'.

There is no way of knowing what the Coroner thought of the crusading journalists. Whether he was intimidated or simply hoped to drag them into the morass, he made a strategic decision to involve them directly the next time he held an inquest inside the Cascades Female Factory. All three editors were with him when he entered the gates on 26 March to determine why 31-year-old Barbara Henning died two months after she disembarked from the *Atwick*. The editor of the *Colonial Times* was there unofficially 'by the kind permission of the Coroner', but the other two editors were actual members of the jury, and the editor of *Murray's Review* was elected foreman. The staff at the Female Factory must have known that this would be no routine inquest, with everyone simply saying like Sarah Rafferty that they did the best they could but the woman died anyway. Josiah Spode as principal superintendent responsible for all convict institutions was on the premises that day, but spent the entire time closeted with John Hutchinson in the superintendent's 'private apartment', leaving everything to his wife Mary Hutchinson the matron, William Cato the assistant superintendent, and Cato's wife Elizabeth, the assistant matron and midwife. The Female Factory was far too large an institution to be run effectively by such a small core of paid civilian staff—in the week of the Henning inquest Hutchinson reported a population of 321 women and 60 children—and the day-to-day running of the place depended upon the reliability and effectiveness of co-opted prisoners like the hospital nurse Sarah Rafferty.

From the moment the jury entered, the Coroner's control began to slip. Instead of going directly to the hospital and conducting their examination of the body, as he suggested, the jury decided they had an obligation to tour the entire site, because 'there was a very great excitement in the public mind, which ought to be allayed'. Over the next two hours the men tramped through the compound, opening doors and seeing for themselves the conditions under which the prisoners and their children lived. They saw, the *Colonial Times* told its readers, 'the work-rooms for the crime class, where a very little wool is picked, and the rooms below, where as little is spun', scarcely a place of punishment 'in a crowded apartment, where the women have an unlimited license of tongue'. They learned that women hated having their hair cut off, but 'the bad effects of this is obviated, by the substitution of false hair, when the women leave the Factory. The washing yard is light and airy, and seemed to us the best place about the building; the hospital too, was clean and well arranged.'

What shocked the men were the dark cells for solitary confinement, 'most frightful dungeons, such as we read of as appertaining only to the Spanish Inquisition. At the end of a narrow yard, you enter a passage, about four feet wide, and into this passage the cells open.' When the outer door was closed the passage was utterly dark, as were the cells 'in which persons cannot well stand upright'. Each cell door was opened once in 24 hours, and the prisoner serving a sentence to the solitary cells on bread and water was then given one pound of bread together with a water tub. When asked how a prisoner in a dark cell could tell the difference between the water tub and a tub 'for nameless purposes', the men 'were informed, *they must feel for them!*' The jury was incensed by the circumstances in which they found a nineteen-year-old Englishwoman from the *Atwick*: 'On the door of the first cell being opened, the stench was so great, as to make the gentlemen immediately near it, retreat into the open air; in this, reclining on what was intended for a bed, at the further end, was a woman, one Margaret Fulford, who had been confined for five days and nights, for refusing to wash more than she was able.'

But it was the visit to the nursery yard which most outraged the editor of the *Colonial Times,* and it was to the experience of being in the nursery that the gentlemen of the jury returned when the official inquest into the death of Barbara Henning eventually got under way. Five witnesses were questioned by the jurors until almost midnight, and the wide-ranging nature of their inquiry is evident from both the newspaper accounts and the transcript forwarded by the Coroner to the Colonial Secretary. The jury, as the Coroner had feared, made it their business to report not just on the cause of Barbara Henning's death, but on how the prison was run, and in particular, on how the mothers and children were cared for. The 'Building', as the compound was often referred to in official correspondence, had opened as a female factory in the final months of 1828. Originally the thick stone perimeter walls enclosed a whisky distillery, which took advantage of the site's location alongside the Hobart Rivulet carrying water down from Mount Wellington. The distillery had been modified for use as a female factory by building internal walls to separate the space into smaller yards with specific functions.

Three of the yards were used to 'classify' women from the third or crime class where they were undergoing punishment, through second class where the diet was better, and up to the first class where they were waiting to be assigned. In the two corners nearest the entry gate were the yards for the nursery and the hospital. Offices were located directly inside the gate, and over the gate was the apartment where the superintendent and his wife the matron lived with their family in a few rooms. Matron Hutchinson, whose attitude was described by the editor of the *Colonial Times* as 'petulant' while she escorted the gentlemen of the jury on their tour of inspection, had given birth to her eighth child a few weeks before the Henning inquest. Three of her children had died at the Female Factory, but whether as she looked down from the window of her apartment into the nursery yard, she felt at times some sort of bond with the suffering mothers and their children, I do not know.

By 1834 a second large enclosure, known as Yard 2 or the washing yard, was added to the original distillery compound because the factory needed space to wash and dry the dirty clothes and bedding sent from recently arrived convict ships, the Orphan Schools, the General Hospital, the men's prison, and other colonial institutions. Carrying water from the rivulet, handling dirty blankets and abysmally stained clothes was back-breaking work, and often disgusting. No wonder magistrates often sentenced women specifically 'to the wash tub' when they wanted to ensure punishment. At the back of Yard 2, and separated by yet another wall, 'solitary working cells' rose in two-storey blocks. Unlike the 'dark cells' in the corner of Yard 1, which so appalled the gentlemen visitors, these working cells had an opening over the doors to let in light, and the incarcerated inmates, though hungry from their paltry rations of bread and water, at least had something to keep themselves occupied as they sat untwisting and picking old rope so that the fibres could be re-used in caulking ships. Encrusted with salt and tar, the ropes were savage on the hands, though less savage to the spirit than being curled up at the back of a stinking dark cell.

The nursery yard, too, was organised according to function. Breast-feeding mothers were housed with their infants in two 'suckling' wards, one above the other, 'small rooms, each about 28 feet by 12'. Barbara Henning and her baby went into the lower room on the ground floor when they arrived from the *Atwick* on 30 January. 'She was very well', testified the wardswoman, 'and the child was very well then'. The upstairs suckling ward was preferable because at least there were 'some vent holes in the ceiling', even though 'they were small, choked with cobwebs, and, in every respect, inadequate to the purposes of ventilation'. The ventilation, explained Assistant Superintendent Cato, 'is effected by tubes through the ceiling and roof'. In the lower room there were of course no openings at all to the roof.

Cato spoke bluntly of what happened when mothers and babies were locked up 'from six in the evening until six in the morning at this time in the year—I have been in the nursery room two or three hours after they have been locked up and I have found it very offensive both from the heat, and from the effluvia arising from their evacuations'. On the night of the inquest there were seventeen mothers and their babies in the lower suckling ward, sixteen mothers and sixteen babies in the upper, 'upwards of 70 human beings' in the two rooms.

Then there was the 'weaning ward', where the infants were introduced to a diet which would end their dependency on mother's breast. Weaning meant separation. Shifted to the 'big nursery', the weaned infants lost sight of their mothers, who left the nursery yard. The convict overseer told the jury that 25 weaned children with ten convict nurses were currently in the ward, but when she first took charge in February, 'there were forty one children, besides nurses there, in the big nursery—fourteen of those children were removed to the orphan school last week', including the Scottish children from the *Atwick*.

For more than seven weeks of summer, from late January until mid-March these boys and girls had been incarcerated within much less space than they shared on the ship. From broad daylight at 6 pm they were locked for twelve hours into the stifling 'big nursery' with its sickening smells and rampant infections, and during the day they had nothing more than a small paved area which Assistant Superintendent Cato made no attempt to defend as a playground. Little light fell on the flagstones except at noonday, he said, 'I think for about four months in the year the sun does not shine on the flags of the nursery yard at all, and during that period the flags are not dry—They are not fit for any (unless with thick shoes) to walk upon—I should think that these circumstances are injurious to the health of the inmates of that yard, especially the children.' The convict overseer told the jury that she had 'placed a rug' on the stones for the toddlers 'to roll on', but there was absolutely nothing for the older children to do.

Being sent to the Orphan School was their only escape, and it must have been with great relief if not real excitement that on 17 March the boys and girls clambered onto a cart to ride across town to their new home. But one child was left behind, more alone than ever, eleven-year-old Mary Henning. Her baby sister had been buried in St David's churchyard three days before, her mother Barbara was now in the hospital where she would die a week later. Barbara Henning had been arrested with her husband Joseph and charged with stealing silk and other goods in Manchester. While she was convicted and sentenced to seven years' transportation, he was acquitted and remained behind in their Liverpool home with two of their four children. Perhaps Joseph kept the boys and Barbara took the girls. Barbara's family background was unknown to the editor of the *Colonial Times*, who spelt her surname incorrectly when reporting the verdict on her death:

> *We find that the deceased, Barbara Hemming, died of diarrhoea and fever, produced by being confined in a crowded unwholesome place, without necessary air and exercise.*

The newspaper's lengthy account of the inquest focused on the tour of the Female Factory, and did not mention the death of Barbara's baby, although the wardswoman from the suckling nursery had told the jury, 'The child was poorly a good bit before her—that child is dead'. Nor did the newspaper take up the cause of poor little Mary, for whom funds might have been raised to send her home to her father. Instead, she languished in the Female Factory for more than a month after her mother's death, perhaps forgotten, perhaps herself ill. On 30 April, after three months' incarceration in the nursery yard, she was finally admitted to the Female Orphan School.

Eleven-year-old Mary Henning was the oldest of the four children transported with English mothers. Two, including her sister, were infants, and the other was a six-year-old boy. Her 'peers' came from the contingent of Scottish children, and hopefully as they shared their time at sea and in the Female Factory they became supportive friends. Two of the Scottish girls were about her age, the ten-year-olds Margaret Morris and Agnes Hall. Agnes, daughter of the 'incorrigible trafficker' Catherine Chisholm, had spent her childhood trampling the roads of Scotland and shivering in the prisons where her inept mother was periodically confined. She survived the voyage, but in the putrid conditions of the nursery she sickened and died, disappearing into the abstraction of numbers mentioned by the Coroner when he admitted to the Colonial Secretary in late March: 'Of *twenty* deaths which appear to have taken place in the factory within the last three months, *seven* only have been enquired into by me as Coroner, not having *officially* known of more than those 7 having occurred'. For the other children who had been with her since they left their Scottish homeland, there was nothing abstract about Agnes's death, and certainly not for her little brother Alexander who would have to face the Orphan School on his own. So much sickness, so much death, such fear. The Female Factory had been for these free children a terrifying introduction to the colony.

4

FINDING A BEARABLE PLACE

Catherine Chisholm, 'Highland Kate', was not in the Cascades Female Factory to comfort her dying daughter Agnes, or her traumatised seven-year-old son, Alexander. How did she hear the grim news of her daughter's death? And was she granted time off by her master in Melville Street to stand by Agnes's graveside as the words of Christian burial were intoned? So much of a convict's experience under sentence depended on how well she got along with the people to whom she was assigned. Her master was acting as a surrogate gaoler, of course, policing her behaviour and entitled to have her punished for tiny infringements—not crimes, just breaches of 'discipline'. Female convicts, unlike their male counterparts, usually worked in the house and slept there too. Men might find some relief from the constant surveillance of their masters if they worked outside during the day, and spent their nights in an outbuilding at some distance from the family, but the surveillance of female convicts was constant, intrusive, and personal. For women who had spent most of their lives wandering the Scottish countryside or scrounging a crust on the streets of Glasgow and Edinburgh, confinement within the walls of a colonial home must have been difficult, claustrophobic.

Small wonder Catherine Chisholm got into trouble three times in the year of her daughter's death. On 17 July her master, Dr. Fowler, charged her with 'insolence and neglect of duty'. A magistrate upheld the charge, and sentenced Catherine to the Female Factory for a week's solitary confinement on bread and water. Late in November she managed to get herself drunk, and yet for some reason was let off lightly with a reprimand. A fortnight later, she appeared before a less tolerant magistrate, charged with insolence and misconduct, and was sent to the crime class for four months' hard labour, the first and last fortnight to be spent at the wash tub. Catherine, like most of the Scottish convicts had no experience as a domestic servant, and the gestures of disciplined obedience expected by the middle class must have irritated her and many of her shipmates. But some of the *Atwick* convicts found themselves in situations which turned out to be bearable, places where they could negotiate the frictions of everyday life and serve their sentences with a minimum of trouble to themselves and their employers. These are the women with few if any charges on their conduct records.

One of the women with a clear record was a black convict from Barbados, known simply as 'Mary Jane', though when stating her offence, she insisted on speaking a different name, including a surname, 'Real name, Mary Ann Bradford', she said. Born into slavery, Mary Jane was well schooled in the lessons of submission. More surprising is the Highland Scot, Elizabeth Williamson, whose background does not suggest submissiveness, and who went to a family with a history of rapid turnover in its assigned female servants. Even though Elizabeth's record under sentence is a blank page, some insight into her experience of assignment is possible because her master was Thomas James Lempriere, an officer at the Port Arthur penal settlement to which male convicts were sent for further punishment if they re-offended in the colony. During the time Elizabeth was at Port Arthur, Lempriere was keeping a diary which has survived, he was also writing a book later published as *The Penal Settlements of Early Van Diemen's Land*. The Lemprieres were far more than gaolers for Elizabeth Williamson; they helped her put her life back together.

ELIZABETH WILLIAMSON: PICKING UP THE PIECES

Elizabeth was one of the last convicts from the *Atwick* still 'waiting to be withdrawn' from the Female Factory when T.J. Lempriere came into Hobart Town on business in mid-February 1838. Lempriere was a minor official with a grand title, Deputy Assistant Commissary General, glorified name for the storekeeper at Port Arthur. While 'trotting about the Town' to take care of various matters, he went out to the Female Factory to find a replacement for the assigned servant whose rudeness was recorded in his diary: 'Our woman dreadfully insolent to Charlotte [Lempriere's wife]—called her by the most terrible epithets—sent her to the cells'. The next day, a local magistrate 'tried Jane, and sentenced her to ten weeks in the crime class'. Back to the Female Factory went Jane, leaving the family with no female servant until Lempriere could get to town. But the trip was not entirely about business. An affable man, Lempriere went to a ball aboard an English ship, and 'Danced till broad daylight 6 in the morning'. Three days later, he was on the boat headed for home again, 'Brought a female servant. Her name is Elizabeth Williamson.'

Lempriere had little reason to hold out hope for this latest assigned convict, given a raft of bad experiences over the years. In 1825 and 1826 when he and his wife were a recently married couple living in Hobart Town, they went through at least six assigned female servants, most of whom ran off and were returned to the Female Factory—one charged with 'absconding from her master's service on the day of her being assigned to him and making her escape from the factory by getting over the wall the day before yesterday and remaining absent till apprehended this morning by Constable Musselwhite'. After the family left town to live on remote penal stations, running off was no longer a real option. Drink was a more likely escape route, as it was for Ann Forest, predecessor at Port Arthur to the insolent Jane. Lempriere wrote in his diary for July 1837: 'Ann went off and so did Mr Simpson's female servant; found they were at Captain Wilson's, went down and rapped at the window. She did not come home till past 1 am—quite drunk and insisted upon being confined. I sent her as she was to the cells.' Nothing on Elizabeth's convict record suggested she would behave any better than Ann or Jane. 'Very bad character', read her report from the Edinburgh gaol.

And unlike most of the *Atwick* women, Elizabeth Williamson was tried for a crime involving violence. The story emerging from her pre-cognition is that of a tough Highland woman who bashed a man in the face with a candlestick when he tried to leave her house on the edge of Edinburgh's New Town without paying for the use of a room where he had sex. Elizabeth gave her age as 22 when she was arrested; her co-accused, Donald McAllan, said he was 26. They may have left their native Caithness together, lured to the city by dreams of something better than rural poverty. Donald McAllan's 'native place' was recorded as the coastal village of 'Johnny Groats north of Scotland'. His family and Elizabeth's—about whom she said only that she was born in Caithness—may have been farmers left landless by the Highland Clearances. At the time of his arrest McAllan told the magistrate simply that he was unemployed, but when he arrived in Van Diemen's Land and was required to state a 'trade or occupation' before being assigned, he said 'clerk and schoolmaster', and 'schoolmaster' is the occupation written onto the register when he and Elizabeth were eventually granted permission to marry. The tawdry crime, the arrest, trial, conviction, and transportation over the seas may have sent the young schoolmaster spinning into shame, and yet it did not break his tie with Elizabeth. And with no evidence of a prior conviction in Scotland, with her blameless record in Van Diemen's Land, Elizabeth's crime looks in retrospect like an aberrant moment in her life, the violence a sign of her inexperience in the role of whorehouse madam.

Nevertheless, as a surgeon testified, the crime was violent and a man's face was bloodied. The victim identified himself as Peter McLean, a spirits dealer from Glasgow aged 39, who about eight o'clock on a winter's night had met a woman on Clyde Street and gone with her to the house where he found Elizabeth Williamson, Donald McAllan, and another Highland woman with whom he went into a room. Afterwards, he said, he gave her 2 shillings and was going down the passage to the outer door when Elizabeth stopped him and demanded money 'for the use of the room'. He gave her a shilling, but she wanted more. Though McAllan came into the passage and threatened him verbally, it was Elizabeth who 'took a candlestick which she held by the stalk, and struck [McLean] with it upon the upper part of the left side of his face, a severe blow which stunned him at the time, & which cut his nose, the eye, and the cheek & from which & his nose, he lost a large quantity of blood'. As he put his hand to his face, he felt her make 'a dart at his watch chain and broke the chain & tore out the watch from his fob', and then he saw her give the watch to McAllan. The watch was expensive, said McLean, a gold piece 'for which he paid forty five pounds and there were appended to it a gold watch chain for which he paid eight pounds—a gold seal for which he paid two pounds 10/ [shillings] and a silver guard chain for which he paid a pound'. Bruised and robbed, McLean got away from his assailants at last and rushed into the street, crying 'Police'. A watchman happened to be nearby, and before there was 'time for any of the prisoners escaping', two policemen and McLean confronted his assailants, and took Elizabeth straight to the Calton Watch-house. When a policeman tried to take the stolen watch from her, she dashed it upon the floor and broke the glass.

In the evidence gathered for the precognition, witnesses disagreed about what had happened. McAllan denied going into the passageway while Elizabeth was struggling with McLean, and did 'not think that Williamson had a candlestick in her hand, in the passage or in the rooms—there was no use for it as the house was lighted'. According to Elizabeth, she and McLean had a chat while the prostitute was undressing. He told her 'that he had been in another house before coming to hers where he had been ill used', and his watch-guard broken. He asked 'if she was a north country woman and upon her saying that she was he said then I can trust you with my watch, and he gave her the gold watch, gold chain, gold Seal, gold key and silver watch-guard . . . to keep for him till the morning'. After a couple of hours, said Elizabeth, he came out of the room intending to leave without paying, and 'began to try the doors in the passage in order to get out, but as he always went to the wrong door, [Elizabeth] laughed at him and he got angry and raised his umbrella as if to strike her when [Elizabeth] warded it off, and the whale bone points came in contact with his face and scratched and bled it a little'. At their trial, the jury believed neither Elizabeth Williamson nor Donald McAllan and 'by a great majority' found them each guilty of assault and robbery. Both were sentenced to seven years' transportation.

When Elizabeth left Hobart Town for Port Arthur with her new master, Donald McAllan was still at sea on the *Moffat*, and the two of them may not have known they were bound for the same colony and could meet again. One of the worst things about being a convict was losing control over where you lived and worked. It seems unlikely that any female servant would have chosen assignment to a family in Port Arthur. The place had a grim reputation, to which Lempriere contributed in the book he was writing by saying that it 'is, and ought to be, an abode of misery to those whose crimes have sequestered them from the society of their fellow creatures'. Ironically, it was also a place of enchanting beauty. Coming by water, Elizabeth could see for herself the settlement's dramatic setting on a mountainous isthmus with a coastline of 'high perpendicular rocks interrupted on the west side by three or four sandy beaches'.

On the summer's day of her arrival, she may have understood why her master wrote that the first appearance of the penal settlement 'is pleasing and impresses on the mind an idea of cleanliness and regularity. Built on the side of a hill, the houses appear in three rows, one over the other and as regularly built as the locality of the place and the skill of its first architects would admit. All the buildings except the Church and Guard House which are of stone, are of wood and white-washed outside.' The quarters for the commissariat officer, which was to be Elizabeth's home, had a front verandah, wrote Lempriere, 'covered with the Macquarie Harbour grape', picturesque in the summer season but not when the weather turned: 'This house, like the Commandant's, has been badly planned, in other respects it might be comfortable enough, but from being weatherboarded, it is very cold in winter'. Lempriere does not say how many rooms were in the house, but as a single-storey cottage conjoined to the quarters of the medical officer, it must have been a crowded space for eight children, six boys and two girls ranging in age from two to fourteen. Charlotte Lempriere was heavily pregnant, and undoubtedly needed help.

As the only female servant, Elizabeth would have been expected to work hard. In *The Complete Servant* by Samuel and Sarah Adams, published in 1825, the authors describe a female 'servant of all work' as someone born and bred to the task. Such servants 'are taught, from the earliest age, to assist in the management of the house, the care of the younger children, preparing the meals, making the beds, scouring, washing, and in every other branch of domestic business:—In short, no girl ought to undertake, or can be qualified, for such a situation, who has not been thus bred up'. A prisoner whose most recent job experience was running an unsuccessful brothel did not figure in this imagining of how a bourgeois household should be run, but then the settlement of Port Arthur was not a village in England. In order to thrive, everyone in the household needed to be adaptable and make the best of their colonial circumstances without dwelling unduly on models from 'Home'.

T.J. Lempriere knew more about adaptability than most. Born in 1796 to a British banker in Hamburg, Germany, he was six years old when he and his father were interned by the French, and 26 when he emigrated to Van Diemen's Land, where he tried unsuccessfully to be a merchant and banker before turning to the Convict Department for a more regular if poorly remunerated income. Ever-present anxieties about finances were balanced by daily pleasures easily indulged because his job was so undemanding. The diary he was keeping when Elizabeth joined the household creates the impression of a cultivated and convivial man who was enjoying his life. Except on ration days when he was busy, he had plenty of time to spend as he liked. He painted landscapes and portraits, and set up a museum to showcase his collecting as a naturalist. An avid apiarist, he wrote in his diary three days after returning home with Elizabeth: 'In the afternoon took the honey from a fine hive of bees without killing them'. Intelligent and energetic, an enthusiast for knowledge of the world around him, Lempriere had many counterparts across the British Empire, but few emerge as men who took as much pleasure from being with their wives and children as in recording the daily measurement of tides.

Thomas and Charlotte Lempriere had met in 1822 on the ship coming out to Van Diemen's Land, and had married the next year. Charlotte was seven years younger than her husband, and when Elizabeth Williamson came to work for her, she was in her mid-thirties and was nearing the end of her ninth pregnancy in fourteen years. A month after Elizabeth arrived, Lempriere wrote in his diary: 'The Club was to be held at our house today, but Charlotte's approaching accouchement prevented it'.

The next day he took his flock of children across the harbour by boat to a church service at Point Puer, the prison for boys: 'Thunder, lightning & rain on our return—very dark—very unpleasant to be in the boat'. The weather was gloomy, and Charlotte was wearied by pregnancy: 'Charlotte still keeps up, strange she thinks she is going on for her ten months'. In drizzling rain, Lempriere dug potatoes, 'rough whites, capital produce, 100 lbs gave me a ton and a half. The runaway boys paid the praties a visit, but did not take much'. At last on the 30th of March Lempriere could report that the waiting was over:

> *Yesterday morning Charlotte began to complain; Mrs Hoy [wife of the shipwright], who was to have attended her, was unfortunately confined to her bed (on dit) with miscarriage. Charlotte continued ill all day and at 40 minutes past 11 p.m. presented me with another daughter, the image of Popsey [the Lemprieres' youngest daughter]. The afterbirth, however, did not come away and we were in a state of alarm all night. Mrs Cart [wife of the superintendent] kindly stayed the whole time and so did Cart till ½ past 5 this morning. At ½ past 7 I laid down in Tom's bed and had an hour's sleep, which, together with shaving, washing etc. quite restored me. About 9 the doctor found it necessary to remove the placenta by force. Poor Charlotte was in dreadful agony and still continues (12 o'clock) in great pain. She is very weak but thank God there are hopes.*

Elizabeth Williamson must have been helping through this entire ordeal, though Lempriere makes no mention of his convict servant.

Unfortunately the entries in Lempriere's diary stop in September 1838, and we lose their daily insights, but the general sense of a loving family making the most of their strange circumstances is reinforced by the published memoir of Linus Miller, an American citizen transported to Van Diemen's Land after participating in a quixotic invasion of Upper Canada. Miller had been in the penal colony less than a year when he was sent to Port Arthur in 1840 because he had tried to escape from a probation station. For a few weeks he was assigned to the timber detail where men were forced to carry massive logs on their shoulders. Relieved of this excruciating punishment, he started work as a clerk for Lempriere, and before long was assigned as tutor to his children. In the account Miller published in New York as *Notes of an Exile to Van Dieman's* [sic] *Land* (1846), he remembers the Lemprieres with real affection as the sole bright spot in his convict misery:

> *In the capacity of tutor to the accomplished and interesting family of the commissariat officer of the settlement, (assistant commissary General Lempriere), I should have forgotten, had it been possible to do so, that I was an exile, and a stranger in a strange land. Mr. Lempriere was one of those rare specimens of humanity whom nature has endowed with a soul so much larger and more noble than we generally meet with, that it is in vain to attempt doing them justice, and I shall only say of the gentleman, that I shall ever venerate his name and cherish the liveliest recollections of his goodness. To his sovereign he was loyal to a fault; yet, had he been my own countryman, yea, father, I could not have expected better treatment than I received. After all my sufferings, to find such a home, and friends, in such a land, was indeed most fortunate.*

Elizabeth Williamson's blameless conduct record is testimony to her own sense of feeling 'at home' in her master's household—if not, like the well-educated Miller, one of the family—and the Lemprieres must have supported her application for a ticket of leave, which was granted on 29 June 1841, little more than three years after her arrival in the colony, making her one of the first half dozen women from the *Atwick* to receive this indulgence. Now she could work for wages, though this meant leaving the always cash-strapped Lemprieres.

Somehow she met up again with Donald McAllan, whose skills as 'clerk and schoolmaster' had brought him an assignment he also found congenial. Like Elizabeth, he survived his sentence without a single charge on his conduct record. McAllan was assigned to Philip Pitt, who had been in the colony since its beginning, arriving as the six-year-old son of a free settler who came with David Collins to choose the site for Hobart Town. The Pitt family had done well with land grants, and Philip

Pitt was living on the property known as 'Clifton Vale', Hunting Ground, when Donald McAllan was assigned to him. With ten children in the Pitt family and undoubtedly other children of farm workers on the property, McAllan may have run a small school as well as helping Pitt with his correspondence and record-keeping. Since Donald McAllan and Elizabeth Williamson were both literate, they may have been writing letters to each other, and McAllan may have persuaded Pitt to employ Elizabeth as a ticket-of-leave holder. Certainly Pitt must have supported Donald McAllan's application for the ticket of leave he received on 24 February 1842, and also his application three months later to marry Elizabeth. This 'indulgence' was granted in June 1842, and on 7 July they were married in the manse of Hobart Town's Presbyterian clergyman, according to the rites and ceremonies of the Church of Scotland.

If McAllan had been free, Elizabeth could have been assigned to him and they might have set up housekeeping on their own, but he was not, and they may have returned to Clifton Vale until they had both completed their sentences in 1844. After that, they vanish from the record until July 1853 when the death of Donald McAllan, aged 46, is entered into the burial register of St Andrew's Presbyterian Church, Hobart Town. Elizabeth erected a tombstone to commemorate the man to whom she had been united through very tough times and hopefully some happy ones, too, and she ensured that the inscription paid homage to his Scottish origins, recording for posterity that the deceased was the youngest son of Mr George McAllan, Farmer, County of Caithness, Scotland.

It may have been through a Presbyterian network that Elizabeth met her second husband, David Laing, to whom she was married less than ten months after McAllan's death. Laing was a free settler who came to the colony in the early 1840s as a 30-year-old with funds to invest in land. Through entries in the heavy and unwieldy registers of conveyance housed in the basement of the Lands Department office, I have tracked his investments over the next seventeen years, and watched his status rise from carrier to timber merchant and licensed victualler. When he married Elizabeth he was the licensee of one of Hobart Town's most prosperous pubs, the Tasmanian Steam Navigation Hotel, named for a shipping enterprise in which he was a shareholder. On 16 May 1854 Laing and Elizabeth were married in Laing's home in a ceremony conducted by the same Presbyterian clergyman who had married her to McAllan. Unfortunately this second marriage lasted only six years. On 27 April 1860 David Laing, aged 48, died at home of pulmonary congestion. Elizabeth observed the rituals befitting a man of status in his community. She placed a notice of his death in the *Mercury*, and erected (another) tombstone in the St Andrew's burial ground, commemorating David Laing, only son of David and Catherine Laing of Great Coram Street, Brunswick Square, London. Laing's Scottish surname and religion together with his parents' salubrious address raises once more the spectre of Scots on the move after the Clearances 'wiped out the middle ranks of Highland society', as historian Eric Richards says, and may explain why an only son left the British Isles for Van Diemen's Land.

And now his Highland wife was on the move again. Without Laing and without children from either of her marriages, no emotional ties bound Elizabeth Williamson to the colony—and she had the means to leave. Less than a fortnight after Laing's death, his widow was in court to prove and execute a will witnessed three years earlier in which he bequeathed 'all my lands and real Estate, and all my goods monies and personal estate unto my dear wife Elizabeth', who testified that the estate did not exceed in value the sum of £1,700. Ten days later she submitted the requisite inventory, and in the months to follow turned these considerable assets into cash. Seven months after Laing's death, an announcement appeared on the front page of the *Mercury*: Mrs Elizabeth Laing of the Tasmanian Steam Navigation Hotel 'desires to acquaint her Friends and the Public generally, that being about to leave the Colony for England' on the *Isles of the South*, she requests on behalf of the hotel's new licensee 'a continuance of that support so liberally bestowed on her'. And that is my last glimpse of Elizabeth Williamson, who arrived in Hobart Town as a disgraced young woman on a convict transport and sailed back to London 23 years later as a wealthy widow, aged 47. I cannot find her in the census records for Scotland, and wonder whether she may have thought it easier to start a new life somewhere in England. She might have bought another pub, might have married a third time. What I do know is that she was very unusual among the convict women in having the opportunity to return from her land of exile.

JEAN BOYD: FINDING A PLACE TO MAKE A LIFE

While Elizabeth Williamson was one of only two Scottish convicts from the *Atwick* who completed their sentences without a single charge on their conduct records, the few entries for several other women suggest that they too served their time under conditions they found bearable. Among the eighteen *Atwick* convicts with no more than one or two charges, half were Scottish, including Jean Boyd, who until her death in 1875 would live within a few kilometres of the property to which she was initially assigned. The story of her life before transportation predicted no such rootedness to place.

It was winter in the port city of Dundee when a lodger in Donald Fraser's house in Coutties Wynd came down with smallpox. Immediately, said a witness, 'Fraser and his wife and all the lodgers forsook the house leaving McRae alone in it'. Someone fetched Jean Boyd 'to wait upon' the suffering man, but who made the arrangements and whether the patient recovered, no witnesses say. When the inhabitants returned, another lodger complained that a pair of seal-skin trousers and a red handkerchief were missing from his belongings. Jean was accused of the theft after a pawnbroker recalled a woman fitting her description who brought in the clothes at ten o'clock one night, saying that they 'were the property of a man who was ill of fever and who was much in need of money'. Jean 'persevered in her denial of the theft' until her trial four months later, but the jury did not believe her protestations of innocence, and since she had twice been convicted of theft in the two months before this arrest, there may have been little joy in appealing to the circumstances under which a woman might take a pair of saleable trousers from lodgings as some sort of recompense for remaining there alone to nurse a man shunned by everyone else. Her reasons for being inside a house contaminated with smallpox were of no interest to the court.

Jean's life in Dundee does look dire. Why else risk nursing a man with smallpox? And why was she in Dundee anyway? In Van Diemen's Land, she gave her native place as Fisher Hall near Edinburgh, and when examined for her precognition told the magistrate that she was the wife of David Laird, 'formerly a painter in Edinburgh', who 'she believes is presently in Spain he having enlisted as a soldier to go there'. But something had brought her to Dundee (or at least pushed her out of Edinburgh) and for the past year the local police had considered her 'habite and repute a common thief'. Jean Boyd was 'about thirty years of age', and on the skids.

Once she reached Hobart Town, her life changed. The clerk who filled in the spaces under 'trade' on the appropriation list wrote 'dress and stay-maker' beside Jean's name, and the skills which were not earning her a living in Scotland opened a future in Van Diemen's Land. Jean was assigned specifically to *Mrs* Wettenhall. Usually convict women were assigned to the husband in the household even if they worked primarily for the wife, so perhaps Mary, wife of Robert Horatio Wettenhall, had made her own submission to the Assignment Board. The Wettenhalls were farming in a valley of the Carlton River near Sorell in the southeast corner of the island. They had three young children, and were expecting a fourth when Jean joined the household. If there was tension between servant and mistress, it was manageable on both sides until some incident at the end of the year sent Jean to the Cascades Female Factory for three weeks in solitary confinement as punishment for 'Gross insolence and disobedience of orders'. Unlike the Lemprieres, who wanted neither the 'dreadfully insolent' Jane nor the drunken Ann returned to Port Arthur after their stints in the Female Factory, the Wettenhalls brought Jean back to the farm.

No further charge appeared on Jean's record until 8 October the following year when she was reprimanded for 'disorderly conduct'. The fellow servant she would marry six days later faced the magistrate on the same charge, and yet he got off completely, 'discharged'. Had the couple begun celebrating a bit early? indulging their passion for each other? If their 'offence' was the same, why not the punishment? Did a self-confident John Clark escape even a reprimand because he knew how to bargain? knew that as a ticket-of-leave man he could find employment elsewhere, and the Wettenhalls needed him more than he needed them?

Clark had been in the colony for more than eight years and knew his way around the system. Sentenced to transportation for life after stealing a mare and cart, he had arrived on the *Argyle* in 1831, and was sent to the Midlands property of the magistrate and large landowner, John Leake. Although Leake is praised in the *Australian Dictionary of Biography* for his 'success in employing convicts by tempering careful management with encouragement and kindness', Clark chalked up a record of increasing friction with his master. During his first two years he was charged with no breaches of discipline, then given what looks like a stiff sentence for a first offence and relatively minor infringement: 25 lashes for being drunk and neglect of duty. From then on, Leake brought a charge against Clark each year. After almost seven years, some vaguely worded 'improper conduct' occurred of sufficient seriousness for Clark to be sentenced to six months' hard labour 'and then assigned as remote as possible' from Leake's district. The recalcitrant convict was sent to the Grass Tree Hill road gang, and never flogged again.

A few months after Jean Boyd was assigned to the Wettenhalls at Carlton River, Clark was sent there too. This was a new part of the colony for the convict ploughman from Suffolk, a hilly area where land was held by small farmers and not just the large pastoralists like John Leake who dominated the grassy plains of the Midlands. Here was a part of Van Diemen's Land where Clark might realistically imagine a future for himself once he was free. And this time he had a master *with* whom, as well as *for* whom, he could work. Robert Wettenhall, unlike Leake, knew precious little about farming. He had entered the British Navy as a boy, and served twenty years on twelve ships before peace with France meant losing his job. Floundering without a career, now married and a father, he chose the path of many other officers surplus to the needs of a peacetime army and navy, and in 1835 emigrated to Australia. No doubt he had heard on the grapevine that George Arthur, who was then the Lieutenant Governor of Van Diemen's Land, was offering land grants as an inducement, says historian Kirsty Reid, to bring 'a class of individuals with invaluable experience of authority and discipline'. Retired officers might make good masters—but to succeed as farmers they needed help. No wonder Lieutenant Wettenhall valued John Clark, described on the *Argyle*'s appropriation list as 'ploughman and farmer's laborer', born and bred on Suffolk farms and educated into colonial conditions during his years in the Midlands working for Leake. Clark, as would become apparent in the future, was canny when it came to matters of land—and he really knew horses.

Robert Wettenhall, the middle-aged novice—he was in his early forties when he took up farming— in return could offer some very real benefits by way of his position as a master within the assignment system. With Wettenhall's support, John Clark began to receive 'indulgences'. On 16 June 1839, the 'lifer' was granted a ticket of leave, and for the next five years or so, Wettenhall paid him wages. In August 1839, Clark applied to marry Jean Boyd, and in September the marriage was approved by the Convict Department. On 8 October that final confrontation between master and convict servants was resolved by a formal reprimand to Jean, and on 14 October the couple were married in the nearest town, Sorell. On the marriage register, both are said to be aged 31, but if their death certificates are correct, Jean was 34 and John 39. From the time of their marriage, nothing is recorded on their conduct records except 'indulgences', evidence of a systematic determination to cross the divide from convict servants to free settlers. In support of this effort and in exchange no doubt for hard-working reliable service, the Wettenhalls protected the Clarks when their two daughters were born while their mother was still under sentence: Jane in 1840 and Charlotte Copper in 1842.

Thanks to the discreet master and mistress, these babies were not subjected to the draconian measures mandated by the convict system. Their mother was not returned to the Female Factory as 'useless being pregnant', and the girls were kept away from the death-ridden convict nurseries, and from the emotional deprivation of the Orphan Schools. Perhaps because Jean Boyd was sewing rather than cleaning or cooking (the Wettenhalls had at least one other female assigned servant), she could manage her work while looking after her babies. Unlike poor Thomas Vowles, these children were not forcibly weaned, and if they were sick, their parents were there to care for them. How important this must have been for John as well as Jean—no one paid attention to the fathers of babies born in the Female Factory, gave them visiting rights or considered that they too felt love and grief. No wonder the Clarks, though required by law to register the births of their children, did not. By keeping their babies invisible, they kept them safe and free. None of this would have been possible without the help of the Wettenhalls, to whom they must have been deeply grateful, but sometime around 1844 when John had his conditional pardon and Jean was free by servitude, the family at last left the Carlton River property for a farm of their own nearby.

John Clark knew the surrounding countryside from his travels through the district on his master's business (female convicts, like other women on the farms, rarely had reason to go beyond the gate), and in the Bream Creek area he found a beautiful spot on Marion Bay where the whalers Charles and James Bayley were said to have built a house during the 1820s, climbing the hill behind to look out over the water for their prey. When the whales were hunted out and the whalers had moved on, the site became part of a 200-acre grant for one of the first small farms in the district. 'Ashley', fronted by the bay and a well-travelled road, was a smart choice for the horse stud John Clark soon built into a very success-ful business, and within a decade his shrewd eye for land as well as horses was reaping significant rewards. Cash from the horse stud financed exten-sive holdings at the narrow East Bay Neck, where the Forestier Peninsula joins the mainland. Beyond the Forestier, another narrow neck leads to the Tasman Peninsula, home to Port Arthur. East Bay Neck was the perfect place for the pub built by Clark on a site where today the Dun-alley Hotel still commands views over the only road south.

Sadly, as the Clarks prospered, the fortunes of the Wettenhalls declined. Not long after the Clarks went to 'Ashley', the Wettenhalls gave up their farm and took their family of young children to live the isolated life of a lighthouse-keeper on Swan Island, off the colony's northeast coast. They lasted a mere six months before Robert was injured in an attack by a ticket-of-leave man, and they left. After that, they moved from place to place in Van Diemen's Land until eventually they crossed

Bass Strait to spend their final years in the goldfields town of Stawell, northwest of Melbourne. Robert died in 1877, while the widowed Mary lived on another twenty years.

Meanwhile, the Clarks made money and climbed the ladder of class. By the mid-1850s they were living at 'Stroud', a property on the hill overlooking East Bay. Even in its ruined state today, the homestead evokes the achievements of early settlement. At the back is a two-storey brick building, part house, part barn, with the date 1839 carved over the doorway. By the time the Clarks came to 'Stroud', this basic and functional building had been converted into a kitchen and storage area, with sleeping quarters upstairs for servants who worked in the house and on the farm. In front now stood a new single-storeyed homestead looking across the valley, a timber house on a stone base, its rooms finished with lath-and-plaster ceilings, skirting boards, and wallpaper. The Clarks were never an ostentatious family, but they lived comfortably and 'Stroud' bore testimony to their propertied middle-class status. The hilltop house set within a garden must have been deeply satisfying to Jean. The young woman who barely survived her bleak circumstances in Dundee had become the matriarch of a respected family with servants of her own.

Jean Boyd and John Clark were a good match. Their material success as they aged depended on a mutual commitment to work and family. Clark, though obviously a smart businessman, was illiterate. Jean's ability to read and write was crucial as they dealt with the inevitable documentation of their expanding enterprises. In their family, too, the Clarks were fortunate. Though they might have wished for sons to sire a dynasty, they clearly loved their daughters and looked after them well. The girls survived all childhood illnesses, and in a district where as yet there were no schools, they were fortunate to have a mother who could either teach them herself or pay someone else. Though the Clarks may sometimes have feared that marriage would lure their girls away from this district where they were working so hard to establish themselves, they were fortunate on this front too. In 1856 sixteen-year-old Jane married 25-year-old George Scrimger in the 'Stroud' parlour. A husband was entering the Clark family, not taking its eldest daughter away.

The Clarks were giving a home to an orphan. George Scrimger was nine years old when his parents died in Hobart Town within four months of each other, and he might have found himself in the Orphan School if not for his 21-year-old uncle John McWilliams. John's own childhood had been seared by the traumatic fracturing caused by convict transportation. Born in Glasgow to Irish immigrants, he was two years old when his mother was transported to Van Diemen's Land in 1822. Over the next seven years, three of his sisters were transported as well, leaving a fourth at home to help their father look after the two youngest McWilliams children, both boys. Somehow, probably by working their passage on a ship, the boys came out to Australia, and were in Hobart Town before 1833 when their mother died. John was now fourteen, old enough to earn his living and yet young enough to appreciate the caring support of his married sisters, including George Scrimger's mother Margaret. Seven years later when Margaret died of consumption, John repaid her kindness by assuming the role of surrogate father to her orphaned son, and for the rest of their lives, the uncle and nephew stayed connected. John McWilliams was a witness at George Scrimger's marriage to Jane Clark, and would continue to work for the Clarks and live in their extended family until his death, when he was buried in their family vault in the Dunalley cemetery. After transportation tore families apart, some sort of healing occasionally occurred in Van Diemen's Land, thanks to the generous spirit of convict emancipists like the Clarks.

George Scrimger met Jane Clark while working on a trading ketch owned by her father, who may have encouraged the match because he was eager for grandchildren. The dynastic ambitions evident in John Clark's accumulation of land cried out for another generation. His own marriage and fatherhood had been delayed by convict transportation, and if his daughter started having children when she was half the age her mother had been, why, so much the better. A year after the wedding, John Clark got a grandson, George Clark Scrimger. The baby, baptised in the Sorell church where his Clark grandparents had married, was identified as son of a master mariner, and for several years George Scrimger continued to work on his father-in-law's ketch. This was never going to make him rich, or even solidly middle-class, but John Clark would look after the family. In 1863 Clark made a will, dividing his real estate equally between his two daughters; in a codicil he advanced to Jane Clark Scrimger 32 acres of land, including the Dunalley Hotel. A few months later when the fourth Scrimger child (and third daughter) was born, her father was identified as a publican.

John Clark was achieving a vision of family success. By gifting the land and hotel to the Scrimgers, he kept them nearby, and from the verandah of 'Stroud', the Clarks could look proudly across the valley towards their grandchildren. Meanwhile, inside the house, their younger daughter, known as 'Cooper', lived a more constricted life. However lively she may have been as a young girl, she had grown into a spinster approaching 30 by the time her father died in 1870. A story passed down through generations of the family suggests that Cooper's desires were thwarted by her father's vision. Somewhere she met an Irishman named John J. Murphy, most likely at races held on the still visible track Clark built in the valley below the homestead. Cooper wanted to marry him. No, said her father, no Irish Catholics in this family. She might have run away with her lover, but did not. Though she must have loved her father, because she named her first child John Clark Murphy, she defied him nevertheless, and within two years of his death, she married Murphy in the 'Stroud' parlour according to the rites and ceremonies of the Roman Catholic Church.

Had Jean Boyd shared her husband's prejudice? Did she finally cave in when she realised Cooper's heart was set on Murphy, and she would marry no one else? Or had she for years quietly counselled patience, persuading her daughter that John might come round in the end? Hopefully, Jean got along with her newest son-in-law and, during her final five years after John's death, could enjoy Cooper's newfound happiness. John Clark's will ensured that Jean could continue to live at 'Stroud' without feeling dependent on Cooper, whose half of the inheritance included the homestead together with several thousand acres of valuable land. Jean still owned all the furniture and other household goods, and her annuity of £150 a year would pay for the comforts of her daily life.

Jean Boyd, like Elizabeth Williamson, prospered in Van Diemen's Land. Transportation brought opportunities as well as punishment, and these Scottish women knew how to make the best of the cards fortune dealt. Neither left any personal letters or diaries to tell me how they felt, but I see hints of Jean's inner life in the photograph her descendant George Scrimger Whitehouse showed me, the faded image on a *carte de visite*. One day around 1865, when Jean was about 60 and John 65, they took their eight-year-old grandson George Clark Scrimger to a photographer's studio in Hobart Town. John had photographs taken of himself alone and with his grandson. He looks like a cheerful old gentleman well satisfied with his life. Jean in her photograph seems more inward-looking and careworn, a reminder that however successful a life may appear from the outside, the pains of the past never entirely vanish. The externally successful life narratives of Jean Boyd and Elizabeth Williamson should not blind us to the background stories of their fractured lives.

5

'THESE REBELLIOUS HUSSIES'

Elizabeth Williamson and Jean Boyd were exceptional. Few Scottish convicts found their assignments so bearable, and many resisted in the ways always open to servants. They did slovenly work or no work at all, talked back to the women who gave them orders, were unreliable with the children, and generally drove their mistresses to distraction. Before long they were back in a female factory for punishment in the crime class, where they could exchange complaints with others of like mind. Sometimes they banded together, as they did in a bread riot at the Cascades Factory on 4 May 1839, an event brought to public attention by the *Colonial Times* when an unnamed 'Correspondent' told of prisoners in 'open rebellion' because they were given bread made from peas and barley instead of wheat.

Two hundred women created a terrible racket, broke the spinning wheels, 'armed themselves with the iron spindles' and large stones, and threatened to burn the building. Fire engines raced out from town, the chief constable entered the gates with his men, broke down the barricades, 'the rebellion was quelled,—and the building restored to Her Majesty'. The rebels, wrote 'Correspondent', were 'inspired, we presume, by the success of the *Canadian* Patriots', a sneering allusion to the botched effort of men like Elizabeth Williamson's fellow assigned servant Linus Miller, who had recently tried to 'liberate' Upper Canada from the 'tyranny' of British rule. Some of the 'Patriots' had been executed, and others transported to Van Diemen's Land—but what would happen to the rebels at the Female Factory? 'Perhaps a week at the wash-tub!' commented the 'Correspondent'. The editor, adding his comment in brackets, spluttered:

[We have frequently censured the inefficacy of the punishment, awarded to female prisoners at the Factory: what punishment will be sufficient for these rebellious hussies, seeing, that, by their misconduct, many families are inconvenienced, for the want of servants?—Ed.]

One of the 'rebellious hussies' was a Scot from the *Atwick*, Ann Martin, accused of 'Insubordination on the 4th Instant in forcibly violently & in a turbulent manner resisting Mr Hutchinson & with openly refusing to obey his lawful commands'. Her punishment was four days in the solitary cells on bread and water, a day less than the sentence she had received in January for 'making use of obscene language & representing herself to be free'. By the time of the riot, Ann had been in the colony a little more than fifteen months and had been brought before the magistrates on ten charges. Unlike Elizabeth Williamson and Jean Boyd, she showed no signs of settling into her assigned role. A tough young woman from the streets of Edinburgh, the twenty-year-old had been looking after herself and her eleven-year-old sister when they were both arrested in March 1837.

A man had complained to the police of being robbed and assaulted in the rooms where Ann Martin ran a small brothel in Halkerston's Wynd, off the High Street running up to Edinburgh Castle, where the soldier clients were stationed. Two other *Atwick* convicts lived there as well, Margaret McNiven and the house bully, Elizabeth Kelly. Their victim was a forester who had come into the house with a private from the 42nd Regiment of Foot. The men stayed for some time, and then left together, but the forester turned back when he found he had left his handkerchief. Going into the house on his own was a bad mistake. 'Kill the buggar', one of the women yelled, while others held him and somebody thrust her hand into his trousers, tearing out the pocket into which he had sewn four £5 notes and two £1 notes of the Commercial Bank. After Ann Martin, her sister, and her housemates were arrested, a neighbour from the tenement volunteered to testify that 'the practice of the prisoners is to bring people in by their front door, to lock that door, & after robbing them to turn them out at the back door into an adjoining close'.

Ann was not the sort of woman changed by transportation into a reliable servant. The colonists complained incessantly about convicts like her. A few months before the bread riot, the *Colonial Times* ran an article entitled 'Female Servants', by which they meant female assigned convicts:

> *The whole plan of assignment, as regards female servants, is bad and mis-chievous . . . you have no means of choice or selection.—You obtain an order,—and to the Factory you go,—where Mrs Hutchinson, (the Super-intendent himself being very rarely visible) summons some six or seven women, and leaves you to take your choice. Your choice of what? Why, you have no previous information, no guide whatever, but the Matron's dictum. 'Here they are, Sir; take which you please.'*

And of course the *Colonial Times* had a point: who would knowingly take Ann Martin into their home? Her Edinburgh background showed initiative channelled into criminal activity. In Van Diemen's Land her employment record, which eventually ran to 22 charges and required a second page in a supplementary volume, was a history of that same initiative channelled into friction with her employers. It was Mary Hutchinson's job as matron to get women like Ann out of the Female Factory and into the workforce. Warning a prospective employer about her record did not serve the interests of the system.

And if Ann were asked in the Female Factory line-up to say a few words about herself, what story would she tell the free settler? What stories did she tell her fellow prisoners in the crime class? On the long voyage to Van Diemen's Land, did she ever chat with the black convict Mary Jane about life as a slave? George Arthur, the lieutenant governor who came to the penal colony of Van Diemen's Land from a posting in the Caribbean, pondered similarities. 'To the mass of prisoners', he wrote, 'transportation is perfect slavery, and a most severe punishment'. This sense of slavery, he believed, was the key to reform. Coerced labour should awaken shame and spur the convicts to mend their ways. But Mary Jane might have taught Ann Martin a completely different lesson, telling stories of how slave women confined within the houses of Caribbean planters devised tactics to strike back, often through a daily subversion of work, but sometimes through a dramatic gesture as when Mary Jane threw down her master's child and struck it with a piece of wood. The terrain of slavery could serve as the breeding ground for guerrilla warfare.

Most convict women had no such plans for prolonged resistance, and did not think in political terms. Like Ann Martin, they were charged and punished just because they were defying conditions on the day. Their breaches of discipline were easily accommodated as minor irritants within the convict system. There were, however, a few genuinely 'rebellious hussies' who took on the system and pushed its limits. One was the ironically named Mary Sheriff, who was to become the most notorious convict from the *Atwick*.

MARY SHERIFF JOINS THE FLASH MOB

Mary Sheriff was a child of Edinburgh's old town, born in one of the densely populated high-rise tenements surrounding the Grassmarket, the cobbled rectangle where crowds gathered for the market below Edinburgh Castle. It was an exciting, if often rough and dangerous, place of childhood. Mary had lived here all her life, and here she learned the ways of a thief. She was first caught and convicted when she was about thirteen. Four years and three convictions later, she was arrested for the theft which would send her to the High Court of Justiciary and off to Van Diemen's Land.

This time she had stolen a silk handkerchief from a three-year-old girl named Isabella, whose father was a printer. Isabella, who lived mostly with her grandmother, went out to play one afternoon about four o'clock, wearing the handkerchief around her neck. Ten minutes later, when her grandmother called her back inside, the handkerchief was gone, and the little girl said a lassie had taken it from her on the stair. Furious, the grandmother marched off to complain to the police. Not long afterwards, Mary Sheriff offered the handkerchief to a pawnbroker, who thought something was suspicious. The police came, took Mary to the watch-house, and went to get the grandmother and Isabella. As soon as the little girl saw Mary, she said, 'Grannie, that's the lassie, tell her to give me my handkerchief'. At the hearing for Mary's precognition, the magistrate tried to coax Isabella into telling what happened, but she could not 'be got to speak except by her Grandmother putting the questions but she states to her that it was the prisoner who took the handkerchief'. With testimony from the grandmother and the pawnbroker, together with police evidence that she was 'habite and repute a thief', seventeen-year-old Mary was sentenced to seven years' transportation.

Nothing is said in the records about Mary's family or about what sort of work she may have done, if any. Her trade on the description list is given as nursemaid, though a settler choosing her for that work might have been startled to learn that she had stolen a handkerchief from the neck of a small child. Nothing about her appearance was striking. She was 5 foot 1 inch, the average height for convict women, with a sallow complexion, light brown hair and grey eyes. Lists of physical traits tell nothing about personality, of course, or about the way Mary moved through her world. The four dots noted as tattooed on her left arm may hint at membership of some criminal fraternity, a network of those at odds with all authority. Certainly her conduct record in Van Diemen's Land suggests a confrontational young woman.

A month after disembarking from the *Atwick*, Mary stood before the Principal Superintendent of Convicts charged with 'neglect of duty'. First-time offenders were often reprimanded rather than punished, but something about Mary's attitude must have irritated Josiah Spode because he came down hard on her, with a month's sentence at the wash tub. A few days into her next assignment, she went off for the night and was sentenced again to a month at the wash tub. And then, after less than six months in the colony, Mary was charged with stealing a £5 note from Isabella Grahame, whose family had been among the retinue sailing to the colony with Lieutenant Governor Franklin. The *Colonial Times* commented on the crime's 'peculiar circumstances', whatever that might mean, and Mary did not deny the theft, though she was outraged to be cheated by the publican's wife to whom she gave the £5 note for safe-keeping and who returned a mere £1 note the next morning, insisting 'it was the same she had given her'. After this escapade, Mary was sent to the Cascades Female Factory for an entire year, and her original sentence to seven years' transportation was extended by three years.

Few convicts were shut up in a female factory for stretches as long as a year, and yet by the time of the bread riot in May 1839, Mary had spent only three of her fifteen months in Van Diemen's Land outside the prison walls. Her life in the colony had been and would continue to be essentially that of a gaoled prisoner rather than an assigned servant. And she was not alone in defying the system's program for 'reform'. In the female factories she came to know other women who were creating their own subculture. Known to the public as 'the Flash Mob', their 'flash' dress was a fashion statement marking them out as special. Amidst the women of the crime class, condemned to drab prison dress, the Flash Mob sported brightly coloured silk handkerchiefs and embroidered caps, wore rings in their ears and on their hands, and as the archaeologist Eleanor Casella has discovered in her dig at the Ross Female Factory, they carried on a thriving trade in fancy buttons. But they were more than dandies. They were power brokers and sexual predators, and their leader was Ellen Scott.

During the bread riot of May 1839, the charismatic rebel was among the ringleaders labelled 'Amazonian chieftains' by *Murray's Review*. Afterwards, while others were convicted of insubordination, Ellen Scott was charged with 'Violently assaulting Mr Hutchinson with intent to kill or do him some bodily harm'. Her punishment was two years' hard labour not in the Female Factory but in 'her Majesty's Gaol', tacit admission that the assignment system could not accommodate her unremitting resistance. The 48 charges entered onto her record between 1830 and 1843 are evidence that she had no intention of being anyone's domestic servant. Her world lay inside the Female Factory walls where she had friends and wielded power. The gaol sentence removing her from this world was the only real punishment the authorities could inflict, but of course they could not keep her locked up forever, so when that sentence was up they sent her to the northern side of the island, hoping she would be powerless if kept away from her friends inside the Cascades Female Factory. Instead, she simply extended the territory of the Flash Mob. After a brief stay in the home of yet another unsuspecting settler, Ellen got drunk, was sentenced to a month at the wash tub, and then introduced to the Launceston Female Factory, where she met up with many of her old connections who had also been sent there to get them out of Hobart Town. One was Mary Sheriff.

Mary had been banished to the island's 'interior' more than a year earlier, making her way north after a series of short stays with employers who always found her useless, or worse. Her punishments now sent her into the colony's second-largest settlement, Launceston, where a factory had opened in 1834, purpose-built to an octagonal design. Like the Cascades Female Factory, it included a prison, hiring depot, hospital, and nursery. The northern factory was smaller. Its superintendent reported a population of 135 women and twenty children when Ellen Scott made her first entrance in July 1841 (at the same time there were 381 women at the Cascades Factory, though only a few newborn infants because the nursery had been moved outside the prison compound). Mary Sheriff was in the crime class to greet her mentor because her third punishment in the Launceston Factory, this time seven months' hard labour for insolence, had been extended by two months in January after she broke seven panes of glass, probably in the superintendent's apartment at the centre of the panopticon-shaped building. Until this window-breaking, none of the charges against Mary had involved violence, and even in her later convict career, she was never charged by an employer with violence. Her attacks were directed against those who held her prisoner, not against their householder surrogates.

For the next two years, Mary Sheriff, Ellen Scott, and their companions created no end of trouble for the Launceston authorities. Mary was about 21 and had been in the colony three years when she began to terrorise the Launceston Female Factory, but Ellen was an 'old hand', a decade older and a veteran of eleven years in Van Diemen's Land. She had arrived on the *Eliza* in 1830, an eighteen-year-old Irish girl sentenced at the Old Bailey to transportation for life after stealing a watch and chain from a tailor she accosted on the street. Mary Sheriff and Ellen Scott were strutting the Female Factory stage at a time when the assignment system itself had come under public scrutiny both in England and locally. The colony was struggling to cope with radically increased numbers of convicts after transportation to New South Wales stopped in 1840. Colonial complaints about the quality of assigned servants were echoed in London by queries about the moral examples set by the colonists.

At home and abroad everyone was panicking about homosexuality—'unnatural' or 'improper' being the code words in their anxiety-ridden discourse. In 1841 what began as an inquiry into whether the Cascades Female Factory needed a new hospital ballooned into a wide-ranging investigation of women throughout the convict system. Although the findings of the board of inquiry set up by Lieutenant Governor Franklin were never published, the 438-page report with appendices survives, a rich source of testimony from a range of voices, including those of five convict women, three from Launceston and two from Hobart Town. The women were promised conditional pardons in exchange for telling their tales of convict life, and in particular, for stories about the 'unnatural practices' of which Mary Sheriff had already been accused. Her sentence after the window-breaking included a recommendation that she 'be kept in a cell apart from the other women in consequence of strong suspicion of improper conduct with a woman from the Crime Class'.

Oral testimony from the three Launceston witnesses was taken early in 1842. Mary Kirk, an older woman convicted of larceny after arriving in the colony as a free settler with two grown-up daughters, was the most cautious of the story-tellers and spoke in general terms:

> *Unnatural conduct is common among them and has increased much since I came in. I am a grandmother and never in my life heard of such practices as are carried on in the building. There are many well disposed women who come in but after remaining some time they generally become as bad as the worst. A well disposed woman cannot avoid being corrupted as she cannot avoid associating with the others, the flash characters corrupt the others to follow their example.*

Bridget Magahan, who had spent fifteen of her 35 years in Van Diemen's Land, and was serving a second seven-year sentence to transportation for receiving bottles stolen from the government store, added details:

> *During the day time the women generally employ themselves very badly in*
> *low horrible discourse, swearing, telling obscene stories, dancing singing etc.*
> *I have heard it generally talked of that many of the women are in the*
> *habit of indulging in improper practices. I could pick out 8 that I have no*
> *doubt of, but there are others perhaps about ~~15 or 16~~ 30 altogether. I have*
> *been prevented from sleeping at night by some of them, talking improper*
> *discourse, laughing & evidently acting indecently.*

The youngest witness, Eliza Churchill, an Englishwoman in her early twenties who had been in the colony less than two years, was the least experienced and least self-protective of the three witnesses, and named names (which she would later regret):

> *There are many women who will not stay out of the factory when others*
> *with whom they carry on an unnatural connexion are in the building. For*
> *instance Sarah Davis and Marian [Shirley], Catherine Owens & Ellen*
> *Scott, Margaret Carr & Rosanne Holcroft, Mary Ann Simpson &*
> *Eliza Roberts, Mary Sheriff & Sarah Brown, Ann Collins & Catherine*
> *Lowrie. These women are quite jealous of each other. The other women are*
> *afraid to interfere although they dislike such practices, they are never carried*
> *on openly but at night, they are never associated with by the other women,*
> *they generally sit together on one side of the yard.*

They were bullies, said Eliza, and she recalled once when 'a woman named Mary Hennassy had a blanket thrown over her & six shillings taken from her by Mary Sheriff & Betsy Forster'.

Eliza Churchill pictured a closed community controlled not by the gaolers but by thuggish pairings of homosexual women, her account feeding prurient fantasies of those who thought the 'majority of female assigned servants' were nothing more than 'annoying and untractable

[sic] animals', as the *Colonial Times* said in one of its fulminating articles about the Flash Mob. 'If any attempt were made', said Eliza 'to separate the women whose names I have mentioned & others of similar habits a riot would be got up immediately, I heard Ellen Scott say so last night if Catherine Owens were sent to Hobarton'. And indeed a riot was 'got up' in October that same year, with Catherine Owens at its centre.

The *Cornwall Chronicle* reported a 'rumpus' created when 'some refractory women urged on several others to an act of open mutiny'. As usual in the case of Female Factory riots, the newspaper had few details to offer its readers, but an internal account of the incident survives in a document submitted to the board of inquiry by the Assistant Superintendent of Convicts, responsible for convict institutions in the colony's north. The problem, he wrote, began when Catherine Owens, 'an extremely bad character, and one who has always ranked as a leader upon all occasions of misconduct', was locked into a solitary cell to serve the second of two fourteen-day periods of solitary confinement included in a two-month sentence for absconding. In the morning she said she was unwell, and asked to be let out. A doctor came, found nothing wrong, and the door was locked again. In the afternoon, the matron came to check on Catherine, and was seized as soon as she unlocked the cell. Catherine was liberated, and the 85 women in the crime class 'bid defiance to the authorities in the factory, one and all stating they would not allow her to serve the remainder of her sentence in the Cells'.

The police were summoned, but 'were beaten off by the women who had armed themselves with the spindle and leg, from the spinning wheels, bricks taken from the floors and walls of the Building, Knives Forks &c and also Quart Bottles in which some of them had received Medicine'. The police retreated, leaving the inmates to spend a night without food or water. At daybreak, the women began 'breaking the Furniture and windows and attempting to burn the Building'. 'The place,' reported the *Launceston Advertiser*, 'was put under siege, but the insurgents were proof against the pangs of hunger, and after twenty-four hours had elapsed, appeared as resolute and determined as ever'. The constables who tried to enter the crime class were 'quickly compelled to retreat'. The police then decided to enlist the help of convict men held in the prisoners' barracks. Some thirty prisoners and an equal number of constables, armed with sledgehammers and crowbars, 'made a breach through the wall, and came to close quarters with their Amazonian captives. The women fought like demons—and who can doubt it? But they were finally overcome by superior strength, and compelled to capitulate.' Those identified as the ringleaders of the insurrection were removed to the Launceston Gaol, where they were kept in irons until they could be sent by the *Lady Franklin* to Hobart Town.

Mary Sheriff initially benefited from the liberation of Catherine Owens. She was serving a tougher sentence, three months' hard labour, with the first and third months in solitary confinement. A week after Catherine began her fourteen-day ordeal, Mary would have gone into one of the utterly dark confining spaces for a month if not for the ruckus caused by the riot. As usual, she had spent most of 1842 incarcerated, going out to only two assignments from which she was quickly returned for being absent without leave. The difference between her prison life in 1841 and 1842 was that she now was spending long stretches in solitary confinement because she had become more violent. With few solitary cells available in Launceston's Female Factory, she was sometimes punished in the local gaol, where in July she and two companions were charged with 'Misconduct in destroying a Table and two mess kits and making a violent disturbance in the Gaol'. The next month she and another woman were charged with 'Gross insubordination and destroying several articles in the Gaol'. She was then returned to the Female Factory, where the confusion after the riot would eventually settle down, and a solitary cell would become available for her second month of claustrophobic misery. It was a terrible prospect.

The one person who could help her was the doctor. On 26 October when Dr George Maddox came in for his visiting hours, she went to the surgery, said she was ill, and asked him to intercede on her behalf. No, he said, you'll have to go into solitary confinement and if your health suffers, then I will speak to the assistant superintendent. She went away, but came back ten minutes later, begging for his help. No. Mary must have been desperate, frantic at the idea of being closed into the pitch black yet again. She lashed out as she had been doing, not with any long-term plan in mind, but simply driven by fury. When Dr Maddox left the surgery, she and two other women jumped him with a knife. They stabbed him several times, cutting down to the bone within a quarter inch of his right eye. At their trial in the Launceston Supreme Court on 10 January 1843 Mary and the other two were sentenced to death, their sentences commuted to transportation for life.

But then what? The sentence could not mean transportation 'beyond Seas', the exile imposed at her trial in Edinburgh, because she was already 'beyond'. If she were a man, she would have been shipped off to a secondary penal station like Port Arthur, but there was nowhere comparable for women. She had been in both female factories and created nothing but trouble. Now that her name had been published in the newspaper's account of the Supreme Court case, no settler was going to accept an assigned servant who had sharpened a dinner knife into a weapon. One can imagine the sense of frustration in the offices of the Convict Department. Women like Mary Sheriff, Ellen Scott, and Catherine Owens seemed to taunt the men who knew they could not flog females or chain them together in road gangs or exhaust them on treadmills.

The only thing the Principal Superintendent of Convicts could think of was to break up the alliances by separating the women, and so it was that six months after Mary's trial, Josiah Spode recommended to the Colonial Secretary that Ellen Scott 'and several of her refractory associates' who belong to 'a desperate set now in the Factory' be removed 'to one or more of the Gaols in the Interior'. He suggested 'Longford Gaol, where I understand there are Separate Cells for their habitation without causing inconveniences'. As if any prison in the colony might hold these women without 'inconveniences'! The Lieutenant Governor agreed to the proposal, but Longford Gaol was under the control of the sheriff, who blandly (though strategically) raised objections about this and that, the rooms were too small, the gaol was not organised to look after females, more money would be needed for fuel and staff—all matters of expense. As usual, money talked, the sheriff won, and in October the Colonial

Secretary wrote to Spode saying that the Lieutenant Governor—who since August had been Sir John Eardley-Wilmot—'has decided upon abandoning the plan'.

In spite of this rebuff, Principal Superintendent Spode must have found somewhere to keep Mary in a cell apart from other prisoners because there are no charges on her record for more than three years. She may have been sent back to the Cascades Female Factory in 1845 when the two-storey blocks of 'separate apartments' were opened in Yard 3. Certainly she was in Hobart Town in 1846 when she was again sent out to work, absconded of course, and returned to the Factory for yet another six months' punishment. In 1848 a new female factory opened in the Midlands town of Ross, almost halfway between Hobart Town and Launceston, and Mary was one of its early inmates. The superintendent at Ross, a strange doctor named William John Irvine, was fascinated by female homosexuality, and given Mary's reputation he may have welcomed her to Ross as a subject for his 'scientific' study. Mary might have been very annoyed to discover that she served Dr Irvine well, though her stay at Ross was brief. On 25 May 1848 he charged her with 'misconduct in occupying the same bed' as another prisoner, and after six days of the hated solitary confinement, he sent her back down to the Cascades Female Factory. No longer his day-to-day problem, she could be relegated to evidence for his theory about the 'pseudo-male'. In a document entitled 'Report on Unnatural Practices at Ross', he wrote:

> *we have had several women of the species of the pseudo male up here—most of whom were sent away, some of these women I have ascertained by enquiries, were notorious (amongst men of their own rank) when out of the factory & despised, detested, & almost hooted at. I have no doubt you may remember one of the women belonging to the species, concerning which I have been writing, her name was 'Mary Sheriff' per 'Atwick', & she was sent to Hobarton, to be placed in separate treatment.*

In June 1851, more than thirteen years after she arrived in the colony to serve a seven-year sentence, Mary Sheriff was granted a ticket of leave and at last began to live outside the prison walls. Two months later she was given permission to marry, and on 6 October 1851 she was married in Trinity Church, Hobart Town, to George Ford, seaman. Mary was now in her early thirties. If she and George had children, they did not register them with the authorities, but then Mary was unlikely to comply with such personally intrusive regulations. Three years later, on 12 June 1854, Mary Sheriff's conditional pardon was approved, and she disappeared from the public records. Did she sail off with her seafaring husband? to New Zealand perhaps? Somewhere far away from her angry and unhappy years in Van Diemen's Land.

6

TAKING THE CHILDREN AWAY

While their mothers, unruly or compliant, were learning how the assignment system differed from the imprisonment they had known in Scotland, the children of the *Atwick* were facing adjustments of their own. They were not prisoners, and yet their freedom had been compromised and the most intimate contours of their lives forever changed in courtrooms where their mothers were found guilty. Who decided which children would share their mother's sentence to transportation? On what basis were decisions made? The lack of evidence is frustrating. In the booklet of comprehensive instructions addressed by the Admiralty to the ship's master and its surgeon superintendent, no guidelines cover the transportation of prisoners' children. Nothing is said about deciding which children will be fed and clothed at public expense on a long voyage, and then looked after and educated in the colony.

Sometimes children were permitted on board as an act of personal charity. Elizabeth Fry's daughters remembered that after spending all day on a convict ship anchored in the Thames, their benevolent mother and her friends in the Ladies' British Society would rush off to the Admiralty office in Whitehall to plead the cause of children about to be left behind. The passionate philanthropists would try to persuade men behind desks 'that the necessary letters should be dispatched without the loss of a post, ordering the restoration of these poor nurslings to their mothers, before the ship should sail'. Sometimes local charities may have paid for children to be sent to the Thames—it would be much cheaper than maintaining parentless children for years in the workhouse. Nevertheless, most children of *Atwick* mothers were in fact left behind. Of the 83 prisoners' children noted in the convict conduct records, a mere eighteen sailed. Only four of the 32 children of English convicts came aboard. The Scottish mothers fared better, bringing fourteen of their 51 children. This means that at least 65 children were left behind, suffering the traumatic loss of a parent they were unlikely ever to see again, a loss mimicking death and often skewed by the particular cruelty of not knowing what had happened to their illiterate mothers, not knowing whether they were alive or dead. At least the children who sailed would end up in the same part of the world as their mothers, even though they might be separated for years.

On the September day when the *Atwick* made its way down the Thames, that separation was in the future. For the present, the children were being introduced to daily life governed by the rules and regulations of prison discipline, and many must have hated the restrictions during the months they spent locked from sunset to sunrise in the prison below decks housing 150 women of variable character and hygiene. How children passed their days on the voyage is purely a matter for conjecture since Surgeon Superintendent Leonard says nothing in his journal about their routine. Was there a school for them as well as for the women who could not read or write? If so, who taught them, and using what books?

Though none of the children met with any serious accident or suffered an illness important enough to be noted in Dr Leonard's casebook, most were surely knocked about by seasickness in the notoriously choppy English Channel and the Bay of Biscay before they found their 'sea legs'. The healthiness of the children is a tribute to Surgeon Superintendent Leonard's regimen of regular food and exercise in the fresh air—including dancing in the late afternoon—and to the attention he paid to keeping floors, bedding, clothes, and people dry and clean. The ship was also fortunate to be carrying a relatively small number of children. In contrast, when the *Earl Grey* left Dublin with 81 children in December 1849, it must have looked like a floating orphanage. On that voyage transporting 240 female prisoners to Van Diemen's Land, five children died. Of course the high mortality rate must have been affected by the poor diet of famine-ravaged Ireland, whereas most children on the *Atwick* had been nourished on Scottish fare, and even though they often led rackety lives at home, as we shall see, a lower-class diet based on oatmeal offered healthy sustenance.

We have no way of knowing how the children reacted to being taken away from Scotland. Much would have depended on the kinds of lives they had known, and on their prospects for a future without their mothers. Many children left behind were probably cared for by grandparents, or otherwise integrated into their extended families. Some may have ended up in the workhouse. While I can only speculate on the children who did not sail, the pre-transportation lives of *Atwick* children are not entirely a blank page. Circumstances some shared with their mothers come to light in the witness statements of the precognition files, and in three cases the children themselves appear in the documents because mothers involved them in their criminal lives.

THE McGUIRE SISTERS AND THE THEFT OF A GREEK TESTAMENT

Six-year-old Grace McGuire and her baby sister Mary went begging with their mother Grace Logan on a late summer's night in 1836. Most *Atwick* thieves stole in the neighbourhoods where they lived, but Grace was taking her daughters and another woman into one of Glasgow's prosperous enclaves. She had her own tactics for getting inside the houses of the middle class: seeing a tradesman open a gate, she followed him with her entourage up the garden path of a clergyman's house in Bell Grove Place. The tradesman knocked on the front door, and delivered a pair of shoes to the servant who answered. She took the shoes, and, as she later told the magistrate, 'before she had time to shut the door, two women came forward, one of whom was carrying an infant in her arms, and the other leading a little girl'. Grace Logan asked to see the master, and when told that she could not 'as he and the family were at worship', she said she would wait, and marched straight into the front hall. The flustered servant tried to steer the bedraggled group into the kitchen, but Grace 'said she would sit down on the stair and keep her child quiet', so the servant left her in the hallway while she went into the back of the house with the other woman and the little girl.

A few minutes later the anxious servant came back into the hall, and saw the study door wider open than she had left it. Again she asked Grace to come into the kitchen. This time she agreed, and was there when the clergyman's wife came in after prayers. Grace asked for charity, received alms, and the women and children went out the front door. The clergyman's son followed to make sure they actually left the property. As they were walking down the driveway towards the street, he 'heard something drop', and 'on going forward, found upon the ground, a thick folio volume, which turned out to be a Greek Testament belonging to his father'. He shut the gate to keep the women inside the garden, shouted for his father to come guard them, and ran off to get the police. When he returned with an officer, he pointed to Grace and accused her of stealing the large testament, which was kept on a table in his father's study. Grace vehemently denied the accusation, and blamed the little girl, who in turn insisted that her mother had stolen the heavy book and then made her carry it. On the way to the station, the police 'had a good deal of trouble in keeping the Prisoner apart from her daughter; and she repeatedly endeavoured to get the girl to say that it was she the girl, who had taken the Book; but the girl still maintained that her mother had taken it, and given it to her'. Everyone seems to have believed Grace McGuire rather than the mother at whose trial 'it was stated from the Bench, that she had been convicted of theft almost every year since 1829'.

I wonder how these events looked through the little girl's eyes, how she felt when her mother tried to shift the blame, and whether this sort of thing had happened to her before. As one of six children in a seriously dysfunctional family, she needed to be tough to survive. Her father, in his mid-forties, was a weaver living in the Old Wynd, Glasgow. Her mother told the magistrate she was 'a native of Lanarkshire but has been living in Glasgow from her infancy—is thirty nine years of age', had worked in a factory but not recently, 'and has had for sometime no fixed place of residence'. And if Grace Logan was homeless, so too were the children she had with her, and possibly at least some of their other siblings as well. On the September night when Grace and Mary McGuire went begging with their mother, their older sister Margaret was sailing towards

Van Diemen's Land on the convict transport *Westmoreland*. Margaret, aged sixteen, had already left Glasgow for Edinburgh and for three years had been 'on the Town', a fate Grace McGuire ironically escaped through the conviction of her incompetent mother.

AGNES AND ALEXANDER HALL AND THEIR MOTHER'S HOMEMADE COINS

At least Grace McGuire may have had some memory of what it meant to live in a place called 'home'. Ten-year-old Agnes Hall and her seven-year-old brother Alexander did not. Their mother, Catherine Chisholm, was one of the women described by the Procurator Fiscal of Glasgow as 'fully ripe for transportation', and we have two snapshots of the children because their oft-convicted mother was tried twice before the High Court of Justiciary and there are two precognitions, one for a trial in Perth in September 1832, and the other for the trial in Glasgow four years later when she was sentenced to transportation. At the time of her arrest in Perth, Catherine Chisholm told the magistrate that 'she has no place of residence', and 'travels the country with articles of merchandise'. Four years later her daughter Agnes described the same itinerant life, saying she 'goes about the Country with her Mother selling lace. And she & her mother are not often or long in the same Town'. She mentioned nothing about her father, Alexander Hall, a riddle-maker by trade—he made the large coarse sieves for separating corn from chaff or ashes from cinders, and was said to have lived in Main Street, Gorbals, Glasgow, before disappearing 'abroad'.

Catherine Chisholm's life of crime seems to be connected with a breakdown in her marriage. The age of her son, and the fact that he was named for his father, suggest that his parents were still together when Catherine was first convicted in September 1830 and sentenced to four months in the Glasgow Bridewell, the city prison where little Alexander may have been born. Maybe the father took off while Catherine was imprisoned. From then on Catherine and her youngest children were homeless itinerants. Late the next year they were in Perthshire where Catherine was hawking caps and edging at the Doune fair. At the heart of this twice-yearly gathering was a cattle market celebrated by Sir Walter Scott in the opening of his short story 'The Two Drovers' as an occasion when business was 'brisk' and money flew from English buyers 'so merrily about as to gladden the hearts of the Highland farmers'. Unfortunately, money from Catherine Chisholm was coin of her own devising, and for this she was sentenced on 5 January 1832 to eight months in Perth Gaol. Four-year-old Agnes and her baby brother went with her. On 4 September, Catherine and the children were released. They were free for about 48 hours.

Just outside the prison gate they met a friend of Catherine's, a hawker who 'earn[ed] her livelihood by travelling the country with confections'. Together they climbed the stairs to a garret where another newly released prisoner was staying in the room of an aunt who had gone to the countryside for the shearing. The women spent the day drinking whisky, while the children presumably sat around being bored. Afterwards, their mother claimed to remember nothing about what happened in the garret. 'Having fallen and dislocated her arm in the course of that day her recollection failed her in a great measure', and being in pain, she lay on a bed 'with her face to the wall'. Nosy neighbours helpfully filled in details for the police. A woman from the floor below said she 'crept softly up the stair', and through a hole in the centre of the door saw 'a big woman who had two children with her', and another woman who was 'sitting with her side to the door and having a shilling or sixpence in the hollow of her left hand and rubbing it with something in her right hand'. Fascinated, the neighbour tapped on the door of a widow living on the same stair, and whispered to her to come have a look, which she did, squinting through the hole. 'They're auld hands, its no the first time', said one neighbour to the other, 'it's a pity there's so much money in the land while I must want my breakfast'.

When the husband of the downstairs neighbour came home and heard his wife's story, he 'ordered' her to 'to go instantly and inform the officers of Justice' while he kept watch to see that no one escaped. The police came, searched the room, found moulds, an iron spoon with a piece of metal in it, and a stash of counterfeit coin including 71 sixpence pieces. Were the children frightened by this sudden intrusion of strange gruff men, and by the inevitable distress of the women? Did they begin to cry before they too were taken off to the station to watch their mother charged? Only two days had passed since they left the prison, and except for the short walk through the streets of Perth, they apparently spent every hour of their freedom closed up in that locked garret room. Now they were on their way back to prison again, and would stay there for the rest of the year until the judges of the High Court of Justiciary came to Perth on circuit in January 1833. At this trial their mother managed to escape conviction because she was not the woman identified by the neighbours as rubbing pewter sixpences with white powder, and because, ironically, the money found on her person was genuine coin of the realm, earned in prison by washing clothes.

Agnes and Alexander Hall were spending their childhood touring the prisons of Scotland. A year after Catherine escaped punishment in Perth, she was convicted for passing bad coins in Stonehaven, and for the first half of 1834 the children were cooped up in the tollbooth of this village on the coast south of Aberdeen. The next year they were in Stirling's tollbooth for three months, and a month after that release were in Glasgow where on 6 April 1836 Catherine was arrested for the crime which would lead them to Van Diemen's Land. Agnes was about eight years old at this stage, and the only schooling she had ever known was in those communal cells where she listened to women like her mother pass the time by telling each other stories, and plotting their inept plots. The witness statements gathered for Catherine Chisholm's final trial in Scotland reveal how thoroughly Agnes had been drawn into her mother's incorrigible coining.

On the Wednesday night Catherine was arrested, she was working with her daughter and a woman named Betty Scott. About eight o'clock Betty Scott went into a baker's shop in the Trongate, the main shopping area in Glasgow's old town, asked for a 'half quartern' (two-pound) loaf of bread, handed the baker's daughter a sixpence for the threepence-farthing loaf, and was given change. Ten minutes later, Catherine Chisholm entered the same shop and repeated the identical routine. 'Chisholm had scarsely [sic] left the shop', said the baker's daughter in her witness statement, 'when a little girl came in and proposed to purchase a half loaf, asking the price of it, and tendered a sixpence in payment'. Something, perhaps the child's nervousness, made the baker's daughter look closely at this coin. She thought it wasn't quite right, and showed it to the shopman, 'who after looking at it said it was bad, upon which it was returned to the girl'. Then it occurred to the baker's daughter that the sixpences from the two women were also 'very black', and she took them from the till to check. Yes, said the shopman, no doubt about it. And out he went to find the culprits. It wasn't difficult. As he watched, Agnes joined the women 'who were standing close by waiting for her'. He then 'followed the whole party along Trongate to Candleriggs—observed Scott go, first into the Lace Shop of Mr Miller at the foot of Candleriggs—and then into the confectionary shop of Mr Baxter in Candleriggs, while Chisholm & the Girl waited for her till she came out of both of these shops'.

The baker's shopman alerted a passing constable to what was going on, and together they managed to get the women to the police station where John Christie, one of Glasgow's most assiduous police criminal officers, took over. After finding counterfeit coins in the women's clothes, he turned them over to a female attendant for a full body search. Knowing their history as counterfeiters, Christie wanted evidence that they had made the coins they were passing. Betty Scott refused to tell him where she lived, but he found out anyway, perhaps inadvertently from little Agnes, who he took with him when he went to search a garret in the Old Wynd, opening the door with a key from Scott's pocket. By the fireside the police found an iron spoon used for melting pewter. A small piece of metal lay on the mantel, and a piece of sand-cloth under the table. Concealed in the thatch of the roof were a stucco mould and a small black cloth full of coins, the money 'quite glossy, shewing that it had been recently made and put there'.

If Christie hoped Agnes would rat on her mother, he was disappointed. She gave nothing away in the garret, and nothing in the courtroom where she was questioned in front of a magistrate. Agnes said exactly what her mother would have hoped—sometimes when we are in Glasgow we stay with Mrs Lockhart, her husband is an umbrella maker in High Street, we never stay in Mrs Scott's house. The only time I've been in Mrs Scott's house was with the police. I saw them find money, a stucco mould, and a spoon, but I never saw those things before. I never saw my mother or Mrs Scott making shillings or sixpences. And no, I certainly never bought any pewter spoons to be melted down, or took any spoons to Mrs Scott's house, and I don't know what base money is made of or how it is made. All this is truth, said Agnes, but I cannot sign my statement because I cannot write my name. Although Agnes stuck loyally to her family's version of truth, Betty Scott's nephew did not. The boy, who took his meals at his aunt's house because his father had 'been out of work for some time', was happy to offer a detailed description of watching Catherine Chisholm make sixpences in the mould, and later seeing her hide things 'beneath the Thatch at the side of the window'. The lad ignored her warning 'not to tell what he had seen'.

Agnes and Alexander Hall probably stayed with their mother in the Tollbooth of Glasgow all that summer because they had nowhere else to go while waiting more than five months for her trial in the autumn session of the circuit court. Betty Scott, after trying to shift the blame entirely onto Catherine, decided to plead guilty. Catherine pleaded not guilty, said the *Glasgow Herald*, 'but after a short trial' was convicted. Both women were sentenced 'to be transported beyond Seas for seven years', and ordered to be 'detained in the Tolbooth of Glasgow till removed for Transportation'. Catherine and her children would have to wait another year before the *Atwick* sailed. Betty Scott was not on board and may have been one of the fortunate women whose sentences to transportation were actually served in Scottish gaols.

THE McKENNA BROTHERS IN A DEN OF THIEVES

Unlike Agnes and Alexander Hall, who had been on the road or in prison as long as they could remember, James and Charles McKenna had spent their entire lives in a small area of Glasgow's old town within walking distance of a grandmother, aunts, uncles and cousins who visited and feuded with each other. Their parents were both Irish by birth, though their

Street life in the Cowgate, Edinburgh.
(© Peter Stubbs, www.edinphoto.org.uk)

Looking towards Calton Hill and the Edinburgh Gaol.
(© Peter Stubbs, www.edinphoto.org.uk)

Women and children in tenements off High Street, Glasgow.
(© Mitchell Library, Glasgow City Council)

Along the Broomielaw and River Clyde in Glasgow.
(© Mitchell Library, Glasgow City Council)

The harbour at Hobart Town from the Old Wharf.
(© Tasmanian Archive and Heritage Office)

Cascades Female Factory with Mt Wellington in the background.
(© Tasmanian Archive and Heritage Office)

Inside the Cascades Female Factory.
(© Tasmanian Archive and Heritage Office)

Queen's Orphan Schools from New Town Road entrance.
(© W L Crowther Library, Tasmanian Archive and Heritage Office)

Lieutenant-Governor Sir John Franklin inspecting the Male Orphan School 1840.

Owen Stanley sketch, from J. C. Brown, *Poverty is not a Crime* (© Tasmanian Historical Research Association 1972)

Jean Boyd, c.1865.
(Private collection, G. S. Whitehouse)

Jean Boyd's husband, John Clark, c.1865.
(Private collection, G. S. Whitehouse)

Elizabeth Waddell in the 1860s.
(Private Collection, John Laing)

Elizabeth Waddell's husband, Henry Cox in the 1860s.
(Private Collection, John Laing)

Jean Smith c.1855.
(Private collection, Cliff Bennett)

Jean Smith's husband, James Bennett, c.1855.
(Private collection, Cliff Bennett)

Jean Smith's son, James Bennett, junior, farmer aged 81.
(Private collection, Cliff Bennett)

Christian McDougall, alias Margaret Rae, later Margaret Wallace.
(Private collection, Muriel Allison)

Christian McDougall's daughter, Annie Wallace, born in the Female Factory nursery and admitted to the Queen's Orphan School as Mary McDougall.
(Private collection, Muriel Allison)

Mary Bentley's grandson, Walter Peeler, born Barkers Creek, recipient of Victoria Cross during WWI.

(© The National Collection, Australian War Memorial)

Margaret Alexander's home on Hope Island, sketch c.1853 attributed to Mary Morton Allport.

The nephews of Margaret Alexander, James and Robert Sawers, with Hope Island in the background.
(Private collection, Dorothy Baker)

mother, Catherine McBrayne, had come to Glasgow as a child. It was at a McBrayne family dinner that the boys' father, John McKenna, was arrested in 1822 when James was an infant and Charles not yet born. At the home of the McBrayne matriarch, Catherine's mother, the family had been celebrating the upcoming wedding of one of Catherine's sisters. Suddenly, the husband of another sister burst into the house with the police, and pointed a finger at John McKenna. There he is, shouted the furious brother-in-law, there's the man who gave my wife a counterfeit note and sent her out to buy whisky! As McKenna was led away, other guests at the ruined dinner table threw insults not at the prisoner but at the brother-in-law who dobbed him in, a husband distressed on behalf of his gaoled wife and their five young children. Eventually Catherine's sister, the star witness against her husband, was released—and John McKenna was sentenced to fourteen years' transportation. He served six years and nine months, though he seems to have stayed in the British Isles, perhaps on a hulk in the Thames or a gaol or a combination of the two, because his name appears on no list of transportees actually sent to Australia. While he was away, his four children grew from infancy into childhood without a father. Catherine must have needed the help of her widowed mother and the extended McBrayne clan, hoping that one sister would forgive the ruined wedding festivities, and another the trauma of arrest and imprisonment.

John McKenna before his conviction had been working in the cotton industry, first as dyer and then bleacher, and at the same time he was part of a network shifting counterfeit money between Glasgow and Belfast. His years as a prisoner seem to have sapped his energy and broken his spirit. Although he was not 70 years old as he claimed when he and most of his family were transported in 1837, he may have felt very old, and he comes across as a weak man whose wife dominated the family. Two teenage sons were working, and sometimes Catherine may have been employed as she said in a warehouse, but to make ends meet, the family depended on an arrangement with Agnes and Christian Gilmour, who would also sail on the *Atwick*. The Gilmour sisters were prostitutes who brought their targets to the McKennas' and for a price had use of the family's second room.

This meant broken sleep for children who had to be moved. In 1836, when two precognitions offer snapshots of the family, there were four McKenna children in the household: Mary Ann, aged about sixteen; John, fifteen; James, fourteen; and Charles (the legacy of his father's return from transportation), five. John and James gave their wages to their mother each Saturday, and slept wherever they were told. Mary Ann may not have worked for wages, but played roles assigned to her in performances directed by her mother. Two of these became the subject of precognitions. The first, starring nineteen-year-old Christian Gilmour, took place on the last Saturday in September 1836, when a middle-aged engineer from Glasgow met Christian in a spirits cellar in the High Street, and then 'stupefied with liquor', as he later admitted, went with her along Callowgate to Callow Mouth and into a house in Deacons Close. It was almost midnight, and Catherine McBrayne was sitting by the fireside with a niece and the niece's husband, who had dropped by to visit at an hour when the McBrayne clan apparently exchanged hospitality. The McKenna children were also in the room, but the engineer didn't notice them. Their father wasn't there because he and Catherine had recently been fined £1 each for keeping 'a noted bad house for entertainment of thieves and other bad characters'. Unable to pay the fine, he had gone to gaol.

Agnes Gilmour took a lighted candle to show her sister and the engineer into the room with a bed, and the man gave her money to go out to buy whisky. And then, like a bolt from the blue, he came to his senses and realised the danger he was in. Jumping out of bed and into his clothes, he was trying to get out the front door when he was viciously attacked by the sisters and the visitors, and he was sure that Christian was the one who riffled his pockets and removed two £5 notes, tearing his trousers from pocket to knee.

Dazed and drunk, the engineer wandered down the High Street where he was spotted by a policeman who noticed the torn trousers. Together they went back to the house in Deacons Close, where they found only the Gilmour sisters sitting by the fire. In the inner room were two boys 'in bed and asleep as it appeared', and everything looked normal, domestic, not the scene of prostitution and theft. The policeman thought that one of the 'boys may be about ten and the other about twelve years, of age', though John and James were actually in their mid-teens. James, the boy guessed by the policeman to be about ten, told the magistrate when questioned about the night's events, that he was a tobacco stripper aged about fourteen, though when he sailed on the *Atwick* a year later, his age was lowered to thirteen. Like Agnes Hall, James McKenna knew how to give evidence before a magistrate. In his version of the attack, no one in his family was to blame. He was sitting by the fire, he said, when Christian Gilmour came in with the engineer, and he later saw the man try to leave. Christian 'followed him towards the door, and said "Surely you're no gan awa' that way" ', and he 'distinctly saw her thrust her hand into his right pocket and take something from it'. A sixpence fell to the floor and James rushed after it, but Christian made him give it to her.

James's brother and sister were also questioned. While John simply agreed with James, Mary Ann added a narrative of her own. She was at home, she said, when Christian and the man came in, but after the man paid to use the inner room, she was sent by her mother with 2 shillings to a pawnbroker's to retrieve her mother's dress and a pair of shoes belonging to the cousin who was visiting. She found the pawnbroker's door shut (it was well after midnight by now), and had started back when she met her mother, who took the money and told her to go home. After giving evidence to exonerate themselves and send Christian for trial, Catherine McBrayne and her children were released from custody, and the McKenna family, including the father, were reunited in their criminalised home space. Reunited temporarily, that is.

A chain of disasters began about nine o'clock on Saturday night three weeks after Christian was arrested. Mary Ann McKenna opened the door to their landlord who handed her a piece of paper (which no one in that household could read), and told her that if they hadn't left by Monday he would have them evicted. For more than a year, the McKennas had paid 5 shillings 10 pence a month for their two-roomed 'house'. Recently they had 'fallen into arrear of about a month's Rent', and this gave the landlord an excuse to get them out, though his real concern was the rumour he had heard of a robbery and of the McKennas 'abusing the property very much by breaking glass & so forth'. On Monday when he returned to make good his threat, he found everyone gone, 'and there was still in the House an old grate, a bedstead & some articles of very little value'. By then the parents were in gaol and the children dispersed. The McKennas had not moved house. They had simply left what they had behind. This was a very poor family.

Catherine McBrayne's Irish temper had flared when her daughter told her about the eviction order. No one was going to put her out, she'd leave of her own accord that very night! She stamped across the hall to a neighbour, James McQueen, and asked whether he 'would allow her two boys, when they came home, to remain in [his] house till she would send for them, and [McQueen] said he did not object to putting them up for one night but that she must get lodgings for them as soon as possible'. Then he went out for a drink, and when his wife returned about half past eleven from shopping (this was a world of night people), she met John and James McKenna, 'who enquired if she knew where their mother was'. No, she said, but they could come in, and 'they lay down on the floor and fell asleep, and they remained in the house till next morning'. Not long after the teenaged breadwinners in this family fell asleep on the neighbour's floor, their parents and sister returned to the house for one last sting. Somehow they had made contact with Agnes Gilmour, who 'inveigled' (as the *Glasgow Herald* put it) a drunken cattle-dealer from the Highlands into the house, a man named William Greig. This time it was Mary Ann McKenna who showed them into the back room, and Mary Ann who was sent out to buy the whisky of which Greig drank a little before he immediately 'became quite insensible'. Drugged no doubt. Next morning he came to consciousness in an empty house with an empty pocketbook.

If the McKennas had been lucky folk, that would have been the end of the matter. Down the stairs with their ill-gotten gains, never to return. Greig would have had no clue where to look for them. But this was reckoning without a neighbour who had had enough of their shenanigans. Just because James McQueen let the McKenna boys sleep on his floor did not mean he had any compunction about helping the police nab their parents. McQueen awoke early on Sunday morning to hear Greig tramping up and down the stairs. I've been robbed in the McKennas of £37 11 shillings, Greig told McQueen, who took him straight to the Calton police. McQueen then did what he could to help the police with their enquiries, confirming that 'of late' the McKennas 'have kept Agnes Gilmour and her sister going about the house, and many thefts have been committed in the house by them, on the persons of men whom they enticed into the house, at least many persons complained of thefts'. McQueen must have come across as an effective and reliable witness during the precognition hearing, because he was asked to give evidence for the very brief High Court trial at which only four witnesses besides the police were called. Statements from the accused were tabled. Agnes Gilmour blamed the McKennas, Catherine McBrayne blamed Agnes Gilmour, and John McKenna said he left the house immediately after being ordered out by the landlord and never went back. The jury found all three guilty, and sentenced each to seven years' transportation.

It was cold in the courtroom where this trial was heard early in January 1837, and according to the *Glasgow Herald* 'the Court was a good deal annoyed by the continual coughing of the audience'. The visiting judges on circuit from Edinburgh reprimanded the Glaswegians: 'Lord Meadow-bank remarked, that people affected with colds, and who had nothing to do there, certainly did not consult their own welfare by remaining in Court, while they subjected the business to continual interruptions'. Some of those coughing people airily dismissed as having 'nothing to do there' were relatives of the accused, including perhaps the McKenna children, anxious about their future. Where had they been living since Catherine and John were arrested almost three months earlier? And where was four-year-old Charles all this time? He is never mentioned in the precognitions. Was he invisible to the witnesses because he was asleep in a corner when the thefts occurred? or was he staying somewhere else, at his grandmother's perhaps, or with another relative? And then, after the sentencing sealed the family's fate, through what process was the decision made for James as well as Charles to sail for Van

Diemen's Land, and for Mary Ann and John to stay in Glasgow? So many blank spots in the stories, so many gaps in the lives.

THE UNINITIATED CHILDREN

The children of Grace Logan, Catherine Chisholm and Catherine McBrayne were growing to consciousness at the edges of poverty where criminal activities and lawful work were intertwined as part of the daily mix. The other Scottish children on the *Atwick* may have been less well-tutored in unlawful ways. Margaret Callaghan was six years old, the same age as Grace McGuire, and like Agnes Hall she had a mother transported for uttering base coin, but the precognition of Margaret's unmarried mother, Elizabeth Brown, makes no mention of a daughter. No little girl was with the less than clever woman who on a Friday, Saturday, and Monday went into the same shop in the Edinburgh old town and used a bad sixpence to pay the spirits dealer for a half gill of whisky. Arrested on the third occasion, Elizabeth Brown muttered as she walked with a policeman to the station, 'what a stupid woman I am, to be taken in for this sixpence when I am quite sober, if I had been drunk, it would have been nothing'. Questioned before the magistrate, she denied knowing that the coin was bad, said that 'she goes about selling butter and Eggs and thinks she may have got it in the way of her trade'. Where was Margaret Callaghan while her mother was wandering the countryside? Was someone else looking after her? Did she have any idea that her mother had been passing bad coins since before she was born?

Similar questions could be asked of Joseph Douglas, whose unmarried mother, Jean Smith, had left Ireland for Glasgow's cotton mills, but turned to prostitution when she could get no other work. Joseph was about three years old when his mother was arrested for theft late on a winter's night, and she may have left him alone in her lodgings before she went out. Or he may have been in Ireland with relatives who agreed to care for him temporarily but were in no position to take on his long-term upbringing. All we know for sure is that Margaret Callaghan and Joseph Douglas were the children of mothers with no stable home life or occupation, and their fathers were not on hand to help.

Caroline Perry was not yet born when her unmarried mother, Janet Bonar, was arrested. Janet herself was still living at home with her own mother in Greenock, the seaport west of Glasgow where Jess Mitchell had stolen from the elderly lodging-keeper before heading back to the Highlands on the *Rob Roy*. At the time of her arrest, Janet said she was 'going eighteen years of age', which means she would have been thirteen or fourteen when first convicted of theft in February 1832. According to the local superintendent of police, she had been 'habite and repute' a thief 'for the last two years at least'. One autumn afternoon about four o'clock Janet walked out into the countryside with Sally Clark, another of the *Atwick* convicts. They were on their way to rob a woman who rented a room in a farmhouse while her sailor husband was at sea. Strangers strolling down country tracks were always noticed by the locals, and Janet with the 'red tartan mantle over her head' was easily remembered. No one actually saw whether it was Janet or Sally who lifted the sash of the farmhouse window, and climbed into the room to gather up whatever was lying around. The thieves went right back to town, sold what they could of the pathetic loot they'd carried away, and got drunk. The only booty Janet took home was an unfinished pair of stockings, which the police found. Initially Janet and Sally blamed each other for the housebreaking, but before their trial, both changed their pleas to guilty and were sentenced to seven years' transportation. Janet gave birth in prison.

Another five children all came from the same family, and that in itself is a puzzlement. Somehow, Margaret Christie arranged to leave Aberdeen with children listed by Surgeon Superintendent Leonard as Isabella, aged fourteen; Bathia, thirteen; Margaret, ten; James, eight; and Cosmo, four. Their father, Cosmo Mourice or Morrice—a surname anglicised in Australia to Morris—was a man of the sea who may have stopped sailing into Aberdeen about the time his youngest son and namesake was born in 1833. Loss of income could explain why Margaret Christie began to steal, her first conviction for a petty theft coming a few months after her youngest child's birth. By the time of her final arrest in 1836, the local police could testify that they considered her 'habite and repute a thief', and she may not have disagreed. When nabbed for stealing a cotton quilt and light printed cotton gown from an unlocked garret drying room, she admitted the theft at once. With this theft and her prior convictions, the outcome of her trial five months later was never in doubt, and whatever Lord Mackenzie said in his 'serious admonition' when sentencing her may have seemed supremely irrelevant to her circumstances.

Margaret Christie was arrested in early July 1836 and tried in October. Then almost a year passed before she and the children sailed on the *Atwick*. The two oldest girls, Isabella and Bathia, may have been working in one of the Aberdeen mills—certainly there is nothing to suggest that like their mother they were thieves, or that she in any way involved them in her petty crimes, and even in the past, their legitimate wages may have supported younger siblings while their mother was locked away. The girls may have played a more significant role than their mother in keeping the siblings together and getting them onto the boat leaving Aberdeen. And what about their father? If Margaret had described herself as a widow when she reached Van Diemen's Land, she would have had the option of finding a reliable breadwinner to marry, but she did not. No record suggests that the father was dead—but nothing suggests that he helped his children either.

None of the Scottish children transported with their mothers left supportive environments at home. Even the McKenna brothers, who lived with both parents and in close contact with their mother's extended family, were not well prepared for lives in Scotland's industrial future. James McKenna must have chosen deliberately to sail on the *Atwick* instead of remaining in Glasgow with his older brother and sister. Already he was earning wages as a tobacco stripper. But he was illiterate. Called to give witness statements, he could not sign his name. Looking around him in the tobacco warehouse, he may have seen visions of nothing but repeated drudgery for the long years ahead. At least going to Van Diemen's Land would be an adventure. Isabella and Bathia Morrice were also old enough to be working and probably were in a town where girls often entered the mills when they were as young as eight. They too could certainly have chosen to stay behind, but they didn't. Children too young to work had no options. They went with their mothers or remained behind according to forces over which they had no control. And how did the mothers who took children imagine their future in Australia? It seems unlikely that a mother could have even the foggiest notion of what would happen to the children once they arrived. If the future was a mystery, that in itself might be attractive. The present in Scotland was all too well known.

7

ORPHANS OF THE *ATWICK*

Mothers lost parental control over children who clambered up rope ladders onto the *Atwick* or were carried on board. Authorities appointed by the state took over decisions about where their children would live, and how. On the ship, they learned to follow the daily rules and regulations imposed by the surgeon superintendent. Once on shore, as we have already seen, they were initiated into the life of a penal colony by staring at high walls in the nursery yard of the Cascades Female Factory. Eventually, after weeks locked up with the summer stench of sickness and death, the older children were released into their new role as 'orphans'. On 17 March 1838 the orphans of the *Atwick* walked back out through the forbidding prison gates, and climbed onto a cart. How alluring the sights and sounds of everyday life must have seemed as they trundled through the streets of Hobart Town. Were any of the boys or girls tempted to jump down and run away? But where would they go? In a foreign place, where they knew no one, knew nothing about the lay of the land, jumping off the cart would mean plunging into the unknown. Seriously scary and risky. At least they had each other. In the six months since they sailed down the Thames, they had shared experiences which set them apart, and hopefully bound them together. The coming years in the Queen's Orphan Schools would be less soul-destroying for the child who did not feel utterly abandoned and alone.

Architecturally, the schools which would be their new home looked daunting. Like so many nineteenth-century institutions designed to house the poor, sick, and helpless throughout Britain and the Empire, they were not intended to foster a sense of family or domesticity. Two double-storeyed buildings stood, as they do today, at the end of an avenue flanked at its entrance by substantial stone guardhouses. Between the buildings of the schools for boys and girls stands St John's Anglican Church, where the orphans would file into a wide balcony, while assigned convicts went into a matching balcony on the other side where they were separated, male and female, with guards stationed in between. On the ground floor the free parishioners could keep their eyes directed towards the clergy-man as they worshipped. If they did not look upwards, they could avoid eye contact with prisoners and with the confined children. As elsewhere in the penal colony, architecture conveyed a message about order and control. Reality was a different matter. We have two tales of disrupted life in the Orphan Schools during the time the *Atwick* children were there, two episodes conveying a flavour of their experience. One involves a feud between masters which affected the *Atwick* boys during their first months in the boys school, and the other tells an unsavoury story about a headmaster and some of the older girls a few years later.

FEUDING MASTERS

Six sons of Scottish convicts from the *Atwick* were admitted into the Male School (known colloquially and more fittingly as the Boys' School) on 17 March 1838: the McKenna brothers, James aged thirteen, and Charles, five; the Morris brothers, James aged eight, and Cosmo, four; Alexander Hall, aged seven, and Joseph Douglas, four. It seems likely that none of these boys had ever been to school or experienced any other formal gathering of children, and suddenly here they were, living in the midst of 220 boys. The lives of these boys were controlled by the master of the Boys' School, John Offer, and by the headmaster of the entire institution, the Reverend T.B. Naylor, who was also the clergyman for the church.

John Offer had been appointed as master of the Boys' School the year before, and it was becoming apparent that he had very firm ideas about how the school should be run. Many of his proposals seem humane, and he might have proved an important reforming influence if his personal-ity had been more congenial. Unfortunately, he and the headmaster were both seriously stubborn and self-righteous men, and instead of spending their time and resources on looking after their charges, they concentrated with ferocious intensity on their feud. During 1838 and 1839 the Colonial Secretary was inundated with reams of accusations and counter-accusations submitted by Offer and Naylor through his office as each man attempted to persuade Lieutenant Governor Franklin that he alone was the epitome of right-thinking and righteousness. Irritating though this excessive and cantankerous correspondence must have been for those to whom it was addressed, its legacy is ironically valuable. Between them, the master and headmaster reveal the world they oversaw.

John Offer's complaints against the headmaster tell us how the 'orphaned' boys from the *Atwick* lived. They all wore leather trousers with unlined moleskin jackets. The trousers, according to the master, 'prove but little warmth—chafe the skin—cannot be cleaned—when wet are excessively cold and flabby—and at all times emit an offensive smell—from the highly muscular nature of the skin—a child's dress should be warm flexible and washable, uniformity is also desirable, and they should be supplied with caps for everyday wear'. The boys slept in hammocks, ate standing up (the master suggested benches for the dining room), used water closets which 'fill the building with offensive effluvia', and were expected to wash daily in two small horse troughs where 'the excessive coldness of the water makes them averse to washing and frequent chastisement is required in order to preserve personal cleanliness'. In the one and only schoolroom, boys from the ages of five (or younger) to fourteen (or older) sat on backless benches studying lessons sent out to the colony by the British and Foreign School Society. No library of books encouraged them to improve their reading or to learn more about the world, and yet the *Atwick* boys probably benefitted from learning the basics of reading, writing, and arithmetic.

Schoolroom lessons occupied the boys only part time. According to John Offer, 'every alternate day from ½ past 8 to 12 and from ½ past one to ½ past 4 (allowing for the Saturday afternoon being a half holiday)', they worked with one of the trade instructors employed to prepare them for apprenticeships in shoemaking, tailoring, and carpentry, trades of use in a colony with no call for tobacco strippers like James McKenna.

Though Master Offer was highly critical of 'the experiment of teaching Trades' and thought the boys learned little, the headmaster vigorously defended the initiative, arguing that the aim was not to produce 'complete masters of the trades' but 'useful *apprentices*'. As evidence of the program's success, he pointed to the willingness of masters to apprentice the Orphan School boys without the usual premiums of £50 or more. The apprenticeship program for all its undoubted failings offered some pathway to earn a living in the future.

In an institution where daily life was governed by immutable routines, and half-day holidays did not mean permission to roam beyond the fences, the incandescent hostility between the headmaster and the master of the Boys' School affected everyone. Matters came to a head during 1839. On 11 April the master, without the headmaster's permission, went into town for three hours to buy a book he said was needed for teaching, a book he was buying because the school would not. Whatever John Offer's motivation, to leave the grounds without permission was forbidden in his terms of employment, and he knew it. This defiant breach of regulations played straight into the hands of the headmaster, who pressed formal charges leading to a board of inquiry. Both men told their stories to the local press, who lapped up the scandal until in the end the Lieutenant Governor must have been heartily sick of their interminable squabble. No one attempted to dissuade the headmaster when he threatened to resign, and as for the master, his exoneration by the board of inquiry proved a pyrrhic victory. Unable to leave well enough alone, he triumphantly threatened further accusations against the headmaster, and to his apparent surprise was fired. The Orphan School, like the Augean stables and the Cascades Female Factory, needed a vigorous new broom, and to get on with the sweeping, another Anglican clergyman was appointed headmaster, the Rev. Thomas Ewing.

Over the months while the Boys' School was descending into conflict and confusion, the girls must have been curious to hear what was going on. Servants gossiped, and brothers came to visit sisters one evening each week. James Morris would have brought news to tell his older sister Margaret, and although four-year-old Cosmo Morris was too little to understand much of the power struggle, he could have regaled Margaret with tales of the floggings for which the master became notorious—even to an adult bystander, 31 lashes on a boy's bare back seemed 'barbarous'. Girls were not flogged in their schoolroom where, like the boys, they were given basic lessons in reading, writing, and arithmetic. They too spent considerable time learning a trade, which in the gendered world of colonial work meant domestic service. They practised laundry skills by washing their own clothes and the boys' undergarments, but were spared having to cope with the heavy blankets, which were carted across town to the Cascades Female Factory where they were treated so roughly by women sentenced to the wash tub that according to the master, they 'returned from the Female House of Correction frequently wringing wet—dirty—and stinking from lying damp in heaps—also neither ironed nor mangled; and generally torn'.

When Rev. Ewing became headmaster in August 1839, the rancour and bitterness infecting the staff dissipated, and as conditions improved for the staff, hopefully the daily life of the children became less stressed. In January 1840, two years after the *Atwick*'s arrival, the first of her 'orphans' left the schools. James McKenna, who was fifteen or sixteen by then, was sent out to serve a four-year apprenticeship in Hobart Town. Boys were usually younger when apprenticed, about fourteen, and I wonder whether James chose to stay because he at last had an opportunity to learn how to read and write, even if the schooling seems abysmal from today's standpoint, and whether he actually enjoyed the opportunity to work at a variety of trades before being apprenticed. Perhaps even the predictability of a monotonous routine suited him after the rackety life the McKenna children had led in Glasgow. What happened to James after his apprenticeship, I have been unable to discover. It seems likely that he left the colony to try his fortune elsewhere.

The first *Atwick* 'orphan' to be reunited with a mother was Alexander Hall, who was 'discharged to his mother' on 30 September 1840. Although Catherine Chisholm did not yet have a ticket of leave, and had notched up several charges on her conduct record, she had been granted permission to marry, and in less than a fortnight after her wedding she extracted her nine-year-old son from the Orphan School. At last the counterfeiter 'ripe for transportation' had a home to offer the little boy who had spent most of his childhood on the road or in the gaols of Scotland. Catherine, regardless of her inept counterfeiting, had always kept her children with her, and for her to retrieve Alexander so soon suggests how much she missed him—and grieved no doubt for his dead sister Agnes.

A BESOTTED HEADMASTER

The year after Alexander Hall went home with his mother, Margaret Morris was apprenticed to one of her older sisters, but before she left, she became embroiled in a scandal swirling around the headmaster. Rev. Ewing had indiscreetly yielded to an obsession. In July 1841 a private fantasy world affecting the daily life of Margaret and her circle of friends became the subject of a board of inquiry appointed to investigate rumours that the headmaster was 'carrying on a criminal conversation with one of the girls aged fourteen', a girl named Ellen Wilson. The matron of the Girls' School told the board that 'for the last twelve months Mr Ewing has constantly had the big girls up in his garden or in his house'. Ewing had given Ellen a key to the locked gate separating his private garden from the grounds of the institution, and she and her friends came and went as they wished. According to thirteen-year-old Mary Ann Woods, who had been in the school since she was four, he 'used to have the big girls up in his garden to make roads'. They also wandered up the hill into the bush where they could not be seen by Mrs Ewing or any of the servants in the parsonage below. The girls told the board that Ewing liked to go off with Ellen, whose secret life fascinated them. 'Ellen Wilson told me about a month ago that Mr Ewing had given her a sleepy cake. It was in the bush, and she said she went to sleep immediately upon eating it.' There were games, too, 'we used often to play at "Hide and seek"—when I used to see Mr Ewing take away Ellen Wilson when it was their turn to hide—into the Bush—away from the other girls—'.

Ellen told John Learmonth, the Orphan School doctor, about these games when he examined her body for evidence of 'criminal conversation':

She said it was quite true that repeatedly whilst playing at 'Hide and Seek' in the bush Mr Ewing had laid her down beside him—that he had untied her frock and put his hands into her bosom—and also that he had put his hands up her clothes as far as her 'place'—and felt her stomach and told her that she ought to put a board upon it—that he has got over her and put his mouth to her mouth—I asked her if she had ever seen Mr Ewing take his trowsers down—she said she had not—I asked her if he ever hurt her or put any thing into her—she said no—I asked her if he ever spoke to her on these occasions—she said no—That on one occasion he had put a newspaper over her face so that she could not see him—he could see her 'place' then as he had raised her clothes so high—.

When questioned by the board of inquiry, Ellen told the gentlemen that three Saturdays ago Rev. Ewing 'laid me down on the ground and got upon me':

Mary Ann Read and Susan Cullyford saw Mr Ewing lay me down on the ground—we were playing at 'Hide & Seek'—at the time Mr Ewing laid me down he beckoned those girls to go away—It was in a bush house— Margaret Morris came into the bush house at the time and brought Mr Ewing an insect—she went away and told the other girls that Mr Ewing was sitting with his legs across me—He pulled up my clothes and was feeling all about my body—He never pulled his trousers down—.

The headmaster's lust entertained his charges throughout the Orphan Schools. 'The boys have songs about it', said the cook, and one of the boys 'tells such a straightforward story' about surprising Ewing with Ellen in the bush 'that I do not know what to make of it'. Cocky with privilege, Ellen Wilson and her friends came to feel a special sense of entitlement, as the beadle discovered when he came upon them inside the church at a time when they should not have been there. 'I was running after this Wilson with my cane when Margaret Morris called at me not to hurt her—for "*that is Mr Ewings girl*"—This speech struck me and afterwards I paid more attention to what was going on—when I learned that it was all known amongst the boys—'.

Strutting their claims of privilege, the girls exposed a secret world to public view, and unwittingly brought it crashing down. Gossip reached the matron, who spelled out the accusations in a note to Ewing. The reaction was swift. Besotted lover was transformed in an instant into powerful, self-protective official. After toying with Ellen Wilson for months, he turned on her. She was summoned to appear before the headmaster and matron in the most intimidating space of the Orphan Schools, the Committee Room. There he accused her of spreading 'a Report in the School that I had taken improper liberties with her'. No, no, said Ellen, I said nothing of the sort, it was Sarah Lawson who said those things. Sarah was sent for and accused of scandalmongering. She stood her ground, telling the headmaster to his face 'that not only had Wilson admitted the buttoning up of the trows-ers but that I had told her to put her hand in'. Ellen—who was said to be 'afraid' of Mr Ewing—denied this, and the other girls called by Sarah to support her, 'broke down in their evidence'. Ewing treated the situation as a breach of trust on the part of Ellen and her friends. 'This girl Wilson has been always a favourite of mine & Mrs Ewing from her apparently modest demeanour', but she has 'presumed much on my regard'. No more. On that winter's day in the coldness of the Committee Room, 'I gave her a severe reproval before the Matron and begged that neither herself or any of the other girls should be allowed to come up to the house again'. The recalcitrant Sarah Lawson was punished 'for the falsehood' of her story. Ewing hoped he had put a stop to the scandalous gossip.

He had not. When Dr Learmonth heard the rumour some days later, he went to the matron 'and asked her if there was any foundation for the report—she said there was'. The next day, Learmonth confronted Ewing, and told him that this allegation 'so injurious to himself and the Schools' should be thoroughly investigated. I have already conducted an investigation, said Ewing, and thought the matter was at an end. It isn't, said Learmonth, let me examine Ellen Wilson, hear what she has to say, and determine whether she is indeed a virgin. Reluctantly Ewing agreed. The next morning Learmonth conducted the medical examination which enabled him to certify 'that reports of any person having had connection with her are totally false'.

Learmonth then wrote out multiple copies of this certificate of virginity, and delivered them to Ewing, telling the headmaster bluntly that 'I was sorry I could not do much for him—that I had heard a very bad story from the girl, Ellen Wilson, which I related to him—however I said I would give him a certificate . . . I urged him to go into town to Mr Montagu [the Colonial Secretary] in the morning, who was his friend, to tell him the whole story—.' Ewing thought this would only invite further scandal, and proposed instead to send Ellen far away, apprenticing her 'to Captain Smith at Recherche Bay'. Learmonth went home and brooded. 'In the course of that evening I made up my mind that it must be made known either by him or by myself and went out early next morning for the purpose of urging Mr Ewing to see Mr Montagu.' Ewing, however, had already gone into town. The night before he had confided in his wife, and she too had urged him to consult Montagu. After he did so, the board of inquiry was inevitable.

But in spite of the damning evidence from the girls, the matron, the doctor, and other employees, the board treated Ewing gently. They listened to his claim that he cared for orphans who had 'no other friend to look to for kindness', and that it was a 'great fondness for children' which led him to bring the girls into his garden, treat them to delicacies, and invite them to his birthday party (the most recent included games of 'Blind Man's Bluff' played with officers from the Royal Navy's exploration ships *Erebus* and *Terror*). In the end the board offered only a restrained rebuke, saying 'we cannot acquit Mr Ewing of certain extent of imprudence in his conduct towards, and treatment of the elder girls of the School, which has not been we think, consistent with his position of Head Master of the Establishment'. Colonial Secretary Montagu passed on the Lieutenant Governor's similarly restrained comments: 'His Excellency cannot approve of your having permitted the girls to amuse themselves on your grounds, and although he has no doubt that you were activated by a kindly feeling and a good motive, yet he can, at the same time, entertain no doubt that your kindness to them has been injudicious, and has given rise to the unpleasant reports which have led to the recent investigation'. Eight years later, another lieutenant governor struggling again with problems posed by the Orphan Schools would comment to the Home Secretary in London that 'having perused all the correspondence and evidence in the matter, I must say that in my opinion [Ewing] was very mildly dealt with'. And so he was. He kept his position as headmaster for another three years, and even when replaced to his great indignation by the retiring commandant at Port Arthur, he continued as clergyman for the parish, enjoying the elegant parsonage surrounded by the garden of his licentious playground.

The future of girls whose lives were affected by his indulgent passion went unmentioned as the officials corresponded with each other. Perhaps not coincidentally, several apprenticeships for the older girls were finalised in the week the board of inquiry was meeting. On 11 July 1841, Mary Henning was apprenticed, the English girl whose mother and baby sister had died in the Female Factory within a few weeks of leaving the *Atwick*. Mary's master during her apprenticeship was John Price, a high-ranking convict administrator who in 1857 would be set upon and murdered by convicts in Victoria, a man whose cruelty became legendary through his depiction as Maurice Frere in Marcus Clarke's *For the Term of his Natural Life*. Mary's apprenticeship ended early when she married a district constable, John Partridge, on 21 November 1843. She was seventeen and he was 30. For more than ten years she had a family again, giving birth to four children as she went with her husband to Port Arthur, Oatlands, and finally to Launceston where she died in 1856 at the age of 29, two years younger than her mother had been at the time of her death in the Female Factory. Short though Mary's life was, it offered her dead mother and sister a connectedness to the land they had known so briefly, a connectedness continuing today through the families of her Australian descendants, and given the circumstances of Mary's first months in Van Diemen's Land, her survival beyond the Female Factory was in itself an achievement.

THE MORRIS SISTERS

Margaret Morris's circumstances were quite different from Mary Henning's—or from those of the other *Atwick* children. She had two older sisters who had escaped the Orphan Schools altogether, and were now in a position to help her. Isabella and Bertha ('Bathia' had quickly rid herself of that exotic name) were listed by the surgeon superintendent as aged fourteen and thirteen when they arrived, and might well have been admitted to the Orphan Schools along with their brothers and Margaret, but they were not. If, as I suspect, they had been working from a young age and were the ones who cared for the younger children while their mother was imprisoned in Aberdeen, they were tough-minded independent teenagers who would never voluntarily subject themselves to the dispiriting routines of the Orphan Schools. And I doubt whether there was any pressure on them to do so. Officials were always looking for ways to cut costs. Why feed, house, and clothe girls able and ready to fend for themselves?

The 'free' Morris girls could have found work easily among those settlers who preferred to pay wages rather than entrust their households and especially their children to prisoners. And soon, if they wished, they could marry. A radical gender imbalance in the pioneering colony was very much to their advantage. In 1838, according to official statistics, the population of Van Diemen's Land was 45,836. This included 31,974 males (15,905 free and 16,069 convicts) and just 13,872 females (11,808 free and 2,064 convicts). Under these circumstances, either of the Morris sisters might have married a man who was already established and could point to his proven record as a provider—though such a prospective groom might well be a much older widower with children. In any case, Isabella and Bertha were not attracted to caution. Both chose young men just emerging from the convict system.

Isabella had been in Hobart Town little more than two years when she married Henry Hicks, recently 'free by servitude', on 9 March 1840 in St David's Church. As a married woman, Isabella gained the status needed to apply for an apprentice from the Orphan Schools and a year later, she brought home her sister Margaret, who may have been meeting her brother-in-law for the first time. Henry Hicks was sixteen when he arrived on the *Emperor Alexander* in 1833 to serve a seven-year sentence for breaking into a warehouse on the wharf in Bristol and stealing two casks of butter. Reported twice for theft on the voyage out, he was accused of shoplifting by his first master in Van Diemen's Land. Sent to the boys' prison at Point Puer, across the harbour from the second-ary punishment station at Port Arthur, he was constantly in trouble for bucking the system, being insolent or absent from work, swearing, refus-ing to be searched, throwing stones. Henry while courting Isabella may have said little about his pedigree as ruffian and thief, and the occu-pation of 'shipwright' entered on the marriage register could have fed into fond memories of her mariner father and a childhood by the sea in Aberdeen. The Hobart Town waterfront offered plenty of work for men who knew ships, and perhaps the young husband was gainfully employed and only supplementing his wages when he was arrested on 29 May 1842 for 'gambling on the Hampton [Hampden] Road on Sunday' and fined 40 shillings, a blow no doubt to the weekly budget of a family which now included at least one baby daughter as well as the apprenticed Margaret. This was not to be Henry's last arrest.

While Isabella seems to have remained in Hobart Town from the time she left the *Atwick*, Bertha ventured further afield, and her marriage three years after Isabella's wedding took place in the Court House at Oatlands, the regional administrative centre 84 kilometres north of Hobart Town. Bertha's husband, James Berwick, had held a ticket of leave for less than four months, and had five years of his fourteen years' sentence yet to serve. Berwick was a survivor of one of the worst convict shipwrecks, the 1835 wreck of the scurvy-ridden *George III*, which foundered near the end of its long voyage when it hit reefs at the southeast entrance to the D'Entrecasteaux Channel. Its 133 dead included a woman, three children, two crew and 127 convicts. Youth may have been on the side of Berwick, one of the 81 convict survivors, who was about eighteen years old. During the voyage he had been second captain of the boys' prison, winning praise from the surgeon superintendent for being very good and 'serviceable', an interesting choice of words which leads the historian Michael Roe to speculate that Berwick may have owed his later appoint-ment in the convict constabulary to his record as an informer. As Roe points out, Berwick kept this appointment as a constable for more than three years even though his conduct record shows that he was regularly charged with insolence, misconduct, and using obscene language. A year before his marriage he had at last been dismissed from the police, and when he and Bertha married, he was an overseer of convict work gangs.

Theoretically, Bertha's family might all have been at her wedding. Her mother, like the bridegroom, had been granted a ticket of leave in January 1843 and could have gone immediately to the Orphan School to be reunited with her two sons. But she did not. She waited until 5 May—four days after Bertha's wedding—before she retrieved Cosmo, now aged nine, leaving James behind. How must the thirteen-year-old have felt when he knew that he was the only member of his family still locked up in an institution? It wasn't until October that he was finally 'discharged to his mother'. Was it merely a coincidence that unless he was discharged, he would soon be apprenticed? Did his mother expect him to find work and hand over his wages? Whatever the relation between mother and son, James seems to disappear from the family records once he left the Orphan School. Maybe he went straight down to the waterfront and found a ship to work his passage on, escaping the island altogether, maybe even going back to Scotland.

If Cosmo lived with his mother immediately after being discharged from the Orphan School, the arrangement did not last for long, because on 12 June 1845 he was living with his sister Bertha when tragedy struck her family in the Hobart suburb of New Town. The Berwicks' second child, a two-month-old girl, died. Grief-stricken, Bertha told the coroner and jury at the inquest that 'the last time I saw her alive was last night about half past nine o'clock'. The Berwicks slept together in one bed, the father closest to the wall, then the mother, then the baby and her two-year-old sister Sarah. 'I gave the child the breast in the night but at what time I cannot say.' There was no light when Bertha awoke at six, but her brother Cosmo 'was just getting one—I took the child up and I then discovered that the child was dead—the child was not cold—her little sister was close to her'. The father, now overseer at the New Town Probation Station, told the same sad tale, and like his wife testified that they had had nothing to drink the night before. 'Nothing to my knowledge has been the matter with the child since its birth,' said James Berwick, and the doctor at a time before the recognition of Sudden Infant Death Syndrome could suggest only that 'it might have been suffocated by the breast'. Speculation certain to make Bertha feel terrible.

The next year brought grief to Isabella's family. On 23 September 1846 Henry Hicks was tried at the Supreme Court, charged with 'stealing a cask of [whale] oil (ninety gallons), the property of Mr F.A. Downing of the "New Wharf"'. How mortifying for Isabella to know that gossipy Hobart Town would read in the *Colonial Times* of her husband's conviction and second sentence to seven years' transportation. 'The prisoner', according to the newspaper, 'directed a carter, named Walter Cleary, to take the cask to Mr Bird's, the tanner, who paid him, Cleary, £6 18 [shillings] for the oil'. For the next four years, until Henry was eligible for his ticket of leave, Isabella would be the sole breadwinner for herself and the three children born in her first six years of marriage. What could she do? She and her sister Bertha were both illiterate, could not even sign their names on the marriage register. In other circumstances, a young woman in Isabella's predicament might turn to her mother for help, but Margaret Christie had never shown any signs of being of practical use to her children. And before Henry Hicks got his ticket of leave, Margaret Christie had herself been sentenced again.

On Tuesday 23 October 1849, a neighbour may have read to Isabella the newspaper account of her mother's most recent disgrace:

> *Margaret [Christie] Morris stood indicted with having stolen a glass tumbler, the property of Charles Cox.*
>
> *It appeared from the evidence that on the 1st instant, the prisoner, accompanied by a man, went into the Salutation Inn, and partook of some beer. The man departed first, and the woman a quarter of an hour afterwards. The landlord immediately afterwards missed a tumbler of the value of 9 [pence], and pursued the woman, upon whose person the stolen property was found. She said that the glass was her own, but luckily it had a small cross upon the bottom of it, which Mr Cox identified as his own private mark. The jury returned a verdict of Guilty.*

And then, pouring salt into the wounds, the judge's comment. His Honour 'stated that the prisoner bore a very bad character, that she had been convicted a great many times, and the most lenient sentence he could pass was transportation for seven years'.

At least Margaret Christie's trial came too late in the year to spoil the wedding of her youngest daughter and namesake, Margaret Morris, who was married on 4 July 1849 in the elegant country church at Longford, built as testimony to the wealth of large landowners in the colony's north. Margaret may have been working on one of their properties when she met a convict transported from Liverpool at the age of twenty to serve a ten-year sentence for embezzling from his master. The gaol report sent with David Brookshaw commented on his 'good disposition' and acknowledged 'connexions respectable', but before his sentence to trans-portation, this young man who could both read and write had already served a year in gaol for housebreaking.

He had been in Van Diemen's Land for nine years when he and Mar-garet were married, and with only three charges on his conduct record, now had a conditional pardon (at one stage he, like James Berwick, had been a police constable but he was dismissed after he came into Hobart Town without permission, presumably got drunk, and left his gun at a public house). Within a year of their marriage, Brookshaw was free by servitude, and could legally take his young bride out of the colony and over Bass Strait to Melbourne where their first child, a son named for his father, was born in 1850. The following year a daughter was born, and Margaret named her Mary Isabella, honouring the older sister who had extracted her from the Orphan School and given her a home. This baby mattered so much to Margaret Brookshaw as a link to her older sister that the young mother travelled steerage class from Melbourne to Launceston on the *Yarra Yarra* and then on to Hobart Town by coach to have the baby baptised when she was six months old. Margaret brought her two-year-old son as well, but their father, identified on the baptismal register as a cabinet-maker, stayed at home.

Isabella Hicks must have been delighted to see her younger sister and to witness a baby being baptised in her name. Life was looking better for her own family as well. Henry's second sentence to transportation would expire in a couple of months, and already as a prisoner with a conditional pardon, he could earn wages to help support his growing family of three girls and one boy. Sadly, the period of stability for the Hicks family was short-lived. Less than two years after Margaret's visit, the *Colonial Times* reported:

DAYLIGHT DEPREDATIONS. On Saturday a fellow in the garb of a seaman, or a Water Policeman, was observed to be 'taking care of' a drunken man in the vicinity of the Custom House; on being approached it was ascertained that he was 'easing' the man of his property, but pretended to be his friend. This not being believed, the 'friends' were taken into custody, one for being drunk, and the other for robbing him. Yesterday, detective constable Morley charged Henry Hicks with stealing a leather bag, a chain, and 22s. [shillings], the property of William Dickinson.

At his trial in the Supreme Court, Henry Hicks was described by the newspaper as 'a man of forbidding mien, habited in a blue shirt', who insisted 'that he had been drinking at a public-house, with Dickenson, and he intended merely to take care of the property'. The judge was speechless with 'indignation at his presuming to say that he was innocent. His Honour dwelt in terms of appropriate severity upon the facts of the case and the aggravating circumstances connected with the prisoner's crime, especially referring to his taking advantage of a man like the prosecutor, who was drunk to such a degree, as not to know where he was.' The judge then sentenced the thief to his third term of seven years' transportation, 'intimating that he should recommend that the prisoner be removed as quickly as possible to a penal settlement'. And so Henry Hicks, now almost 40 years old, was sent to Port Arthur, across the harbour from Point Puer where he had spent years of his youth.

Isabella Hicks and her four children, noted the convict conduct record, were at Mrs Berwick's in Campbell Street, Hobart. Homelessness must have been mortifying for Isabella, as well as placing emotional and financial strains on a household already crowded with six Berwick children.

The most recent addition was Cosmo, named for his uncle in the family of Morris siblings who still stuck together. Bertha marked the place for signature with an 'X' when she registered this birth, but the next Berwick baby would be registered by his oldest sister, Sarah, who could sign her name—evidence that her parents sent their children to school, and that is not surprising because among the three husbands of the Morris sisters, James Berwick was the most ambitious.

Six months after Henry Hicks was carted off to Port Arthur, Berwick wrote a letter to Hobart's municipal council, 'soliciting employment under the corporation, and enclosing testimonies'. His application was successful, and he became a city turncock, responsible for controlling water between the mains and supply pipes. He had started on a career which would take him to positions of considerable responsibility within the Water Department. Soon the Berwicks were renting a house in Campbell Street of sufficiently high rateable value to qualify James for jury service, a marker of middle-class status also evident when he joined the Freemasons. In contrast to his brother-in-law Henry Hicks, who figured in the newspapers as a criminal, James Berwick's appearances betokened respectability. The convict emancipist could be proud to know that Hobartians were reading his name as steward for the annual dinner and grand ball held at the Theatre Royal on 5 September 1859 for brethren of the Tasmanian Primitive Lodge.

And as the years passed, the Berwick children kept coming. The last of twelve, another Isabella, was born on 19 June 1867. Bertha Morris Berwick was 45 years old, and had been giving birth for 24 years. All her children except the baby who died in the family bed survived infancy, but her first-born son Thomas died the year before his sister Isabella was born. He was eighteen years old when a notice in the *Mercury* lamented the death of a young man who 'was serving his apprenticeship on this journal and was a most promising youth'.

In spite of the signs of stability and respectable status, the Berwicks were not a happy family. On 2 June 1873, a fortnight before the sixth birthday of their youngest child, James Berwick placed an advertisement in the *Mercury*:

I hereby caution all persons giving credit to any one on my account without my written authority. I also caution any person harbouring my wife, she having left her home without my consent.

The next day Bertha answered with a front-page advertisement of her own:

In reference to an advertisement signed 'James Berwick, Brisbane-street' (which appeared in today's Mercury*) I may inform the public that I, with my family, have left 'his home' without his consent, but not without a good deal of provocation, which the whole of my large family and any of my friends can testify to; and I may also state that the public need not be afraid of my contracting any debts in his name.*

The Berwick marriage was finished.

Bertha found a place for herself and the children in nearby Murray Street, where disaster struck almost immediately. Her angry husband might have called it a sign of God's wrath visited upon a rebellious wife when the Berwicks' sixth son Joseph contracted a virulent fever and died. He was fourteen years old. Devastated though Bertha must have been— and the fever may have spread to other children in the household—she did not return to her husband.

Her grief continued. A month after Joseph died, two notices appeared in the *Mercury* of 12 August: one announced that on 10 August Mrs James Berwick, junior, had been delivered 'of a daughter (prematurely)'; the second announced the death of 'Minnie, only daughter of Mr James Berwick, junior'. Bertha may have remembered the grief she felt as a young mother when her namesake daughter died almost 30 years earlier. James junior and his wife had been married the year before. The death of their first child and the more general Berwick family woes may have determined the young couple to get away from Van Diemen's Land and start afresh somewhere else. With the distinctive surname 'Berwick', James junior may also have wanted to live in a place where he could not be confused with his father. Whatever his motives, James moved to Melbourne, taking his mother with him as well as his wife.

For Bertha, leaving Van Diemen's Land meant separation from Isabella, who was now 50. The sisters had shared so many trials and tribulations from the time of their childhood in Aberdeen, to the voyage into strangeness and the problems of looking after themselves without family or friends when they reached Van Diemen's Land, through the years of having babies and coping with difficult husbands. Isabella's husband Henry Hicks had recently died, and Bertha may have tried to persuade her sister to come with her to Melbourne, but Isabella stayed on the island where most of her children were still living, though her second daughter, Margaret, had been a restless girl who left home to see the world when she was quite young. She had married a grocer in Brisbane, and probably never saw her mother again. In 1905, when she herself was widowed, Isabella's daughter would sail with three of her own daughters to San Francisco to join her son, and would live the rest of her life in California. Her descendants today are Americans—and so the saga of the Morris family of Aberdeen takes another geographical turn.

Bertha Berwick was moving a much shorter distance, but the metropole of post-goldrush Melbourne was nevertheless a strikingly different world from the one she had known in Van Diemen's Land. At least she had a sister there to welcome her. Over many cups of tea, Margaret Brookshaw may have regaled Bertha with stories of living through the goldrush, giving birth to eight children over the nineteen years between 1850 and 1869, and watching the last two die in early childhood, including little Bertha, who died when she was three. Sadly, Margaret's husband, like Bertha's, turned out to be a violent man. His behaviour became public in a newspaper item of May 1855 entitled 'Assault and Maliciously Damaging Property'. David Brookshaw had taken 'a bottle of grog' into the tent of a woman camped on the Collingwood Flat, 'and on the lady refusing to join him in a glass, not only threatened but did pull her tent down'. On the same night, he assaulted a man 'with what he took to be a loaded whip'. The case was heard at the District Court, where Brookshaw was fined £10 for destroying the tent and sentenced to three months' gaol with hard labour for the assault.

Not surprisingly, Brookshaw also bashed his wife and children about. Two years before Bertha Berwick informed the readers of the *Mercury* that she had left her husband 'without his consent, but not without a good deal of provocation', her younger sister Margaret went to court, as the Melbourne *Argus* reported on 12 August 1871:

> *David Brookshaw, a drunken cabinetmaker, who continually ill-used and threatened his wife and family, was ordered to find two sureties in £50 each, that he would keep the peace for 12 months, or go to gaol for that period. The wife said she and her son could support the family.*

All three Morris sisters had difficult marriages, although ironically there is no evidence that the thrice-transported petty criminal Henry Hicks was violent to his family or to anyone else. But in their three large families—Isabella had five children, Bertha twelve, and Margaret eight—the sisters never followed the example of their own mother, Margaret Christie, who gave up on aspirations to respectability. They stayed out of gaol and, unlike Margaret Christie, remained involved in the lives of their children.

Bertha was the first of the sisters to die. Her son James of Grant Street, South Melbourne, registered the death of his mother on 29 January 1890, aged 65, in the home of her daughter in the inner-city suburb of Carlton. James identified his mother as a housewife born in Aberdeen, but reported only the surname, Morris, of his grandparents. Bertha's brother Cosmo, the youngest of the Morris siblings, had died three years before at the age of 55. A shipwright like his father and his brother-in-law Henry Hicks, Cosmo had left Van Diemen's Land for Victoria at the time of the goldrush. Later he went north to Queensland, and once was arrested and fined in Brisbane for drunkenness in the company of other carousing men. The next year he married a young immigrant woman from Lancashire, and they returned south to Melbourne where they were living with their fifteen-year-old daughter in an inner-city suburb not far from his sisters Bertha and Margaret when Cosmo died on 4 July 1887. His wife in registering the death gave his place of birth as Aberdeen and identified his parents as Cosmo Morris and Margaret Morris 'formerly

Christy', but she evaded any whiff of a convict connection by replacing his Tasmanian childhood with an assertion that he had been in Victoria for 52 years. The clerk at the registry office presumably did not notice he was placing Cosmo in the colony before its first settlement.

When the oldest Morris sister, Isabella Hicks, died in the final months of the nineteenth century, the informant for her death was an official of the New Town Charitable Institution, in which more than half the aged patients had been transported as convicts. Ironically, this institution stood within the grounds of the Queen's Orphan Schools. Isabella, who had escaped institutionalisation as an 'orphan' spent her final days a stone's throw from the buildings where her youngest sister and brothers had slept. But this was not the story Isabella's children told when they paid for two notices of her death to be published in the *Mercury*:

> *HICKS. On November 22, 1899, at her late residence, 168 Argyle Street, Hobart, Isabella Hicks, late of Aberdeen, Scotland, relict of the late Henry Hicks, Senior, in the 76th year of her age.*

Her death in a pauper establishment has been erased, and she is returned in text to 'her late residence'.

The circumstances of Margaret Brookshaw's death appear kinder. After an illness of only seven weeks, the youngest of the Morris sisters died on 6 August 1902 in the South Melbourne home of her eldest son, Joel David. He had been a young man of 21 in 1871 when his mother went to court for a restraining order against her violent father, saying that 'she and her son could support the family'. Joel David Brookshaw may have given some thought to how he would tell her story in the information to be recorded on the death certificate. She was a widow, he said, aged 72, her father was James Morris, mariner, 'other particulars' (name of mother) 'not known'. He relocated her birthplace from Aberdeen to Norfolk, England, and reduced her time in Tasmania to two years, just long enough to acknowledge her place of marriage, but not enough to raise questions about whether she was a convict. At the beginning of the twentieth century, fear of a 'convict stain' was real, and Joel David Brookshaw was creating a paper trail which would delete his grandmother, the convict Margaret Christie, from the Morris family saga. No one need know that his own mother, together with his aunts and uncles, came to Australia as children on a convict ship.

THE LAST ORPHANS

In 1842, the year before James and Cosmo Morris left the Male Orphan School to rejoin their sisters, Charles McKenna was 'discharged to his father'. At first this seems a little puzzling. How could the Orphan School hand over a child to a convict father without a ticket of leave, a convict who had notched up a string of charges on his conduct record, had his sentence to transportation extended two years for 'Larceny under £5', and had just spent three months doing hard labour on the Glenorchy road gang? John McKenna had no means to support nine-year-old Charles, and neither did Charles's older brother James, who was still working out his apprenticeship. The one member of the family in a position to earn money was Charles's mother, Catherine McBrayne, whose conduct record had been flawless except for a charge for 'indecent conduct in the street'. Her application for a ticket of leave, granted in February 1842, was lodged in New Norfolk, the settlement up the River Derwent. If John McKenna was allowed to go out to the Orphan School to arrange his son's discharge, he must have been organising travel arrangements to send the boy to his mother in New Norfolk, while the father himself returned to life in the prisoners' barracks of Hobart Town. Whether the McKenna parents ever lived together again seems doubtful. John McKenna died among the male convict paupers on the Tasman Peninsula at Impression Bay in 1853, and before then, the rest of the family may have left the colony.

While Catherine McBrayne apparently arranged for Charles to be retrieved as soon as she could support him, Grace Logan seems to have been in no hurry to release her daughters, Grace and Mary McGuire. She had made her way slowly through the system, incurring fifteen charges for a string of petty offences—being absent without leave, lying drunk in Liverpool Street, being in a disorderly house after hours, representing herself to be free, begging in the streets, behaving in an insolent manner. Somewhere along the line she had teamed up with a man named John Faulkner, transported from Gloucester for poaching deer. Like Grace, Faulkner said at the time of his arrival on the *Eden* in 1836 that he was married with six children. In August 1841 he applied to marry Grace, but the application was not approved, either because there was a question about his marital status (Grace herself was widowed when George McGuire died in Glasgow the year after she was transported) or, more likely, because Grace's conduct record showed no evidence of 'reform' (Faulkner's record in contrast was unblemished). Seven months later, Faulkner applied again, this time successfully, and on 2 July 1842 Grace Logan, widow aged 39—she said she was 40 when she arrived four years earlier—married John Faulkner, widower aged 42, at Trinity Church, Hobart Town.

But they left the girls in the Female Orphan School. Almost three years later, on 11 January 1845, Grace at last retrieved them. The older daughter, Grace McGuire, had been in the Orphan School for nearly seven years, and was almost old enough to be apprenticed. Was the timing of the 'orphan's' release a coincidence? Was Grace Logan expecting her daughter to go out to work and then compliantly hand over her earnings? If so, she was probably disappointed. That stubborn six-year-old who long ago had stood up for herself when falsely accused by her mother in the clergyman's garden was now thirteen, and most likely delighted at the prospect of running her own life.

Within a year or two of release from the Orphan School, Grace McGuire met an Irish convict named Henry Landy who was seventeen years old when he arrived on the *Egyptian* in 1840. In July 1847 Henry was free by servitude, and two years later he and Grace McGuire had escaped the penal isle for a new life in Melbourne where they were married in St Joseph's Catholic Church on 6 May 1849. Their first child was born in Melbourne just as the goldrush began, and the births of their next ten children were registered in the goldfields towns of central Victoria. At the end of her life, this child of the Glasgow streets returned to Melbourne where she died in 1893 and is buried in the Melbourne General Cemetery.

With the McGuire sisters gone from the Orphan schools, only two *Atwick* transportees remained: Margaret Callaghan and Joseph Douglas, the children of unmarried mothers. Margaret and Joseph stayed in the schools until they were old enough to be apprenticed. Both served longer periods as 'orphans' than their mothers did as convicts. Margaret's age is entered as six on the admissions register, which would make her fourteen when she was apprenticed in 1846. Her mother, Elizabeth Brown, had been sent north to the Launceston area within a few months of disembarking, and her 25 charges, most for being drunk, form the pattern of an alcoholic. In January 1844 she would have been free by servitude, and after that she disappears from public record, perhaps because she changed her name. Whether she ever saw her little girl again, I do not know, but at least it looks as if Margaret Callaghan had found some sort of family life in the Orphan School because she chose to return to its church in 1860 to be married by her old headmaster, Rev. Ewing. Margaret married a widowed farmer, Thomas Lane, and their four children were born in Tasmania.

Margaret Callaghan's mother looks like a careless woman, careless about her daughter, careless about herself. Jean Smith, the mother of Joseph Douglas, was someone entirely different, and I will return later to her story, but it is not a story which includes her first-born son. Joseph was only four years old when he was separated from his mother after they entered the Cascades Female Factory from the *Atwick* in 1838, and like Margaret Callaghan, he probably never saw her again. With no one in the world to care for him, he remained subject to the Orphan School's austere discipline for more than ten years before he was apprenticed to a settler named James Crear and went to work on his substantial property 'Clynvale', at Cleveland in the Midlands, not far from where his mother was living with her husband and their growing family of children. After his apprenticeship, Joseph seems to have stayed in the area. Within the networks of farming activities in the Midlands, of buying and selling sheep and bartering for feed and produce, did Joseph Douglas ever unknowingly encounter his half-brothers, this child genuinely transformed by transportation into an orphan?

8

MOTHERHOOD UNDER SENTENCE

Almost all the Scottish convicts were still of childbearing age when they arrived in Van Diemen's Land, and their sentences of seven years or more inevitably affected their reproductive lives. Escaping the dangers of childbirth may have come as a relief to some of the women, while others were probably put off by the prospect of motherhood within the convict system. Enduring life as assigned servants was bad enough without having to spend months locked up in the stench of a convict nursery amidst sick and dying children. And yet, in spite of the risks and the difficulties and the unpleasantness, women under sentence continued to give birth. Some of course had no choice, had been coerced into sex. An image of masters as sexual predators was being fostered at this time by those in England and the colonies who wanted to get rid of the assignment system, and some women were undoubtedly abused in the households where they worked. How many, we will never know. The register of births might yield clues if the names of the fathers were routinely entered in the column provided, but they weren't. A child born in a female factory had no father as far as the Registrar General's Department was concerned. Babies from the convict nurseries were stigmatised from the beginning, their births designating them the illegitimate offspring of immoral mothers.

The convict system was a brutal impediment to forming families. This situation made matters worse for children born to women who themselves had little experience of loving and supportive family. Many of the convicts who became mothers under sentence had been fending for themselves on the streets where as girls of twelve or thirteen they began thieving. They were unlikely to start thinking 'family' in any positive sense when a master labelled them 'useless being pregnant', and returned them to a female factory where they were forced to don the demeaning garb of the crime class and eat the inadequate rations befitting punishment for the 'crime' of motherhood under sentence. No one was going to teach them 'mothering' skills inside the prison walls, and those who remembered their own mothers as women from whom to escape were ill prepared to think constructively about how best to protect children born into the convict system. A prison setting is no place to break cycles of abuse. Disturbed young convicts were likely to make disturbed mothers. Agnes Campbell Robertson was one of these.

AN UNDIAGNOSED PATHOLOGY: AGNES CAMPBELL ROBERTSON

There is something very strange and disconcerting about Agnes Campbell Robertson and her relationship to children. Even though no one who wrote up her records of crime and punishment ever suggested that she was suffering from a pathology, the patterns of her behaviour are disturbing. At the time of her crimes in Scotland, Agnes herself was on the cusp of childhood. When arrested on New Year's Eve 1834, she told the authorities that she was about sixteen, and had only recently come to Glasgow from Paisley where she lived with her father. At the first of her two trials before the High Court of Justiciary, Agnes was indicted for stealing clothes 'from the persons of young children of very tender years . . . by means of decoying or seducing such children to a great distance from their homes'. After waiting in prison for almost four months, she was tried, pleaded guilty, and sentenced to a further fifteen months in Glasgow's Bridewell. Less than three months after her release in July 1836, she began again to steal from children. These thefts continued intermittently for six weeks until she was arrested on 12 November 1836 and charged with the eight thefts for which she would be sentenced to fourteen years' transportation.

A crime known specifically as 'child-stripping' had become a matter of public concern and colours the *Glasgow Herald*'s report of Agnes's second arrest:

A female is at present in custody, in the Gorbals Police Office, charged with an immense number of acts of stripping children, a crime which has of late become exceedingly common . . .. This female seems to have carried on the practice to an extent, and with a heartlessness, never before known. On one occasion . . . (a wet cold day) she wiled a little boy from Gorbals to Calton, took away his stockings, shoes, and nearly all his upper dress, and left him. The poor thing, in consequence, caught cold, and died soon after. Numerous other instances of her callousness have come to light.

'Heartlessness', 'callousness', words of unequivocal condemnation. However inconsequential the value of the items stolen, these were no ordinary property crimes because the thief preyed upon small children. What impelled Agnes to lure the children away, spend time with them, often with the physical contact of actually carrying them in her arms, then undress and abandon them?

Agnes Campbell Robertson did not steal in order to eat. Though she probably had no formal education and could not sign her name, she did have a trade, as she told the woman to whom she sold one victim's tartan frock, giving her correct name, and saying that she 'was a Straw Hat Maker'. If she was employed at the time of the thefts, this might explain why she could afford to keep the stolen clothes as fetishes or trophies, and why she met most of the children around five in the afternoon, including three-year-old John McLean whose death had so outraged the newspapers, even though he actually died of measles. John's mother, in her witness statement for the precognition, recalled the afternoon when her son went outside 'about ten minutes past 5 o'clock'. While he was playing with two neighbour boys, 'a girl had come up to him, and desired him to go with her and she would buy him a horse and a coach, and sweeties and raisins'. Agnes lured children through their desires for toys and sweet food. She promised another boy 'a Poney & some barley sugar', and to the girls she promised dolls, a string of beads, apples, and a tart. John agreed to go, Agnes picked him up, and over the next hour and more, she carried him several kilometres away from his home in Laurieston, taking him across the bridge over the River Clyde into the old parts of Glasgow, crossing the open spaces of Glasgow Green, and walking north to the industrial suburb of Calton. There she set him down, took off his black cloth dress, brown linen overall, and his shoes. Then she left him on the cold dark street. John's mother was the first witness at Agnes's trial, and one can imagine the jury's response to her tale of woe.

The second witness told the story of finding the frightened little boy. The wife of a cotton-spinner heard 'a child crying in the thro' going close near her House', and first 'thought it some of the neighbours children who were crying, but having at length gone out she felt in the dark a little Boy having a shirt, stockings & Handkerchief on his person'. She brought him inside, and asked his name, which he knew, but he couldn't tell her where he lived. She then 'put a large shawl upon the Boy and carried him thro the Streets expecting that he should be able to point out his residence, but he could not and she took him home to her House'. There 'he cried himself sick, and having fallen asleep she put him to bed'. Many people came in to see him, and at last a young man went across the river to the Gorbals Police Office where they knew about his disappearance, and the boy's aunt came to fetch him. How could the jury fail to be moved by this story, ending as it does in the death of the child? But was Agnes herself moved? Was she suddenly confronted with the consequences of her behaviour, and devastated at the hurt she had caused? So many questions, so few answers, for understanding Agnes—and the children.

The trustingness of these city children is puzzling, Agnes did not drag them away; they went with her. One child did sound a warning, an eight-year-old girl who told her five-year-old playmate not to go with Agnes, as her 'mother had often cautioned [her] not to go with strangers for fear of being stripped'. The parents may have hoped their children would be protected in the respectable neighbourhoods where they lived. Agnes never took children from rough neighbourhoods, children with street sense. Her victims came from intact families, where the fathers were tradesmen or small shopkeepers. The children were dressed by mothers who paid attention to clothes, as we can tell from the items Agnes stole, gold earrings from a four-year-old, the fashionable tartan frocks three of them wore, a boy's 'Tuscan Hat trimmed with Buff ribbons' and a girl's 'striped Tuscany Dunstable Bonnet trimmed with pink ribbons'. These were the clothes of the aspiring middle class, not the recycled detritus of second-hand shops. Four-year-old Margaret Buchanan, who told her story in the courtroom at Agnes's trial, had been horrified when taken to a 'dirty, dirty, House' where Agnes drank some whisky. Margaret, the daughter of a manufacturer, was unacquainted with the seamier side of Glasgow tenements, and perhaps it was the sheer shock of the foreign that made her submit when Agnes 'stripped off' her leather boots, tartan frock and linen pinafore.

Two of the fifteen witnesses at Agnes's trial—a trial going into detail unheard of for cases of theft in an English court like London's Old Bailey—bore testimony to what Agnes did with her ill-gotten gains. After stealing from John McLean, Agnes went back to her lodgings, told her landlady 'she had got [the clothes] from her Aunt', and asked a sixteen-year-old girl who was visiting to sell them, which she did, returning 9 pence to Agnes who then bought 'some strong-beer' to treat the girl, her landlady, and her landlord. A few days later, Agnes gave the girl 'a pair of Gold Ear-Rings, [as] a present and said she had got them from a sweetheart of hers'. They may have been gold, but they were obviously for a child, and the girl gave them to the landlady's little daughter. Agnes comes across as bereft of real friends.

Although she pleaded not guilty at her trial, her initial confession was already on the record and was read out to the court after the children and their parents were heard (the accused themselves were not examined in the courtroom). According to the *Glasgow Courier*, Agnes's own counsel 'declined addressing the Jury'— as if there were no point. When Lord Meadowbank 'asked the Gentlemen of the Jury if it was necessary for him to sum up the evidence', they said no and without retiring to consider their decision 'instantly returned a verdict of guilty. The prisoner was then adjudged to 14 years' transportation. On receiving sentence, [she] dropped down in a swoon at the bar.'

Agnes was a thief, no doubt about that, and she was cruel. She also seems to have been driven by some pathology compelling her again and again to make friends with young children, frighten them by taking off their clothes, and then abandon them. The children at first found her fascinating. They remembered her clothes in detail, a 'green Gown, light handkerchief, checked apron, white stockings and black slippers', said one; she 'had on a red shawl and had red cheeks & wore green slippers', said another. What had happened to Agnes to turn her into a predator, to entrap her within compulsively repetitive behaviour? This is a question I continue to find troubling as I track her through the records of the convict system.

Upon arrival in Hobart Town, Agnes the 'Straw bonnet maker' was assigned to a merchant named John Johnson with a shop in Liverpool Street. Johnson specialised in bonnets 'of the latest and newest fashion', and his advertisements in the *Colonial Times* touted the very same Dunstable and Tuscan bonnets Agnes knew so well because she had been stealing them from children. Knowledgeable as Agnes might have been and quite possibly skilled, too, she was far from an ideal worker. In April, May, and June of the year she arrived, she wandered off from her master's premises. A charge of 'absent without leave' in April sent her to the Cascades Female Factory for ten days in the dark cells; in May when she was gone for two nights, she went back to the cells for another ten days, this time on bread and water; and in June when she stayed away for five days, she went to the solitary working cells for a month. The Principal Superintendent of Convicts recommended that she afterwards be 'assigned in the Country', although for some reason her exile extended no further than the suburb of New Town. In October she was reprimanded for absenting herself from her new master, Captain Read, and in December she was back in the cells for another ten days on bread and water after being away all night. As on the streets of Glasgow, she seems locked into a cycle of compulsive repetition, walking away from her work, being punished, going back, and walking off again. And then in March 1839 the cycle was broken with a brazen theft using a child as a prop.

For this crime, Agnes was arrested with Catherine Bain, a red-headed Scot convicted in her native Aberdeen and transported on the *Westmoreland* a little more than a year before the *Atwick* sailed. Like Agnes,

Catherine was punished repeatedly for going off from the places to which she was assigned, and the two serial absconders may have cooked up their scheme while under punishment in the Female Factory. Both were consummate actors. In a penal colony where shopkeepers had reason to treat unknown customers with caution, the young women fooled the shopman of an emporium known as Wellington House in central Hobart Town where everything was sold from 'slops' (cheap rough clothing) to the 'fancy goods' attractive to prosperous customers. They entered the shop under the guise of a mistress whose servant was carrying her child. Catherine the mistress 'asked to be shown some half-mourning prints', while 'Robertson said nothing but walked about with the child'. Catherine tried charging dress materials to the account of Captain Read, Agnes's erstwhile master and now hers. The shopman, reported the *Colonial Times*, 'said that he could not do so without an order, which she said she had not got; she then purchased, and paid for, two pairs of gloves and a ribbon; during this time, the child nursed by Robertson, was crying, and she walked in and out of the shop as though soothing the child, although most probably conveying goods out to a confederate'. Was Agnes pinching the baby as she moved back and forth from the counter to the accomplice waiting outside? She must have made several trips over some extended time because the haul was impressive: '35 yards of print, 2 lbs silk thread, and 17 pairs of gloves'.

With this considerable loot, the thieves left the shop, and adjourned with their accomplice to a public house nearby. Seeing people in the taproom, 'they went into the parlour, where [the publican] was lying on the sofa reading the paper; as they made a considerable noise, he looked up and saw the women' throw a 'quantity of prints upon the table'. They borrowed a pair of scissors and 'commenced cutting it up and dividing it amongst them'. Not surprisingly, the publican suspected 'that all was not right', and when the women left, he contacted the police, who seem to have had little trouble locating the culprits. At their trial, Agnes and Catherine mounted no defence, though the accomplice—who was not a convict—attempted to get an alibi from a woman whose unfortunate surname was 'Shark'. All three were found guilty. Agnes was sentenced to three years' hard labour in the Female Factory, her conduct to be reported in two years. She was also reprimanded for 'Absenting herself without leave & taking her mistresses child with her'.

Agnes was sent to the crime class at the Cascades Factory, where she ate the meagre and unvaried diet, wore a jacket with a large yellow 'C' on both sleeves and on her petticoat, and slogged away at whatever hard labour was available for punishment, unpalatable tasks like washing filthy blankets from the Colonial Hospital and Orphan Schools. She stayed out of trouble, showing no interest in the defiant subculture run by Ellen Scott, Mary Sheriff and the Flash Mob. She was in the crime class during the bread riot of May 1839, but apparently took no part and seems more of a loner. When her case was reviewed after two years, the Lieutenant Governor remitted the unexpired portion of her sentence to imprisonment, and she was assigned to a master.

Once outside, she began to abscond again. Less than a fortnight into her new employment—after more than two years locked behind prison walls—she was charged with being absent without leave, and sent back to the Female Factory for six weeks at the wash tub. In mid-August she was assigned to another employer who charged her in late September with being absent without leave, and back she went for a month in the separate working cells. About the beginning of November she went to yet another employer who in late December charged her with being absent without leave, for which she was sentenced to '3 months at the wash tub then assigned in the Interior'. And so the straw bonnet maker, a city girl whose trade had long ceased to matter in the situations to which she was assigned, was sent out to work on a farm at the Black Brush in the hills behind Brighton, to the east of Hobart Town. After less than a month she made her way back into town, perhaps with help from the man who fathered her child born in December while Agnes was serving a nine-month sentence for the absconding. When she gave birth to a daughter, Agnes Campbell Robertson had been in the colony for nearly five years, of which she had spent almost three and a half in prison.

After the birth of her baby, she changed. Four and a half years passed before she was again charged with anything. Agnes seems to have found her metier when she entered the nursery with her baby. She would have lived there for at least nine months during 1842 while breastfeeding, but it looks as if she stayed on afterwards, and was actually assigned to work at the nursery, because in June 1844 a notice was published twice in the *Hobart Town Gazette* to say that permission had been granted for Charles Berkins, a convict constable transported on the *England*, to marry Agnes Campbell Robinson (sic), *Atwick*, in service at the Female Nursery, Dynnyrne, Hobart Town. For some reason, they didn't marry.

In September that year Agnes was granted a ticket of leave, and assuming that she found a job (looking after children?), could have made a home for herself and her little girl. Another man applied to marry her, but didn't, in 1845—he was the third applicant; the first had been refused in 1841 when her record was too bad for the 'indulgence' to be granted. In 1846 Agnes registered the birth of a second daughter, identifying the father as a licensed victualler named John Connolly. The next year another licensed victualler applied to marry her, and on 23 March 1847 Agnes Campbell Robinson (sic), aged 26, married George Farris, aged 42, in the Bethesda chapel of St George's Church, Battery Point, with her shipmate and fellow Scot, Catherine Forsyth, as a witness. Agnes does not seem to have settled readily into the domestic routines of marriage, and it would have been surprising if she had. Everything about her says restless, unstable. She lured children only to abandon them on the streets of Glasgow, absconded from one master after another, and left one man after another, the men who applied to marry her or spent time with her while she was 'absent without leave', the men who fathered her first two children.

Tensions in Agnes's early married life were translated by her convict status into breaches of discipline. As a ticket-of-leave holder, she could earn wages but was still under surveillance, and required to return each night to her registered 'abode'. A month after the wedding, she was hauled before the convict authorities and reprimanded for unspecified misconduct, and little more than two months later she was reprimanded for being 'Absent from her authorized place of residence'. At the same hearing she was sentenced to a month's hard labour for 'Refusing in presence of the magistrate to return to her place of residence'—refusing in other words to return to her husband. Apparently she preferred prison to home.

There may have been good reasons for this. Agnes was not the only one in this marriage without experience of domesticity. George Farris had been in the colony for 23 years before he married. He had come free as a young man, and seven years after his arrival was still depending upon credit to stock his small shop in Hobart Town. In 1834 he was arrested for forgery and tried with a man identified in the *Hobart Town Courier* as W. Saib Ralph, a soldier in the British Army during the Peninsular War who had served under Wellington and 'behaved with much courage'. The newspaper claimed, improbably, that he 'is the son of the sister of the great Indian Prince Tippoo Saib', the legendary Sultan of Mysore against whom the British fought four wars. Farris pleaded guilty at his trial and was sentenced to transportation for life. Four months into his sentence he was punished at Port Arthur for 'not performing his work on the plea of inability', but that was the single blot on his conduct record. Farris settled into the institutionalised male world of Port Arthur, where in 1838 he became a police constable. In 1842 he received a ticket of leave, in 1843 was recommended at the beginning of the year for a conditional pardon, and at the end for an absolute pardon. And then, free to go wherever he liked in the colonies, he moved across the harbour to take up an appointment as assistant superintendent at Point Puer, the boys' prison. This was a mistake. The superintendent did not like his new assistant, and after three months fired Farris.

Shocked and desperate, he petitioned the Lieutenant Governor: 'owing to the supercilious treatment I experienced from the Superintendent, and the incompetence I witnessed and attempted to remedy [my appointment] has ended disastrously as I have been deprived of my situation and am now without employment of any kind'. No one was going to stand up for a recently released convict in an argument with a senior officer, and Farris was faced with finding other work at a time when the economy had taken a drastic downturn. He went into Hobart Town, and in November 1846 acquired the licence for a pub in the Old Market

Place, near the harbour. Three months later, he applied to marry Agnes. Did she know that her future husband was insolvent?

Money woes must have added to the other difficulties facing this unlikely couple in the early months of their marriage, but in August 1847 when she was released from her month's hard labour for refusing to return to her place of residence, Agnes went back to Farris or at least she was with him five months later for the census of January 1848. So was one female child, aged over two and under seven, an age which fits Agnes's first child born in 1842. Her second child, daughter of John Connolly, would have been younger. Where was she? With her father? Dead? There is only one further sighting of Agnes. A month after the census, on Valentine's Day a year after George Farris applied to marry her, Agnes gave birth to a third daughter. The birth was registered by a friend. 'Agnes Campbell Robertson' is the name listed in the register as mother and then repeated as father. Why was this? Was the friend deliberately refusing to name the father? Had Agnes asked her to? Why did the clerk in the Registrar General's office comply? And where did Agnes go after this? She and George Farris simply disappear from the records. Did they leave the colony? Together? What happened to the children? The storyline simply stops. I cannot find her anywhere.

STARTING A FAMILY IN A CONVICT NURSERY: ELIZABETH WADDELL

Having children is not the same thing as starting a family, and yet families with long-lasting bonds *were* started while mothers were under sentence. Faced with all the impediments the convict system could throw at them, some women and men managed under dire circumstances to create families which lasted. The enduring attachment between the convicts Elizabeth Waddell and Henry Cox is one such tribute to trust and love.

At the time they met in Hobart Town, Elizabeth certainly did not look like a promising parent. When examined in Glasgow for her precognition in February 1837, she said she had worked some time ago as a piecer in a cotton mill, and was eighteen years old, which would make her about sixteen when first convicted. In retrospect, Elizabeth's behaviour during the three months before her final arrest looks chaotic and self-destructive, leading inexorably if unintentionally to transportation. The first of at least five thefts was a family affair, impelled perhaps by anger against a mother who could not or did not meet her needs.

On 8 December 1836 Elizabeth showed up on the doorstep of her mother's cousin in the village of Airdrie, 18 kilometres east of Glasgow. She said she had left the city because she was hunting a girl who had taken her gown, and she asked the cousin if she could 'sleep in the house all night'. This was a family of handloom weavers, and the son, who was a couple of years older than his cousin Elizabeth, was the proud owner of a silver watch hanging on a nail inside the kitchen bed. Next morning Elizabeth took the watch when she left the house. Back in the Glasgow old town, she ran into another weaver who when later questioned would say he knew her a little and 'went with her to a public house and treated her to a dram'. She then showed him the watch and said it 'was her uncle's who lived in Airdrie and that she had got up that morning in her uncle's house and left it taking the watch with her'. She asked him to sell the stolen watch (fewer questions would be asked of a man with a watch), and he agreed. He got 10 shillings for it, of which 'she returned him 2/6 for his trouble'.

Though the other thefts had nothing directly to do with her family, they continued to involve betrayals of trust. A fortnight after stealing her cousin's watch, she was caught thieving in inner Glasgow, was tried in the Calton police court, and sentenced to 30 days' imprisonment in the local Bridewell. A day or so after her release, she was still in Calton when she talked her way into a job as servant to a glazier and his wife. The glazier worked from home, and in a room adjoining the kitchen another woman 'was at work tambouring' (embroidering) on the afternoon Elizabeth took advantage of her employers' temporary absence to sneak out of the house, taking with her the family's blankets from the kitchen bed, 'two pairs of Scotch blankets, one pair having red borders and the other blue'. Why did she do this? She had employment and a place to live, but instead of working, she stole and went straight to a second-hand shop to sell the blankets for 7 shillings.

A week later she had left Calton for nearby Bridgeton, where she stopped at the door of a woman with an infant child whose pensioner husband was twice her age. She 'pretended she was destitute and had got no victuals for two days', and 'out of sympathy' the woman took her in, 'gave her her dinner and some yarn to wind and at night she was allowed to sleep in the house'. The next evening, the woman went out for an hour, and when she returned, she 'found that Waddell had absconded leaving the infant in the cradle crying' and her few precious possessions gone—a printed cotton gown, two shawls, and a pair of earrings she described as gold though the broker to whom Elizabeth sold them dismissed them as brass. The useless pensioner husband slept dead drunk through the theft and the cries of the child.

Less than a fortnight later, Elizabeth Waddell tried her luck with another woman also living in Bridgeton. She asked for work, and 'as she was ill off, and out of compassion', the woman 'engaged her to serve her and take care of the children, on the rate of 1/ [shilling] a week, & her meat'. The next afternoon, the woman left Elizabeth to look after the baby while she went to enquire about work at a local mill. The minute her employer was gone, Elizabeth bundled up clothes, took an umbrella, put on her mistress's mantle, and walked out the door. A neighbour, hearing 'the cries of the child . . . was led to go to the House & found the infant laying on the floor as it had fallen out of the cradle'. Elizabeth went to the house of a girl she knew, and asked her to pawn a 'merino gown, tartan shawl, white silk shawl and striped apron' which she said she got from an aunt in Calton. The girl agreed, and took the stolen goods into the shop of a clothes-dealer while Elizabeth hovered outside the door. The woman in the shop later said she had not noticed Elizabeth, 'and she would not have bought any thing from her as she and her husband were some time ago put to trouble about a flannel petticoat they bought from her which turned out to have been stolen'.

Unlike Elizabeth's earlier victims, some of whom may not even have bothered to go to the police, this outraged mother went looking for the culprit and 'after anxious enquiry succeeded in finding the prisoner and got her apprehended . . . in Princes Street, Glasgow, by Robert Stewart one of the Glasgow Police watchmen and taken to the Police Office'. The woman walked along with them to the station, and on the way heard Elizabeth confess to 'having stolen all the articles missed'. Indeed, she was actually dressed in the stolen clothes, wearing her erstwhile employer's green printed gown with blue-striped apron and a black handkerchief. She had no other clothes, and would have been consigned to prison garb if not for the kind-heartedness of her victim who requested that she be allowed to continue wearing them.

Elizabeth was genuinely destitute. When questioned before the magistrate, she said that she 'resides in the house of her mother who is the wife of George Mathieson cotton spinner situated in Wilson's Land, Kirk Street, Calton near Glasgow'. But this was not true. Elizabeth did not live with her mother. She was on the streets, going from one household to another, stealing as she went. How long she had been doing this is not clear, though the sergeant-major of the Calton police who had witnessed her two trials at the local police court for theft, had considered her 'habite and repute a thief' for almost two years since her first conviction in May 1835.

Elizabeth seems to have been very much on her own, not integrated into a family. Even her surname was improvised from her unstable background, as she explained to the magistrate: 'though her father's name was Waddle, yet she sometimes goes by the name of Cunningham from her mother having been married at one time to a person of that name, but she was never known by the name of Mathieson'. Within a week of her arrest, Elizabeth was questioned three times as earlier victims came in to make their statements, and she admitted each theft, named the brokers to whom she sold goods and the prices she received. Her case was straightforward, and the sentence to seven years' transportation inevitable.

Elizabeth had little reason to mourn her exile. What she needed was a chance to take control of her life, and ironically, transportation gave her that opportunity, even though for years the control would be heavily circumscribed by the dictates of her convict status. Soon after disembarking from the *Atwick*, she was assigned to Richard Brown, a cooper who lived and worked at the Old Wharf in the area along the waterfront where Elizabeth probably met Henry Cox, who was to be the father of her eight children and her partner until death. Cox had been nineteen years old when he arrived in Van Diemen's Land on the *Georgiana* on 1 February 1833, almost exactly five years before the *Atwick* dropped anchor. He must have been in a state of shock. A mere two months before his ship left, he and another farm worker had been arrested for a theft in Chiddingly, a village in East Sussex. The thefts were paltry—two hats, a knife, a 2-shilling piece—but the sentence was brutal: transportation for life.

In Van Diemen's Land he was sent to apply his farming skills on a 3,000-acre property on the River Clyde in the Hamilton district. The estate, known as 'Lawrenny', belonged to Edward Lord, one of the colony's earliest and most controversial settlers. Lord was in England at this time, and the property was under the control of a manager, with whom Cox got along fairly well for the first year and a half, his only punishment a reprimand for being absent without leave. Then on 23 August 1834 something happened. Cox was hauled before a local magistrate on 'suspicion of felony', committed to trial, and sent down to Hobart Town. There his case was dropped 'by the Attorney General in consequence of the want of legal evidence to support the charge', but a 'violent suspicion of felony' remained in the minds of officers in the Convict Department, and he was punished anyway, sentenced to be worked twelve months on the brutal Spring Hill road party. Five months into that sentence he was charged with 'improper conduct in pilfering from a fellow prisoner' and sentenced to eight months' imprisonment with hard labour in addition to his current sentence on the road gang. By May 1836 the twenty months of gruelling labour were over, and he was again assigned to private service. After less than two months, he was charged on 25 July 1836 with disobedience of orders and sentenced to be flogged. Twenty-five lashes. Four years, almost to the very day, had passed since his arrest in Sussex.

For a 'lifer' facing years in the system this was a bad beginning, and promised more physical punishment to come. And then unexpectedly the direction of Cox's life changed, a change signalled by blankness on his conduct record. Never again was he charged with even the slightest breach of discipline. It would be another five years before he got a ticket of leave, so he was working without wages all this time, but he was also working without conflict, and the reason for this may be that he came in from the countryside and was assigned to a master in Hobart Town who taught him a trade which would stand him in good stead, the trade of a cooper. Coopers were essential for shipbuilding, a major local industry. Their trade was skilled, and they were much in demand in an economy dependent upon barrels to move goods around. The master who taught Cox the trade gave him a future. And by stabilising his daily life into the routines of valued work rather than punishment for crime, the master probably brought relief to a bitter young man, lifting some of the burden of anger, so that when Cox met Elizabeth Waddell on the Old Wharf where the coopers worked by the harbour, he could be open to the softer emotions of love.

Henry and Elizabeth met very soon after she arrived. She was twenty or 21, and Henry about four years older. Before long they were lovers, which probably explains why Elizabeth was charged on 26 March 1838 with being absent all night without leave. She paid for her night's pleasure with four days in the solitary cells on bread and water. Less than a year later their first child was born, a girl named Henrietta after her father. It seems unlikely that Henry Cox ever saw his daughter because after she was weaned, Elizabeth had to leave her behind in the convict nursery where she died. We know about her only because an entry in the burial register for St David's Church notes the burial on 5 March 1840 of Henrietta Waddle, aged twelve months, convict's child. Did Elizabeth and Henry stand together at the grave as Rev. William Bedford yet again intoned the words of burial over a child from the convict nursery, a child with no experience of family?

In the months after Henrietta's death, the grieving parents may have seen little of each other. Henry Cox was still working down on the wharf, while Elizabeth was assigned to a lawyer who lived in a more salubrious part of town. Being apart must have been difficult. Not surprisingly, Elizabeth was punished in early November for absconding, and at the beginning of December for being drunk. Both times she was sent to the solitary cells—in the first instance for fourteen long days—and then returned to her master. In mid-July the next year she was 'returned to the Crown, being pregnant', and three months later gave birth in the Female Factory hospital to their second daughter, Agnes. At least Elizabeth did not have to take baby Agnes to the house in Liverpool Street where Henrietta died, because the nursery had now moved to Dynnyrne House, closer to the Female Factory in South Hobart.

As long as she was breastfeeding Agnes, Elizabeth would not be assigned, but she must have dreaded the thought of abandoning a second baby to the perils of the nursery. And somehow, Elizabeth did manage to take Agnes away. I can only guess how this happened. Henry Cox at last had a ticket of leave and could support his baby daughter. Even so, giving a baby from the convict nursery into the care of her unmarried ticket-of-leave father depended on the goodwill of the matron, Harriett Slee, and I suspect that Mrs Slee helped Elizabeth and Henry in much the same way as the Wettenhalls helped Jean Boyd and John Clark: she overlooked the regulations and thought about the welfare of a family. Mrs Slee, unlike most of her male colleagues, believed that convict women made good mothers—and she said so on the public record.

The matron must have approved the arrangements made by Elizabeth and Henry for their daughter's care, but what were those arrangements? Who cared for the baby while the parents worked? Where did she sleep at night? Did the master to whom Elizabeth was assigned allow the baby to live with her? Or did Henry arrange for someone to look after her during the day and then take her home with him at night? Of course he might have paid to have her boarded out entirely, sent to a 'baby farmer', but I don't think that Matron Slee would have approved, and she must have had confidence in the arrangements—and in the parents—because she was taking a professional risk. If the baby died and the newspapers got hold of the story during an inquest, the matron could be in the firing line for allowing a convict's child to leave the nursery. Whatever the arrangements for baby Agnes, all children in the colony were vulnerable, and even the most caring parents could not always stave off death. In the autumn of 1843 Elizabeth went to the office of the Registrar General to inform the civil authorities that Agnes Waddell, cooper's daughter aged eighteen months, had died on 10 April of quinsy, a complication of tonsillitis.

Elizabeth and Henry had been lovers for five years when their second daughter died, years marked by long periods of separation while Elizabeth was locked up to give birth and breastfeed her babies, and then seared by grief when the babies died. It was a trying prelude to marriage, but the clock was ticking off the years of Elizabeth's sentence, and on 1 July 1843, not quite three months after Agnes's death, she was granted a ticket of leave. The next month, Henry the 'lifer' applied to the convict authorities for permission to marry Elizabeth. For seven years now his record had been entirely clean, not a single charge for even the slightest misdemeanour. Permission was granted, and on 18 September Henry Cox, cooper aged 30, married Elizabeth Waddell, spinster aged 26, in Holy Trinity Church. The ceremony was performed by the clergyman who had buried their daughter five months earlier.

Nine months after the marriage, the couple's third child was born. Elizabeth went again to the Registrar General's office and ensured that this child would be recognised within the structure of family, not of convict regulations: George, son of Henry Cox, cooper, and of Elizabeth, formerly Waddell, of Patrick Street, entered the public record. The following month Elizabeth and Henry stood with their baby in front of the congregation at Holy Trinity, and through the public ritual of baptism took another step closer towards belonging to a community not as prisoners but as parents. The next decade may have been the happiest in Elizabeth's life. Baby George was a new beginning for her. Two months before his birth, she was freed, her sentence complete, her old life of theft gone forever. Her first boy was born in a home, not a prison. And he lived. As did the next three boys born at two-year intervals. The house no doubt became crowded, and paying for this increasing brood was tough on the parents. When Elizabeth registered the birth of her fourth son in 1850, she identified his father as cooper and herself as servant. Did she sometimes remember wistfully her two lost daughters? Did she ever fantasise about having girls around the house? They could have helped a mother who must have been working very hard.

How physically robust was she in December 1854 when she gave birth to her fifth son and seventh child, Charles? It's impossible to know how her teenage years of prison and destitution affected her later health, though even a thriving toddler might have succumbed to the measles from which Charles died when he was fourteen months old. His parents grieved, and when their last child was born in 1856, they again named him Charles. He died as well, aged sixteen months, of inflammation of the chest. For a fourth time the parents stood beside the grave of a child who had lived long enough to have a real personality, and to be sorely missed, three graves in the burial ground of Holy Trinity, and that first grave at St David's.

Whether to escape the sadness of their little boys' deaths or for other reasons, the Coxes soon moved from their house up the hill in Patrick Street down to the docks, and in 1858 they were renting a house from Richard Brown, the cooper to whom Elizabeth was first assigned and who may have taught Henry his trade. The house, valued at £20, was probably a wooden structure in the tenement behind the stone warehouse where Brown had a store as well as his cooperage. After two years, they moved again, perhaps because business around the Old Wharf had slowed after the construction of a new wharf across the harbour. The work available to 46-year-old Henry Cox may have been less regular than it once was, and this might explain why he decided to join the government service, even though it meant moving the family across the island to Launceston, where a position was available for a cooper-storeman in the bonded warehouse of the Customs Department. For the boys, the journey itself must have been exciting. Unlike their parents who had sailed across the world to reach Van Diemen's Land, these 'native-born' lads had never been far from their place of birth in Hobart Town.

Was Elizabeth, now in her early forties, apprehensive about starting over somewhere new? Whatever her fears, she could not foresee the accident vividly recounted in the Launceston *Examiner* on 9 November 1861, less than two years after the move:

Last Thursday afternoon as Henry Cox, a storeman at the Bonded Ware-house, was engaged in piling up some chests of tea, a portion of an unusually high stack of malt in bags fell down, completely burying him. Bond, the assistant storeman, was close by, and was surrounded by bags, but for-tunately was not hurt; and having managed to extricate himself, ran out and called for assistance, which was promptly rendered, and poor Cox was extricated. It was then found that his leg was broken just above the ancle [sic], and his face and body were much bruised. Mr Dickins immediately rode up for Dr Grant, who on arriving at the spot directed that Cox, who was in great pain, should be conveyed home, where the doctor attended to his broken limb.

'The limb', reported the newspaper three days later, 'is so inflamed it has been found impossible to splinter it'. Henry must have been in agony for days or weeks, and Elizabeth beside herself with worry that the leg might not heal. She could scarcely feed the family of growing boys on her wages as a cleaner at the Grammar School. She got a job for her second son William as 'boots' to the boarders, but this would have brought in little more than pocket money, though every bit helped.

Thankfully, Henry Cox recovered and went limping back to the job described by his descendant Gwenda Webb in her account of the family as a 'comparatively humble' appointment which involved opening casks for the Customs officials who imposed duty on goods shipped to Launces-ton. He also had to move and stack the goods, a dangerous job for a man his age, as the accident proved, but the wages were dependable, and his reliable record acted as a recommendation for his oldest son, George, to join the Customs Department as a cooper in 1864. George, unlike his parents, had been to school, and Elizabeth must have been very proud to send him off to register the birth of his youngest brother, signing his name with a flourish in the column where she had always placed an 'X'. George was bound for far higher positions than his illiterate father ever achieved.

How satisfying for Elizabeth to watch her sons move into stable employment, knowing that she and Henry had given their boys the family support and stability missing from her own childhood. The sons stayed near their parents as they grew into manhood. Henry set up a cooperage beside the family home in George Street, where the third son, James, learned to follow his father's trade. The second son, William, went to work for a local merchant, and the youngest son, John, for the Post Office. In 1867 the Coxes' oldest son George married, and their first grandchild was born. The family had a girl again, a baby named Elizabeth Ann. What pleasure her namesake must have brought Elizabeth Waddell as she became increasingly ill with the cancer of the womb from which she would die in March 1870, aged 53. How ironic that the womb from which her cherished children had come should be the seat of death. Elizabeth was buried in a family plot where a handsome white stone stood surrounded by a cast-iron fence. Even in death, Elizabeth had a place in the family where she was recognised, remembered, where she mattered. She had come a long way from the lonely and destitute thief wandering in and out of other people's lives in Glasgow, taking as she went, always on the move, on the run.

9

THE VAGARIES OF FREEDOM

Freedom came in stages for the convicts of the *Atwick*: ticket of leave; conditional pardon; certificate of freedom or absolute pardon. With a ticket of leave, granted locally by the lieutenant governor, a woman could work for wages in a specified district but had to return at night to her 'authorised' place of residence. The next stage, a conditional pardon, had to be approved in London. With this piece of paper, a woman was free to live wherever she liked in Van Diemen's Land or sometimes in any of the colonies. The final stage for most convicts was the certificate of freedom, a document certifying that they had served out their sentences and were 'free by servitude'. They could go wherever they liked, could even go Home—though how they might pay for the return voyage was another matter, and as far as I can tell, Elizabeth Williamson was the only convict from the *Atwick* who made that return journey. A woman transported 'for the term of her natural life' would never be eligible for a certificate of freedom, and the only way she could enjoy complete freedom of movement was to petition Her Majesty the Queen for an absolute pardon, a gift rarely bestowed.

EARLY RELEASE

'What is the shortest period within which a woman can obtain a Ticket of Leave?', Principal Superintendent of Convicts Josiah Spode was asked when testifying before the Board of Inquiry into Female Prison Discipline in December 1841. He replied: 'Four, six and eight years—according to their sentences of seven, fourteen years and life; but it has been the practice latterly to grant Tickets earlier to very well conducted females'. 'Very well conducted', a slippery phrase, leaving plenty of room for interpretation. And who were the interpreters? The most important was the lieutenant governor, who granted tickets of leave and made recommendations on applications for conditional or absolute pardons. The lieutenant governor was advised, of course, by Principal Superintendent Spode and other officials who consulted a convict's entry in the volumes of conduct records before passing her application along to the next rung of bureaucracy, but none of the lieutenant governors were simply rubber stamps for departmental advice. All involved themselves in micro-managing convict rewards and punishments, as notations on conduct records make clear.

What remains invisible is the involvement of masters and mistresses. Their recommendations, while not filed for posterity, undoubtedly influenced decision-making within a small community where names and networks were like currency, sometimes debased, sometimes of exceedingly high value. An intervention from a well-connected master seems the only way to explain why Catherine Adams, the first *Atwick* convict to receive her ticket of leave, was granted this indulgence on 24 December 1840 when she had been in the colony for less than three years. What made her special?

Catherine seems unremarkable, an unmarried Irishwoman nearing 30, tried at the Old Bailey and convicted of stealing a pair of shoes. We know from the appropriation list that she was assigned to 'Mr Hobbs, Swanport'. James Hobbs had been a boy when he sailed with his widowed mother—an American loyalist who had married a British naval officer—and four sisters on the *Ocean*, the supply ship accompanying the *Calcutta* on the voyage culminating in the settlement of Hobart Town. Through his sisters' marriages, Hobbs was related to men prominent in the colony. His own claim to fame was a circumnavigation of the island by open boat in 1824, a dangerous and difficult voyage of exploration in search of territory suitable for settlement. In return for services rendered, he was given a land grant and a lucrative government appointment as wharfinger in Hobart Town, an appointment he held until his resignation the year Catherine Adams received her ticket of leave. By the time she was assigned to him, Hobbs was concentrating on his east coast property, 'Ravensdale', at Little Swanport, and that is where Catherine was sent as a 'servant of all work'.

While at 'Ravensdale', Catherine was never charged with any breach of discipline, and given her totally blank conduct record up to that point, the early ticket of leave would remain an inexplicable mystery if not for another set of records, the admissions register of the Queen's Orphan Schools. On 11 July 1842, Richard Adams was admitted, the son of Catherine Adams, *Atwick*. Thirteen children were transferred that day from the convict nursery to the infant school. Most were two years old, but Richard was three, which means he was born in 1839, the year after the *Atwick* arrived. If he had been born in the Female Factory hospital, his mother's conduct record would have noted, 'delivered of an illegitimate child', and there could have been no early ticket of leave for Catherine. It looks as if Richard was born at 'Ravensdale', his birth unrecorded, and stayed there until his mother got her ticket at the end of 1840. Another piece of information may be relevant here. In October 1840, advertisements appeared in the *Colonial Times* offering for rent a house called 'Roseway', situated on the banks of the New Town Rivulet, 'now in the occupation of J. Hobbs, Esq.'. Were the wife and family of James Hobbs moving from Hobart Town to 'Ravensdale'? Was the convict 'indulgence' an opportunity for the master to rid himself of his convict mistress and illegitimate son?

Where did the mother go with her toddler when they left 'Ravensdale'? If Richard was not yet weaned, they may have been admitted to the convict nursery at Dynnyrne House. This would explain how Richard got into the convict system and ended up at the Orphan School, and why Catherine was listed as an inmate in the House of Correction at the time of the convict muster on 31 December 1841. She was not there for punishment because there was still no charge on her conduct record, though that would change radically in 1842, a year of separation and trauma for the mother and child.

Suddenly the ticket-of-leave holder with an unblemished record was punished four times for misconduct. In March 1842 she was accused of 'coming to town without a pass' (her ticket of leave restricted her to the Oatlands district, far from 'Ravensdale' as well as Hobart Town). The punishment was unusually severe for a first-time offender: six months' hard labour in the Cascades Female Factory. In July, Richard entered the Orphan School. On 21 September Catherine's sentence to six months' hard labour was complete. The next day she was charged again with misconduct. Punishment: two months' hard labour. At the end of November, she finished that sentence and on 5 December was charged twice on the same day with misconduct, her first sentence of two months extended by another two. On 5 April 1843, those two sentences were over. The next day Richard died in the Orphan School of scarlet fever. A week later his mother was sentenced to punishment for the fifth and last time, charged with being 'absent from her place of residence and found in Bed with a man'. No reference of course to grief for the death of her only child. Punishment: three months' hard labour. In the past year she had spent just a few days outside the stark regime of the crime class, and she had lost her son. Catherine's early ticket of leave had proved a poisoned chalice, an ironic 'indulgence'.

The second *Atwick* convict to receive her ticket of leave is also a surprise. Margaret Alexander, to whose story I will later return, was a Scot sentenced in her native Stirling to seven years' transportation on 18 April 1837. When her ticket of leave was granted on 17 February 1841, she would have been within two months of the regulatory four years into her sentence—if punishments for five charges by four employers had not extended her existing term of transportation by another two years and three months. Maybe she persuaded her fifth employer to write a glowing reference, but even so, a cursory glance at her conduct record would show she was not eligible according to the regulations. Nevertheless, she got her ticket.

Margaret's case is a reminder that the convict system was simultaneously a physical reality and an institutional fiction, sometimes indeed a fantasy. On paper, the institution was all-encompassing and its procedures were systematic, and yet in practice, it was riddled with inconsistencies. Some of them, like the multiple spellings of a convict's name, rarely mattered. Others did. Punishment for breaches of discipline could vary widely from magistrate to magistrate. Even the same magistrate could mete out inconsistent punishments, as if letting some women off more lightly than others for no discernible reason—on paper, that is, leaving us to wonder what the woman looked like and how she 'performed' before her inquisitor. Moreover, in a penal colony utterly dependent upon sur- veillance carried out by ordinary citizens, not all civilians co-operated fully in their role as interim gaolers, and why should they? Why should a farmer waste a day bringing an assigned servant into town to charge her with inso- lence, provide the testimony leading to her week's sentence in the solitary cells of the Female Factory, and then either arrange to have her returned or take a chance with someone new? He was just making more work for himself and his wife. Women assigned in town had more freedom to move about the streets, but they were also more likely to be charged for petty breaches of discipline. Inconsistencies were unavoidable.

Within these inconsistencies, the *Atwick* prisoners moved towards freedom. Between 1841 and the end of 1843, tickets of leave were granted to 74 of the 151 women who sailed (another fifteen women had died). In 1843, after five years in the colony, three women serving fourteen-year sentences and one on a life sentence received their tickets, and the grant- ing of certificates of freedom began that year as well. For some convicts, however, freedom remained a long way off. The rebellious Mary Sheriff would spend thirteen years in Van Diemen's Land before getting even a ticket of leave. And there is a small but significant group of 25 *Atwick* women whose conduct records show no applications for either tickets of leave or conditional pardons.

FENDING FOR HERSELF

Some of these women may have preferred the security of the assign- ment system with its promise of reliable employment, food, clothes, and shelter. Working for wages meant facing competition both from the unwaged assigned servants and from recently arrived free immigrants. The labour market, says economic historian R.M. Hartwell, 'was glutted', and money was tight because the economy had taken a nosedive towards the end of 1840 and was deepening into recession by 1843. Employment opportunities were further limited by a strong gender bias in a predominantly agricultural economy. If wool from the sheep of Van Diemen's Land had fed a serious local textile industry, women with skills acquired in the mills of Scotland would have made valuable employees, but the wool was shipped to England's industrial cities. Most convict women, as historian Kay Daniels concluded, 'neither established businesses nor became independent but exchanged life as a government servant for life as a free servant'.

Some worked at least part time as prostitutes. Even while under sentence, this was a sure way to make money, as Grace Heinbury told the board of inquiry in her statement of 1842: 'All the disorderly Houses that will receive absconded Women are well known in the Factory and women are directed to them when in the Factory'. Prostitution was work generally hidden from the records—though the claim that convict women were prostitutes recurs as a sweeping accusation—but there are hints at this way of life in the inquest inquiring into the death of Eliza Smith. Eliza had gone from the *Atwick* into the convict nursery with her baby daughter, Ann Condon, who died there. Refusing to knuckle down to authority, Eliza was already on her tenth punishment for absenting herself from work when she joined the bread riot of May 1839. With her long string of charges and time added for absconding, Eliza had served more than her original seven-year sentence when she eventually got a ticket of leave in December 1844. Three months later she was dead. She had been living in a house with other women in St John Street, Launceston, and at her inquest they gave evidence. One said that Eliza had 'felt very bad since she came home from the races'; another had seen her 'at the play house last night'. The doctor attributed death to 'her having suddenly left a crowded Theatre, the night being rather chilly—and this sudden engorgement of the lungs together with the presence of fluid in the chest became rapidly fatal'. Eliza's companions might have shared a house while they went out to jobs other than prostitution, but there's no indication that they did.

Some *Atwick* women may have moved from unpaid to paid employment with the same masters as they moved towards freedom, or used good references to find other paid live-in positions. Some teamed up with men they did not marry. Like the prostitutes they are difficult to track, especially if they had no children. Again, an inquest brings one of their stories to light. Wilhelmina Smith Lander was 25 and married when she was arrested for theft in Edinburgh shortly after 'working for some weeks in the country, since she left the House of Refuge about a month ago'. Even before receiving her ticket of leave in November 1845, Wilhelmina had entered into a long-term relationship with a fisherman named Cornelius Dalton, who told the Coroner's jury, 'I was living with her for the last eight years—but I was not married to her'.

At the time of her death, Wilhelmina Smith Lander and Cornelius Dalton rented a room they shared with another man, whose bed was a mattress on the floor. Wilhelmina made money by doing laundry, and she spent the money on drink. 'I used to beat her', Dalton admitted at the inquest, 'thinking to make her keep sober', but beatings had no effect, and 'I have not lifted my hand to her for the last sixteen months'. Two days before her death, said Dalton, 'I found her in the street, she was lying on her face, her forehead on the ground, and her arms stretched out. She was lying flat like.' He carried her home, and laid her on the bed, thinking she was drunk and would sleep it off, but she had had a stroke and never left the bed before she died.

Although Wilhelmina certainly had not prospered during her years of freedom, she had at the very least a roof over her head and a man to whom she could feel securely connected, a man who would pick her up from the street and carry her home to bed, even if he hated her drinking and thought she was lying there drunk. In the final immobilised nights of her life, after the stroke had deprived her of movement and speech, Cornelius Dalton lay in the bed by her side. Comfort may come in small gestures.

While teaming up with a man inevitably meant gambling on the future, the stakes were particularly high for convict women as they grew older under sentence and faced years of fending for themselves in a society with few opportunities for single women. Not everyone rushed to marry, however. Sarah Stevenson was an eligible 23-year-old when she arrived in Van Diemen's Land. She might have spent much of her sentence married and having children, but she did not. She was almost 30 and had been in the colony for more than six years when she married Samuel Hopkinson in April 1844. Only 64 of the *Atwick* women had married by this time—not quite half the number still alive. No applications to marry (always lodged in the name of the man) were made for 39 of the *Atwick* women. Other women were either refused permission, or for some reason changed their minds. Sarah's own background may have made her wary about taking on marriage. She had not left behind a happy family life in Edinburgh.

A FAMILY FALLS APART: SARAH STEVENSON AND SAMUEL HOPKINSON

Sarah's mother told the Edinburgh magistrate at the precognition hearing that her daughter 'has behaved very ill for about four years & has been punished for stealing . . . when she gets out of confinement she comes back to her fathers house, and [my] mind is never so easy as when Sarah is in confinement'. Her father, a tanner, said that he 'has done all that he could to get her to behave' and about a year before 'got her into the Magdalene Asylum [for 'reclaiming' prostitutes], but she would not remain'. Fed up with his daughter's constant pilfering, he went to the police 'to give information against her'. Sarah, in her own statement before the magistrate, painted her mother as an alcoholic who sent the daughter out to pawn or sell household goods in order to buy drink. Other witnesses made it clear that it was Sarah, and not her mother, who wanted money for grog. Sarah emerges from the witness statements of the precognition as a young woman without motivation, trapped by alcohol. At some stage before her trial she decided to plead guilty, authorising 'her counsel to sign this confession in respect she cannot write'.

Sarah spent more than a year imprisoned in Edinburgh between the time of her arrest and her transfer to the *Atwick*. The gaol report accompanying her to Van Diemen's Land said that while her behaviour had been 'irregular for some time', she was 'industrious in prison and of quiet disposition'. When asked to state her offence in her own words, Sarah said she had been transported for 'stealing articles—prosecuted by my father'; she had been imprisoned three times, and had been 'on the Town' for two years. On the *Atwick*'s description list, she is identified as a 'farm servant', surprising for a prostitute who had been working the streets of Edinburgh. But then, she had not always lived in the city. As she told the examining magistrate, she was born in Dalkeith, and may have spent her childhood in the countryside of this Midlothian parish. Had the family moved into Edinburgh hoping to improve their fortunes? Whatever her past, Sarah used the opportunities opened by transportation to get out of town. Questioned about her 'trade' for the appropriation list, she elaborated the skills which would take her away from settlements: 'Farm servant, milk, butter, wash, iron'. Most of the convict women tried to stay in Hobart Town, but not Sarah.

And so she was assigned up-country to 'Mrs Dr Sharland' whose husband, the district surgeon in Bothwell, belonged to a prosperous and well-established family of landowners, his father having explored much of the island while employed by the Survey Department. For some reason the arrangements did not work out, and when Sarah was charged with her first offence in July, she was working for another master who reported her as absent without leave, and requested that she be 'returned to government'. Sarah was resisting the servant's role prescribed as her punishment. During her first year in the colony she had four employers, and was returned five times to the Cascades Female Factory to be punished for being absent or out after hours or drunk. By the end of the year, she was facing a long stretch of institutionalisation rather than domestic service because she was pregnant. Her son was born around January 1839, and she named him James, her father's name. Did she ask someone who could write to send a letter back to Edinburgh telling her 'prosecutor' that he was now a grandfather, hoping for some sort of reconciliation at least by mail?

During 1839 only one charge appears on her conduct record. On 9 September she absconded from the nursery, and may have been gone for some time because the punishment was severe, a year's extension to her original sentence. This incident, so crucial to understanding Sarah as a mother, is frustratingly lacking in detail. Did Sarah take James with her when she walked out of the Liverpool Street nursery in the centre of Hobart Town? If so, was this a desperate bid to stay with her baby? The timing seems significant. James was now nine months old, the age of weaning and separation in the convict nurseries. Did Sarah run off with her baby because he was the only person in the world to whom she was emotionally attached? If so, her desperate gesture of mother love was met not with understanding, much less approval, but with further charges of criminality. And she lost James. On 8 March 1841, he was admitted to the infant section of the Orphan School, aged two and a quarter years, and there he died six months later.

That same year, the first of four men asked the Convict Department for permission to marry Sarah Stevenson. Permission refused—as were applications lodged in 1842 and 1843, 'woman's conduct indifferent'. Her offences continued, minor breaches of those regulations intended to keep her working, sober, and celibate. Sarah was sent from one employer to another, often in the country, but never in some place where she felt settled and wanted to serve out the weeks and months of her punishment. At last, in November 1842, six years after her trial, she was granted a ticket of leave. A year later it was suspended after she was charged with 'misconduct in being absent from her authorised place of residence and found at a hut with an assigned servant at night'. Her partner-in-crime, whom we can identify because she eventually married him, was charged with 'misconduct in being absent from his Hut and in company of a ticket of leave woman' and sentenced to three months' hard labour, his punishment a month less than Sarah's. Sexual passion between consenting adults as criminality. Within the convict system, there was no place for sexual or emotional intimacy. Hide your secrets or be punished. How were the lovers discovered in a hut? By accident? More likely, by treachery. There were rewards for informers. Van Diemen's Land might be an open prison—but a prison nevertheless, a penal colony populated by spies and the spied upon.

Sarah was punished one more time after this, for some charge under the vague heading of 'misconduct', which incurred another severe sentence, six months' hard labour and her ticket of leave again suspended. If her sentence had not been extended when she absconded from the nursery, she would have been free by now. And did she know that her lover from the hut had applied to marry her a month before this 'misconduct'? The marriage was approved, though the wedding had to wait until Sarah emerged from her final stint of punishment in the Female Factory. Then, on 26 April 1844, Sarah Stevenson, house servant, married Samuel Hopkinson, widower, tanner, in the Parish Church at Pontville, District of Brighton. Sarah gave her age for the marriage registry as 29, consistent with earlier records. Samuel said he was 44, but if his son was later correct in giving his age at the time of death as 102 years and ten months, he was actually 60, twice Sarah's age. His hair was already grey when he disembarked from the *Elphinstone* two years before Sarah arrived. Identified as a ploughman and shepherd sentenced to life for stealing eight ewes, he said he was married and the father of five children, and his wife kept a public house in the village of Longstone, Derbyshire, in England's starkly beautiful Peak District.

From his convict records, one might imagine that Sarah had chosen well in deciding to move into freedom by attaching her fortunes to Hopkinson's. He had certainly impressed the pious surgeon superintendent on the *Elphinstone*, who described the prisoner as 'uniformly good, an attentive scholar', and even added a supplementary report to say that 'during his passage from England' Hopkinson 'has, as far as the circumstances in which he has been placed afforded opportunity, given Scriptural evidence that he has turned to God by the Faith of the Gospel. A hopeful character.' Just the right sort for assignment to a man with a mission, the 'conciliator' George Augustus Robinson, who was presiding over the unhappy Aboriginal settlement at Wybalenna on Flinders Island. Robinson needed reliable shepherds to look after flocks at various locations on Flinders and the smaller islands nearby, and the isolated life may have suited Hopkinson. For more than a year and a half no mark appeared on his record, and then on 5 February 1838 Robinson in his double role of victim and magistrate accused him of 'Having a linen towel supposed to be stolen from G A Robinson', and for this 'supposed' theft sentenced Hopkinson to two weeks in irons. Even in his own journal, Robinson never claimed to have proved the theft: 'This morning Hopkins [sic] was sentenced [to] fourteen days in irons for having a towel in his possession supposed to have been stolen'. Hopkinson was back on the main island of Van Diemen's Land when next charged in 1841 for 'having cattle in his possession and not being able satisfactorily to account for them'. He was sentenced to six months' hard labour in chains, a sentence later remitted by the Lieutenant Governor, who was unpersuaded by the evidence and less inclined than the 'conciliator' Robinson to punish on suspicion.

When Samuel Hopkinson married Sarah Stevenson, he had been in the colony for eight years, and had been punished just twice, once by Robinson and once for being sprung with Sarah in the hut. His record was much better than Sarah's, with nothing to suggest that he shared her fondness for drink. Even though he was serving a life sentence and would never be free to return to England, he had a ticket of leave and could look forward to a conditional pardon. Both he and Sarah had skills suited to bush life, and during the early years of their marriage when they disappear from the public record, they were most likely living in the bush, working hard and saving assiduously with the goal of buying a place of their own, which they did within ten years.

It was as landowner in the district of Buckingham that Samuel Hopkinson's name appeared on a list of electors published in the *Courier* on 17 October 1853. Five years later, on a property valuation roll printed in the *Hobart Town Gazette*, he was named as the owner of two properties in Glenorchy, north of Hobart Town where the plains undulate up from the River Derwent towards the lower reaches of the Mount Wellington range. Villages were scattered along the river, with large properties on the plains, and small farms back in the heavily timbered valleys, often difficult to reach. Up the valley of the Abbotsfield rivulet, on the edge of settlement and the edge of the law, the Hopkinsons lived on a 25-acre farm, known as the Old Brewery. When the farm was sold again in 1867, the hype of real estate advertising could not conceal the isolation of the place. 'A snug little farm', it was called, with 'a never-failing creek of pure water', a farm offering 'a certain independence for any industrious man'. Perfect for a man who dealt in livestock of dubious origin.

Hopkinson's toehold on respectability derived from the ownership of land—he had divided the Old Brewery, and was renting one section—but his questionable business practices ensured the appearance of his name in the newspapers for less savoury reasons as well. A man charged with stealing a bull and bullock said he bought them from Hopkinson. An insolvency case named Hopkinson as a man of questionable veracity. A neighbour charged him with assault, saying that one day 'he was on the road at Glenorchy, with two of his servants, who were driving three sheep; they met the defendant, who was on horseback; he said to witness, appining [sic] to him a very opprobrious epithet, "You've got my sheep, and if you do not give them to me I'll murder you". He then attempted to ride witness down, and having dismounted he assaulted him by striking him, and attempted to throw him over the fence.' Hopkinson was fined. In 1859 he was gaoled for larceny. A doctor in Hobart Town, answering a house call late one night, tied his horse outside the patient's door, and when he was ready to ride home fifteen minutes later, the saddle was gone. A policeman, presumably acting on a tip, went out to the Old Brewery, where he found the saddle. The judge 'considered the case a very clear one and sentenced the prisoner to twelve months' imprisonment with hard labor'. Hopkinson was sent to Port Arthur.

This left Sarah on the isolated farm with three daughters, the oldest no more than eleven, and a three-year-old son. When Hopkinson's first wife was left to fend for herself with five children in the wilds of Derbyshire, she at least had a pub to run. Sarah was no dealer in stolen livestock, and may have feared visits from ruffians who frequented her husband's company. Whether she feared someone in particular or was frightened by her general vulnerability, she left the Old Brewery and took the children to live in a cave they shared with a couple and a single man. When Hopkinson returned to the valley after his year's incarceration, he was furious (jealous?) and charged the other three adults in this unlikely commune 'with stealing a saw, a grindstone, bed tick, and other articles'. He told the court: 'I left my wife and family at home with the things, and while I was at Port Arthur they went to live with the prisoners in a cave in the rocks'. The stolen 'things' seem so sadly paltry. A saw. The sort of homemade mattress called a 'bed tick'. A grindstone. The vengeful white-haired patriarch called upon his young daughters to substantiate the crime. According to the newspaper, Ruth 'aged about 13', told the court that when they went to live 'in a cave in the rocks at the back of Mr. Lowes"', she saw one of the accused men 'taking the bed tick away in a cart from her father's house, and saw the grindstone produced in the cave'. Her sister Sarah, 'a little girl, about 12 years of age', said she saw the other man 'take the grindstone away from her father's house to the cave on the hill, and also the bedding, but . . . did not see the bed tick'. The case rested solely on the testimony of these daughters sucked into their father's misguided mission. 'The Bench said it was impossible that the Magistrates could convict on this evidence, and ordered the prisoner to be discharged.'

Sarah was not in court. She had left Hopkinson, probably after a blazing row—did she fear for her life? It turned out a year later that she was living 'down the Huon', a rugged forest region south of Hobart Town, dominated by emancipists, ex-convicts turned tenant farmers or timber-cutters and sawyers. She may have fled Hopkinson hoping never to be found, and he was not the one who found her. He was in gaol again when the police tracked her down. Another of his dicey livestock deals had come unstuck, perhaps because he had had a falling-out with his tenant, Abraham Avery. In April 1862 Avery told the Supreme Court that he had stopped to talk with two men driving ten or fifteen sheep in the direction of Hopkinson's and noticed the brand, JB. Knowing that those drovers owned no sheep, he told the rural police what he had seen, and they came out to have a look at the Old Brewery, where they found 'ten carcases and a half, of mutton hanging up in the barn, and two sheeps' hearts and some liver in the house'. A week after this initial discovery, a police constable dug up 'thirteen sheeps' heads, the ears from which had been cut off'. Other bits were found in a dung heap, and while searching the rivulet which ran alongside the family garden the constable spotted 'two bags containing 15 sheepskins branded JB, covered over with wattle boughs'. A settler named John Burrows had lost 100 sheep from a run near the Sorell Creek in the New Norfolk district, and the branding-iron he produced in the Supreme Court matched the brands on the skins. The men were found guilty, and stood before the colony's chief justice for sentencing. Hopkinson, reported the *Mercury*, 'pleaded for mercy on account of his age (72) and his having four small children'. The chief justice observed in response:

> . . . *it was a sad thing to have to pass sentence on a man of grey hairs, and far advanced in years. The prisoner arrived here under sentence for sheep-stealing: after that he had 41 cattle in his possession of which he could give no satisfactory account. In 1859 he was convicted of feloniously receiving a saddle; and now he was convicted of receiving stolen sheep, the carcasses of which were found on his premises. Justice must be done, and the wholesale system of plunder such as this, was such as the settlers must be protected from, he therefore sentenced him to six years penal servitude.*

Protecting the settlers meant leaving the Hopkinson children unprotected. A few days later, their father's solicitor, John Woodcock Graves, junior, applied for the Hopkinson children to be admitted to the Queen's Orphan Schools. Graves, remembered as a friend of Truganini in her final years, was the son of free settlers, but like the Hopkinson children, he understood how precarious family life could be. His own father, famous as the composer of the hunting song, 'D'ye ken John Peel?', was a dangerously unstable man. A diagnosis of 'mania' sent Graves senior to the New Norfolk Asylum in 1841. A month after his release, his wife managed to get three of their children admitted to the Orphan Schools, and to get a job there herself as hospital nurse. At the end of the year, J.W. Graves, junior, aged twelve, joined his mother and siblings, and remained in the Boys' School for the next four years. Grim though the Orphan Schools undoubtedly were in many ways, they had offered refuge to a mother and her children, and now Graves turned to the schools to protect the children of Sarah Stevenson, applying on behalf of Ruth, fourteen; Sarah, eleven; Margaret, eight; and William, five—'who are at present almost naked and without any protection and means of support'. Perhaps memories of his own childhood, threatened and fearful, made the lawyer particularly sensitive to their plight: 'When your worship learns that three of these children are girls, and that they are living in a lonely hut far back in the bush, you will at once understand to what dangers they are exposed'. The police magistrate sent someone out to the Old Brewery to check on the children, and a note on their file adds details to the picture Graves had painted:

> *Hopkinson lived on a small piece of ground supposed to be his own property but I have ascertained that in reality it belongs to Mr G Crisp who holds a judgment . . . upon it for more than its value[;] his conviction therefore leaves his unfortunate children utterly without means and as their mother has long ago deserted them and gone to live with some man it is not known whither, they are as unprotected as they are destitute.*

And then a later note, closing the file: 'The application is cancelled, the mother having taken the children with her down the Huon'.

'Down the Huon', into another backwoods world, much further from Hobart Town and more remote than the Old Brewery. In the heavily forested valleys running down to the Huon River lived people described by the first Anglican Bishop of Tasmania as convict emancipists who 'cast off their religious ordinances and loved to lead solitary lives, wandering away from towns and settlements, forming little groups in the bush where they could remain unnoticed and unreproved'. Sarah Stevenson may have enjoyed the rough and independent life of a sawyers' camp, but it was hardly the place for children, especially adolescent girls, and the man with whom Sarah had been living may have been less than thrilled when he suddenly acquired a family. How long Sarah and the children stayed in the area or how they lived, I do not know.

My next glimpse of the family comes more than three years later when the daughter Sarah Hopkinson, now aged about sixteen, was arrested with another girl for stealing a pair of carpet slippers. Under the heading 'Juvenile Delinquents', the *Mercury* reported that the girls were remanded for trial on 25 September 1865. Two days later the 'Juvenile Shoplifters' were tried, found guilty and punished with tough sentences of twelve months' hard labour for Sarah, and two years for the other girl. Sarah's mother had served much lighter sentences for her first convictions in Edinburgh 30 years earlier, but the colonial magistrate was intent on making a point, and 'in passing sentence severely lectured the girls, and said it was disgraceful that two natives of their age, should be placed in such a position'. Four years later Sarah Hopkinson was back in court again, this time as a witness to an incident in the Black Swan Hotel, Argyle Street, near her lodgings behind the Theatre Royal. She said she had gone to the hotel with a friend named Robert McFarlane to look for her sister. While they were there, two men got into a fight, during which one was stabbed. Three days after Sarah and Robert told the police magistrate what they had seen, they were married in the Wesleyan Church. Samuel Hopkinson, released from prison after his most recent sentence for sheep-stealing, was a witness. Neither Sarah nor her 21-year-old husband could sign their names. Robert McFarlane was a sailor, and Sarah Hopkinson may have married him partly in the hope that he would take her somewhere else, and he probably did because they disappear from sight.

Her sister Margaret disappears as well, and I suspect that she died while 'down the Huon'. Otherwise she would have figured in the story her mother Sarah Stevenson told when she was arrested in 1866, accused of stealing a sofa and table, the property of her landlord. Sarah made much of the landlord's cruelty in turning 'me and my child out by the shoulders; it was a very wet day'. This child was William, who was ten at the time. Margaret would have been thirteen, and most likely living with her mother since her father was still in prison and her sisters were not yet married. But Margaret simply vanishes, probably into an unmarked grave somewhere in the bush.

Ruth Hopkinson was working as a servant in Hobart Town when her mother was tried in the Supreme Court before the same chief justice who had sentenced her father for sheep-stealing. The case turned on whether Sarah had intended to return the landlord's property, or had stolen it. With neither Sarah nor her landlord represented by a lawyer, the trial was chaotic. The chief justice admonished Sarah to 'ask questions, not make statements', and after asking his own questions, said in frustration that the landlord 'was the most confused witness he ever had to deal with'. Ruth Hopkinson was called as a witness because she had helped her mother furnish the room, though she was not living there. Praised by the chief justice for giving 'her evidence in a fair and honest manner', Ruth did not corroborate her mother's claims. The jury, having retired, could not agree. They spent six hours on this minor case, and when they returned at the end of the day, the foreman asked the chief justice whether the verdict had to be unanimous. Yes, he said, this is a criminal case. And so the gentlemen of the jury were conducted to Beaumont's Hotel for the night ('but of course not to embrace spirits'), and when one member of the jury continued to hold out against the other eleven the next day, they were discharged. Sarah was remanded, and apparently released without a second trial.

She was now in her mid-fifties, and would live another twenty years, but how and where she scratched a living is unclear. Occasionally she would come before the police court on charges of using obscene language. Her daughter Ruth and her son both stayed in Hobart Town, and no doubt spent time and money trying to alleviate the poverty of their unreliable parents. Samuel Hopkinson went back to gaol again in 1872 after he stole chickens from one of his neighbours in New Town— and sold them to another. The police magistrate 'said he had known the prisoner for a number of years, and during that time he had borne a very bad character, being particularly fond of appropriating the property of others. He had been charged at different times with sheep-stealing, saddle-stealing and other offences, and he was afraid prisoner had not grown honest in his old age. There was very little doubt as to his guilt, but on account of his advanced age he would be dealt with leniently.' The chicken-thief was almost 90. Four years later, he was arrested on a charge of stealing a goose, but the case was dismissed. The 'hopeful character' from the *Elphinstone* for whom the surgeon superintendent held such high hopes as a man 'turned to God by the Faith of the Gospel' had proved an incorrigible thief. In 1886 he died, said to be a legendary 102 years and ten months, at the home of his son. A year later that long-suffering son, William Hopkinson, aged 22, was able to marry without the burden of his father, and he did not take on the responsibility of his mother in her final years. Sarah Stevenson would live until 1890, a senile old woman cared for by the state in the New Town Charitable Institution. Her turbulent life is a reminder of how very difficult it could be to keep families together.

A RESILIENT MOTHER: JEAN SMITH

Sarah's shipmate, Jean Smith, was more resourceful and resilient. Unlike Sarah, who was living at home and stealing from her family at the time of her arrest, Jean had already struck out into the world on her own, leaving her home in northern Ireland to work in a Glasgow cotton mill. She was in her early twenties and had lost her mill job before she was stopped by a pair of nightwatchmen as she hurried along the Broomielaw wharf at quarter past two on a winter's night. 'Knowing her to be a girl of the Town', one of the watchmen thought it suspicious that she was rushing along with 'her gown up over her head', and asked her to stop. She didn't, and he seized hold of her. His companion asked what she was hiding 'in her bosom'. A cap, she said, and pulled it out. That's not all, said the policeman, 'and he put his hand into her bosom and found a bunch of Banknotes'.

Jean offered each policeman a pound note, which they declined. Then she 'desired them to keep the whole money and not take her to the office'. They ignored this proposition, and walked her back to the station where they watched the lieutenant on duty count out nineteen £1 notes, all snatched from the pocketbook of a man with whom Jean had earlier been dancing in a public house. Jean must have given up on her prospects of a decent life in Glasgow because at her trial she pleaded guilty and authorised her counsel to sign her confession as 'she cannot write'. When she sailed on the *Atwick*, her son, four-year-old Joseph Douglas, went with her. Who his father was or where he was born, her convict records do not say. Once they reached Van Diemen's Land, Joseph went to the Orphan School with the other children on 17 March 1838, and stayed there for ten years until he was old enough to be apprenticed. His mother never retrieved him from institutional confinement, and may not have told her new husband of his existence. Jean Smith was starting a new life.

At first it seemed no more settled than the old. Jean in the role of assigned servant was constantly in trouble for insolence and bad language, for being absent all night without leave, or under the influence of liquor—ten charges in the first two years, all from the same master, who eventually got fed up and refused to have her back. The Principal Superintendent of Convicts decreed that she be 'assigned in the interior'. She was sent inland to Bothwell, and soon she met James Bennett. There must have been an immediate rapport because within a matter of weeks, a few months at the most, they had decided to marry.

James Bennett had a horrifying story to tell. In March 1827 when he was tried at Southampton and sentenced to fourteen years' transportation for sheep-stealing, he was 21 years old. He seems to have left the farm where he grew up and gone to work as a cook and gentleman servant for a man he singled out for mention when he arrived in Hobart Town, 'Squire Daniels, a magistrate'. Whatever talents he had acquired in the house of an English magistrate were of no interest to the convict authorities he encountered in Van Diemen's Land. On the description list he was relegated to 'farm labourer and ploughman', and sent to 'Bowsden', near the Midlands town of Jericho. For the next six and a half years he would be assigned to perhaps the most brutal master in the colony, Dr John Maule Hudspeth, who in addition to farming his 2,700-acre sheep property was the resident medical officer for the district of Oatlands. Hudspeth's brutality came to the attention of Lieutenant Governor George Arthur sometime late in 1834. I haven't found any reference to what happened, but it must have been dramatic because Dr Hudspeth was committed to the New Norfolk Asylum as an insane patient, and Principal Superintendent Josiah Spode was ordered by Arthur to prepare a return showing the punishments meted out to ten of Hudspeth's recent assigned servants, including James Bennett. The 'Return of ten convicts in the service of Dr Hudspeth' survives in the correspondence file of the Colonial Secretary's Office, detailing from their conduct records the charges brought against each—and the punishments. Someone, perhaps the Colonial Secretary, has gone through and with a large emphatic flourish has tallied the number of times each man was flogged. On the last page is written '1436 lashes! eight men'. On the entry for James Bennett, '350 lashes!!'

And that did not include one final lot of 25 lashes inflicted on Bennett during the very week Spode was preparing the 'Return' for the Lieutenant Governor, a punishment ordered by the magistrate Thomas Anstey of nearby 'Anstey Barton'. Anstey was complicit in the cruelty at 'Bowsden'. Brutal though Dr Hudspeth may have been as a master, he followed the procedures promulgated by the Convict Department. He laid charges, the charges were heard, the convicts were punished, and everything was recorded, as Lieutenant Governor Arthur discovered when Spode submitted the return. Horrified by what he learned about conditions at 'Bowsden', Arthur commented at the end of the document, 'it is more distressing than I can describe'. After all his efforts to make the assignment system work, to provide convicts with masters who would reform as well as punish the servants assigned to them, a pathology of cruelty could nevertheless infect a property for years. At 'Bowsden' the infection ran deep, it was not just about a mad master. The final lashes inflicted on the deeply scarred flesh of James Bennett were brought after Hudspeth had been sent to New Norfolk. Bennett was charged with 'insolence to Mr Hudspeth's Overseer and with using profane oaths in the presence and hearing of Mrs Hudspeth's children'. The very atmosphere of 'Bowsden' was rancid.

But at last, by order of the Lieutenant Governor, James Bennett was given the ticket of leave which freed him from this hell. It seems likely that he left the district altogether, and he may have been working for the settler to whom Jean Smith was assigned at the beginning of 1840. On 23 June that year Bennett lodged his application to marry Jean. Supportive and influential references may have been sent as well, because the application was approved in spite of Jean's recent record of frequent punishment, and a month later they were married by a visiting chaplain at the police office in Bothwell. Early the following year Bennett's name appeared on a list of people whose sentences had expired, and yet even though he now was free, his wife for some reason was not assigned to him. On the convict muster taken on 31 December 1841, her employer is listed as a Mr Stonehouse in Launceston, and three months later another employer charged her with insolence, and she was sent to the Launceston Female Factory for a week's solitary confinement. That is the final offence entered on her record, although she would not receive her ticket of leave for another two years.

Where was she during this time? And most intriguing, where was she in 1842 when she gave birth to Robert Charles Bennett within a few months of her final punishment in the Launceston Factory? Perhaps she had at last been assigned to her husband, an 'indulgence' from the Convict Department enabling the Bennetts to give their children a family, an opportunity denied to Elizabeth Waddell and Henry Cox, whose two daughters were born in the Cascades Female Factory and died in the convict nursery without knowing their father. The first Bennett child, concealed from the convict records, never went near a convict nursery and unlike the Coxes' daughters, he lived, lived indeed to the ripe old age of 80, dying in 1922 in Campbell Town, not far north of the area where he spent his early childhood. When his next sibling was born in 1844, Jean had been a ticket-of-leave holder for two months and, confident in her marriage, lost the fear of the convict nursery. The birth of James Bennett, son of James Bennett, was registered in Oatlands, and two years later, the birth of a third son was registered at the same office (meanwhile Jean's first son, Joseph Douglas, remained immured in the Orphan School; he would play no part in this new configuration of family). When the next two Bennett births were registered in 1849 and 1854, a girl and a fourth boy, their father's occupation had moved from labourer to farmer.

An unexpected material trace remains for understanding the Bennetts during these years. When I went to Oatlands to visit one of their many descendants, Cliff Bennett carefully opened the cloth protecting two portraits. Initially they seem to be charcoal drawings made by a skilled artist, but on closer inspection are early photographs meticulously touched up with a charcoal pencil. The Bennetts, though undoubtedly working hard on their small farm, had money to spend on these tokens of their aspirations, portraits to hang on the farmhouse wall, just as the grand landowners of the colony displayed their own family images. Life for the Bennett family was under control, it had direction and meaning. And then on 7 December 1856, disaster struck. James Bennett, aged 50, died. The death was sudden, a bolt from the blue. The next day the Coroner and a jury of six men came to the farmhouse on Axminster Tier to examine the body. There were no marks of injuries, and they agreed that 'he died from natural causes', from 'disease of the heart'. No mention of course of how years of flogging may have weakened his heart and shortened his life.

What was Jean to do? In the portraits, James is a man with fierce eyes, determined, austere. Jean looks warmer, a woman on the verge of an unfashionable smile. They seem to have made a good team, and as parents probably balanced each other, but with James gone, I think Jean panicked. That is the only way I can make sense of her marriage six months later. A quick marriage is in itself perfectly understandable. Jean was 43 years old. She had five children to look after, the oldest was fourteen and the youngest was two. Running the farm was more than she could manage, and yet the rented farm was all she had. The man she married was also a farmer, and he was almost ten years younger than Jean, potentially a good investment as a farm manager. The panic is not in the marriage as such, but on the page of the marriage register and in the character of the new husband.

I would never have found this marriage without the help of Ann Daniel, one of Jean's descendants through whom I learned that she is buried with James Bennett even though she later married a man named Kealy. And sure enough, in the marriage register for St Paul's Catholic Church, Oatlands, I found the marriage of John Kealy, farmer, widower, to Johanna Smith, Lady, widow, on 15 June 1857, not quite six months after the death of James Bennett. Johanna Smith? Lady? An invented name, an invented status. To me, this re-fashioning suggests that Jean was uneasy about what she was doing to her identity as James Bennett's wife, now widow. And I doubt whether any of her Protestant children were in the Catholic Church to hear their mother claim to be someone they had never heard of—and to be a 'Lady' at that! But maybe that was the role she played for Kealy, a role he found enchanting, his fascination in its turn enticing her. We will never know.

Like James Bennett, John Kealy had been transported for sheep-stealing, but other than their crime, Jean's two husbands shared nothing in common, neither temperament nor background. Bennett came from the Protestant yeoman class of southern England, and if he drank, it never interfered with his work (no charge against him at 'Bowsden' involved alcohol). In contrast, the textual trail left by John Kealy, for whom we have no portrait, suggests a stereotypical Irishman. He had grown up and was convicted in County Tipperary. He was short, 5 feet 2 inches, 3 inches shorter than the formidable James Bennett—and just an inch taller than Jean. A Catholic who could neither read nor write, he must have suffered from the terrible poverty inflicted during the Irish famine, an experience shared with his fellow shipmates who sailed from Dublin on the *Hyderabad* in 1849. Kealy had already spent a year in gaol before he was transported. Shortly after he landed he was issued a ticket of leave—and lost it carelessly the next year by missing a muster. His conduct record noted three breaches of discipline, two for being absent without leave, and a third for assaulting a constable while drunk. The quintessentially Irish theme of hard drinking would recur during his marriage.

Kealy had come to the Oatlands area while under sentence, and after receiving his certificate of freedom the year before James Bennett died, he became a tenant on one of the small farms carved out of the 'Anstey Barton' estate where the Bennetts were also farming. Thomas Anstey, the magistrate who had ordered Bennett's floggings at nearby 'Bowsden', had died, and his death had been ironically to the advantage of James Bennett, whose experience in the Midlands would have helped him select a good farm when the estate was parcelled up and rented out. When 'Johanna Smith' married John Kealy, she did not immediately sign over the tenancy to her new husband. On the property valuation rolls printed in the *Hobart Town Gazette* in May 1858, 'Mrs Jane Bennett' is listed as the tenant of a 65-acre farm valued at £48 15 shillings, while John 'Caley' (being illiterate he lacked control over the spellings of his name) is the tenant of an 11-acre farm valued at £8 5 shillings.

If the Bennett farm was part of the allure for Kealy, he had won the prize two years later when the larger farm was listed in his name, and it was he who bid for the freehold title when 'the magnificent estate of Anstey Barton' was sold by public auction on 21 November 1860. The 'extensive domain', wrote a reporter for the *Mercury*, began just west of the Oatlands township and stretched 'over a tract of fertile country, to the extent of upwards of 20,000 acres, dotted here and there by well cultivated and thriving farms, which yield annually no inconsiderable supplies to the granaries of the colony, thanks to the untiring industry of an honest and hard-working body of tenant-yeomen, fostered and encouraged by the Anstey family'. The reporter commented that 'only nine of the existing tenants have become purchasers', but this was hardly surprising given the price of the land. 'Tenant-yeomen' were unlikely to be cashed up, and John Kealy's 'purchase' of Lot 5, 150 acres at £5 an acre, was really the grandiose gesture of an Irish dreamer who certainly did not have £750. This 'purchase' of the only property he ever seems to have owned was subject to a mortgage for which the land itself was security. Kealy could not make the payments required, and within a year title to the mortgaged freehold was transferred to the brother of his next-door neighbour, Richard Sturgeon.

The Kealy/Bennett family reverted to the status of tenants. As the Bennett sons watched the dream of owning their farm evaporate, they may have pondered how differently things might have gone if their father were alive. Their stepfather was turning out to be a real no-hoper. A few months after the farm was sold he got into an argument with Richard Sturgeon, and ended up in court. Kealy claimed breach of contract, saying that he gave Sturgeon grain to be threshed, and it was not. Sturgeon, countering with an argument that the grain was a set-off for rent in lieu of money, won the case—with costs. A week later Kealy was in the police court, charged with having 'ridden a horse so furiously, on the 17th May, as to jeopardize other persons' safety'. Kealy had been galloping on a grey horse down the main street of Oatlands in a race against a woman named Florence McCarthy who was driving a cart as furiously as he was riding. The lives of the other women in her cart were in danger, testified the superintendent of police. 'I called out to him "stop". He would not, but galloped on the harder.' How fast was I going? asked Kealy. Sixteen miles an hour, replied the superintendent. Impossible, said Kealy, the horse won't go more than five miles an hour. Fined, said the bench, £2 and costs. 'The money was instantly paid.' But this was money from a struggling family farm, and Jean and her sons must have been angry. Family tensions escalated during the year until Kealy was brought again before the police court on 12 December 1862, a prisoner in custody, 'charged with beating his wife Jane Caley'. She declined to prosecute, and the charge was withdrawn. But the beating, no doubt, was real.

The Irish husband and wife were drinking. The next year Kealy was in court for outstanding debts to a publican for liquor and for the cost of two nights he and Jean spent at the hotel, a debt offset by what the publican owed the farmer for oats. Kealy's final appearance at the Oatlands courthouse seems to have been in November 1864 when he actually won a case against another neighbour who owed him 7 shillings 6 pence for hay. He also tried, unsuccessfully, to extract £1 10 shillings for an axle tree which turned out not to fit the neighbour's cart wheels. The cases brought by and against Kealy suggest how readily the farmers went to court to settle their disputes over small sums of money. The neighbour who eventually paid Kealy for his hay had been brought before the bench that same day by the Oatlands milkman trying to recover 10 shillings for the sale of a hat, a pair of trousers and a bed tick. The court cases give an insight into an emancipist community with few cash resources. The historian James Boyce has pointed out the irony of creating pre-industrial agricultural communities amongst the emancipists of Van Diemen's Land at the same time 'as the mother country was being rapidly transformed into the first modern industrial society (with her people becoming both a wage-force and a mass consumer market)'. As Boyce says, it is difficult to identify the 'cultural bonds that bound emancipist communities to each other, and to their shared past of servitude', but the former convicts, particularly the Irish like John Kealy who had left behind a land of famine in the 1840s, 'had commonly experienced a depth of trauma comparable with refugee communities today'. Were the children growing up in these emancipist communities aware of the trauma? Maybe not. It is easy to imagine how critical the young Bennetts may have been of their mother and her second husband, and yet Jean was managing the bonds of family well enough to keep her children connected to her, to each other, and to the place where they were born. The Bennetts, according to local lore, became known as the shepherds of the Midlands, acknowledgement of an important role in a community where prosperity depended on sheep.

At some point Kealy gave up farming, and he and Jean moved to Longford, another Midlands town not far from Oatlands. The third of the Bennett children, John, lived there as well, and it was he who registered the death of 'Jane Cailey, labourer's wife', in the home she continued to share with her hapless second husband. And then he returned his mother to Oatlands. Her descendant Cliff Bennett, who showed me the haunting portraits of Jean and James Bennett, took me to see their graves in the old Anglican cemetery on the edge of Lake Dulverton. It must have been the Bennett children who arranged for the simple yet beautiful stone to be erected in memory of James Bennett, died 7 December 1856, aged 50; 'also Jane Kealy', died 26 August 1887, aged 73. The children had reunited their parents.

10

THE LAST SURVIVORS

January 1888 was a month of anniversaries. A century before, the British began their settlement of Australia when convict ships remembered as the First Fleet sailed into Botany Bay, and now half a century had passed since the *Atwick* had disembarked its cargo of women onto the shores of Van Diemen's Land. Although I have found death records for only 55 of the 151 prisoners on the ship, I know that at least thirteen were still alive at the time of this fiftieth anniversary, seven Scottish convicts and six English. All had grown old in the last fifty years, and so much had happened since their arrival that the voyage itself may have receded into memories freed from the raw emotions tearing at them when they first stepped ashore. None of them had achieved notable success in the eyes of the world, and yet even to have attained what we might call the ordinary comforts of daily life is quite impressive, given the difficulties with which they began. This final chapter tells the stories of three Scottish survivors: Christian McDougall and Mary Bentley, who left the island colony which tried to put its convict heritage behind by changing its name to Tasmania; and Margaret Alexander, who found another island to call home. All three would prove physically tough and emotionally resourceful.

CHRISTIAN MCDOUGALL: SURVIVING IN A COUNTRY TOWN

When Christian McDougall was questioned in Glasgow on 14 April 1836 she said she 'sometimes goes by the name Margaret Rae which is her mother's name'. And where was her mother? Christian, who told the magistrate that she was sixteen, had four previous convictions for theft in the past five years, all under the name of Margaret Rae, the mother who was not there. Even if Christian was a couple of years older, as other documents suggest, the convictions began when she was an adolescent, another of the young *Atwick* thieves with no one to care for her. Christian said she was a corset maker, had become ill with some unspecified though undoubtedly contagious fever, and as one of Edinburgh's poor was admitted into the Royal Infirmary. When she recovered and came out, she had 'no regular place of residence' and was 'obliged to sleep in stairs at night', until the wife of a weaver took pity on 'her destitute circumstances' and agreed to 'give her a night or two's lodgings'. Christian repaid the kindness of folk who were themselves poor by stealing the husband's prize possession, the silver watch he kept under his pillow. As a child of the streets, Christian had not learned loyalty. At her trial in September 1836, she pleaded guilty, deciding perhaps like the other young Glasgow convict Mary Ann McAllister that 'she would rather be transported for this crime' as she 'has no person to look after her'.

Christian spent the first year of her sentence in the Glasgow tollbooth, and may have begun to wonder whether she would ever get out of Scotland before instructions finally came to send her down to the convict ship taking on cargo in the Thames. She arrived in Van Diemen's Land as a restless young woman unprepared to transform herself into a compliant servant. Her first master must have returned her quickly to the Female Factory, because she had been in the colony less than six weeks when a second master accused her of being insolent to her mistress. She was reprimanded and 'returned to government', meaning that the employer did not want her back again. Christian would incur eight more charges on her conduct record, brought by seven masters, and all for the same reason: walking away from her work. Twice she 'absconded' for days and nights at a time, her pleasure punished by adding a year to her sentence and sending her back to the crime class for several months. But for Christian, the pleasure may have been more than immediate gratification. Three times in four years, she returned from these illicit adventures pregnant, three times she gave birth in the hospital of the

Cascades Female Factory. Fathers do not seem to have played any part in this story, no one applied to marry her while she was under sentence, and when she did marry, her husband was someone she met after these children were born.

The pattern began in late January 1839, when Christian was sent to the Factory for three months after absconding from the house of the sixth master to whom she had been assigned within her first year. While serving this sentence, her pregnancy became apparent, and about the middle of the year she gave birth to a daughter. After the birth, Christian went with her baby to the convict nursery, which at the time was a house in Liverpool Street, seriously overcrowded and yet healthier than the earlier nursery inside the gloomy prison walls of the Cascades Female Factory. There Christian nursed the baby for nine months, and then was compelled to leave her. Everything about this child's later history suggests that Christian loved her very much, and it must have been heart-wrenching to wean her baby and leave her behind in the nursery where she had seen many children die in the year after they were weaned.

A few months later, Christian was back in the Female Factory to serve a sentence at the wash tub for being absent on Sunday and Monday. If she hoped to become pregnant again during this interlude, she was disappointed. Her next charge, again for absconding, came in July 1841. This time she was indeed pregnant when she came back into the Female Factory for three months in the crime class. After that punishment she managed to get herself assigned to the convict nursery in Liverpool Street, where she was registered at the time of the colony-wide muster in December 1841. Unfortunately, she arrived at the nursery not long after her little girl, now two years old, was transferred to the infant school of the Queen's Orphan Schools. Early in 1842 Christian McDougall gave birth to her second child, another daughter whom she again named 'Mary McDougall'. As soon as the baby was weaned, Christian was sent out on assignment. Repeating her earlier pattern, she left her service for two nights and a day, and was returned to the Female Factory to be punished for absconding. A few months later it would become evident that she was again pregnant. On 30 May 1843 she gave birth to her third child, a son named John. She was in the nursery to breastfeed John when the second 'Mary McDougall' became ill with diarrhoea, the scourge of the nurseries, and died, aged sixteen months.

On 12 December that same year when the second Mary died and John was born, Christian extracted the first Mary from the Orphan School. The timing is puzzling. Christian should have been confined to the convict nursery to breastfeed six-month-old John. Though the four-year-old 'orphan' Mary might have joined her mother and baby brother in the nursery, this seems unlikely because Matron Slee had no reason to take an older child into a building already overcrowded with women and infants. The other possibility is that Christian left the nursery under some arrangement allowing her to look after her own infant and child. Christian had never applied for a ticket of leave or conditional pardon. If her sentence to transportation had not been extended another year as part of two punishments for absconding, she would have been free by servitude in September of that traumatic year, but as it was, she was still under assignment, working without wages. Her unwaged status may have been exactly what was needed at this moment. The unwaged work most likely to meet the approval she needed to take John from the nursery and Mary from the Orphan School would be to look after someone else's children at the same time as her own, perhaps as a wet nurse. In this small community where favours circulated as currency, Matron Slee may have recommended Christian when she was asked for help by a settler whose wife was ill or recently dead. Whatever the arrangements, Christian certainly had her first child with her during her final months as a convict, and there was no absconding. She stayed where she was supposed to be. In June 1844, three months before her extended sentence was complete, the Lieutenant Governor remitted the extensions, and she was free.

If Christian had some ongoing relationship with the father or fathers of her children, this was the time to 'come out' as a family, but nothing of the sort happened, and I suspect that the young woman who missed her mother so much that she used her name had been more interested in mothering than in men. Unfortunately, the mothering was proving difficult. On 21 October 1844, four months after receiving her certificate of freedom, her son John died of consumption (tuberculosis), aged seventeen months. How long had he been ill, and how did she manage to look after him? Worries about how she could work and also take care of the one child she now had left may have influenced her decision to marry Michael Wallace. When and where they met remains unknown, but since he came to Van Diemen's Land in March 1844, seven months before 'John Ray' died, he cannot be the father of the children born to Christian at the Female Factory.

Michael Wallace had arrived from the penal station on Norfolk Island where he had served four years of his seven-year sentence for stealing money in Dublin. He was 29 years old, a Catholic shoemaker from Galway who could read and write. He had already been granted a ticket of leave, and upon arrival was appointed to the police as a convict constable, but because he was still under sentence, he had to apply to the Convict Department if he wanted to marry. This he did in April 1845, asking permission to marry not 'Christian McDougall' but 'Margaret Ray', and that is the name, a variant spelling of her mother's name, under which they were married at St Joseph's Catholic Church on 19 May 1845. Without the help of her descendant Muriel Allison, who sent me copies of documents about the Wallace family collected over years of research, I would have missed this moment when the convict 'Christian McDougall' is transformed into the free woman 'Margaret Wallace', and the illegitimate child born in the Female Factory and admitted to the Orphan School as 'Mary McDougall' turns into 'Annie Wallace'. The Wallace surname gave the little girl respectability, and made her a part of the family, unlike Jean Smith's first son, Joseph Douglas, who was kept away from the Bennetts. On Annie's death certificate her father would be identified as Michael Wallace, shoemaker, a sure sign that this renaming made her feel she belonged.

Getting away from the people and places of their convict past would be the next important step for this new family. On 9 October 1846, little more than a year after the wedding, a certificate of freedom was granted to Michael Wallace, and three weeks later the family left Van Diemen's Land forever. The passenger list of the *Sea Queen* includes Michael and

Mary Wallace (the impulse towards camouflage ran deep), accompanied by an unnamed child. Ironically, the convict emancipists freed themselves from the penal colony on a ship which had sailed from England as a prison, and had just unloaded 169 female transportees. The *Sea Queen* had then advertised for passengers and cargo to make the voyage home, claiming to be a 'fine fast-sailing first-class British barque' with 'excellent accommodation for passengers'. Before heading to London, the *Sea Queen* would cross Bass Strait to pick up more passengers and cargo in the port of Geelong. Would the Wallace family have stayed on the ship all the way back to London if they could afford the fare? An unanswerable question. What we know is that they stopped in the port where they disembarked, and in Geelong made their first home in a place where no one knew their history.

Seven months later, Margaret Wallace gave birth to a baby named Michael James, after his father. For the first time, motherhood would not be entangled with prison discipline. This child did not open his eyes to prison walls, and his mother need not dread a forced weaning and separation. Over the next twelve years, another five children were born, four boys and a girl, all nurtured to adulthood. On 26 July 1853 Christian's oldest child, Annie Wallace (born Mary McDougall), married George Atkins in Geelong when she was just fourteen. About this time, the entire family—including Annie and her new husband—settled in Winchelsea, a village with a population calculated ten years later in *Bailliere's Victorian Gazetteer* as no more than '300 in the township, with 65 dwellings'. The settlement had begun as a ford across the Barwon River between Geelong and Warrnambool, and even in the 1870s with the coming of the railroad which passed through Winchelsea on its way from Melbourne to western Victoria, the town remained small, a good place to bring up children. Christian had found a place where she could feel at home, and here she would live for 50 years.

The Wallace family grew and prospered, and by 1864 the shoemaker owned his own home and workshop on his own land. Then tragedy struck. Michael Wallace went mad, and had to be committed to the Yarra Bend Lunatic Asylum in Melbourne where he died on 16 January 1866.

This must have been a terrible time for Christian. She was 50 years old, and her youngest child was only six. Having her grown-up daughter Annie nearby would be a comfort, and her oldest boys, in their late teens, could help support the family. Christian faced the future by working the unskilled jobs she knew. The council rate books, which show that she held onto the family property as owner and occupier, list her occupation as laundress in 1886, and then as charwoman until the end of her life. In the village where she lived as a widow for almost 40 years, Christian became the matriarch of an extensive family.

Christian's daughter Annie made her a grandmother three times before she herself gave birth to her ninth and final child in 1859, and living near each other in a country town, they could share the pleasures and responsibilities of watching small children grow. Then, in 1881 when Annie was 42 years old and carrying her sixteenth child within 26 years, she was struck down by measles, gave birth prematurely, and died. How Christian must have grieved for this last remaining child from the miseries of her convict years, the baby whose childhood was blighted by confinement in the convict nursery and the Orphan School. But Christian had other children and grandchildren to console her as she moved into the twentieth century and an advanced old age.

She had friends as well, friends whose standing in the community endorsed her own respectable status when the illiterate old woman marked her signature with an 'X' on a will dated 30 October 1901. Four men from Winchelsea put their names to this document ensuring that her estate would be settled as she wished. Her two executors are identified as auctioneer and horse owner, the witnesses as blacksmith and bank manager. The provisions of the will were simple. A loan of £20 was to be repaid to her son Joseph, and then her property and personal estate was to be sold and the proceeds divided equally between her married Wallace daughter, and her two unmarried sons, Joseph and Henry. The ceremony of making and signing the will demonstrated that Christian was still in charge of her own life in this town where she had found a place to set down roots. On a winter's day less than two years later she died of heart failure and lung congestion after an illness of four weeks.

On 19 August 1903 when the Anglican minister intoned the rites of burial, her five living children may have gathered at her grave in the Winchelsea Cemetery. Her youngest child, named John in a ghostly echo of her first son, had died a decade before in his mid-thirties, and it was the next to youngest son, Henry, who registered her death. Death certificates in Victoria asked for considerable information, and when the informant was the child of an emancipist parent, the details give some insight into how much they knew about their parent's convict and pre-transportation history—or how much they were willing to put on public record. Henry, who never married and may have lived with Christian until her death, gave her age as 87. In the column asking for the names of her father and mother and their rank or profession, all he entered was 'Rea' for the father, understandable since that surname in its various spellings appears as her maiden name on the birth registers for her children, as it had on the marriage register. Henry may never have heard the name Christian McDougall, but he knew she was born in Glasgow, was correct in saying that she had married in Tasmania, and had been in the colony of Victoria for about 55 years. Most interesting, he named every one of her nine children, including the two who died in Van Diemen's Land. The 'illegitimate' children born in the Female Factory had been part of the story she told her Wallace children, they had been remembered. And today she is remembered with admiration by her descendants, that lonely destitute girl sleeping on stairways in the tenements of Glasgow who survived to become a pioneer mother in western Victoria.

MARY BENTLEY: SURVIVING ON THE GOLDFIELDS

All but four of the 78 *Atwick* convicts tried in Scotland were serving sentences of seven years. Longer sentences had been imposed upon the 'wilful fire-raiser' Eliza Davidson who would remain in the penal colony for the term of her natural life, and upon three women transported for fourteen years, including the compulsive child-stripper, Agnes Campbell Robertson. Surprisingly, one of these longer sentences was imposed on a thief with no prior convictions, Mary Bentley. I suspect that if Mary had not been arrested with a local thug known as Fitty Wilson, her sentence might have been shorter.

One Saturday night after the local workers had been paid, Wilson orchestrated the robbery of a quarryman on a dim gas-lit street of Dalkeith, the market town 10 kilometres south of Edinburgh. The victim later claimed that Wilson intimidated him into buying a drink in a public house where he did not want to go, and where a prostitute named Mary Bentley appeared. They drank their whisky and as they left were joined by another woman who would also sail on the *Atwick*, Mary McVicar. The quarryman, who had 'heard that Wilson was a thief', grew anxious, but instead of confronting his tormentor directly, asked him to send the women away. Wilson spoke to them, and said he had 'kicked their ar—s', but when the quarryman suddenly realised he was going in the wrong direction and tried to turn back, Wilson seized him by the breast of his coat, tripped up his heels, threw him to the ground, and uttered the traditional threat of highway robbers, 'Your money or your life!' 'Oh man is that it!' cried the terrified victim as Wilson called to the two women who materialised out of the dark. After the man yelled 'murder', Wilson knelt down hard on him to stifle his voice while the women riffled his pockets. Mary Bentley felt coins, and asked for a pair of scissors to cut the pocket, encouraging Wilson to take their victim's 'life as he lay'. The quarryman 'begged of them to save his life and to take all he had'—which they did.

The police had no trouble identifying and arresting the culprits, and instead of processing them in Dalkeith, sent the prisoners straight up to Edinburgh to be examined. There Thomas 'Fitty' Wilson identified himself as a carter aged 21, living with his father in Dalkeith. Mary McVicar said she was nineteen, born in the county of Fife, and living with her stepfather, a weaver in Dalkeith. Mary Bentley said she was 22, born in Linlithgow and living in Dalkeith with her widowed mother. The accused were young adults still living with families too poor to give them a basic education (none could sign their precognitions) or to apprentice them to some trade promising a real income upon which to build a future.

When Mary Bentley arrived in Van Diemen's Land, she stated her offence as highway robbery, named the victim, and said she had been on the town for twelve months, but mentioned nothing about her co-accused. Mary McVicar said nothing about being on the town, but did name the persons with whom she was tried. Gaol reports described both women as 'of irregular habits' and 'indifferent connexions'. Was Mary Bentley silent about her 'connexions' because she consciously intended to re-fashion herself in this new land? After their arrival, there is no evidence that she ever saw Mary McVicar or Fitty Wilson again. Similar breaks with the past seem a recurring pattern among Scottish convicts from the *Atwick*, who rarely show up as witnesses for each other's weddings, or marry other Scots, or live in anything resembling Scottish enclaves. For some of the transportees, especially single childless women under the age of 25, the break imposed by transportation may have come as a relief, even if they had families and friends to miss. What they made of the break depended on their own resilience—and on luck, on being assigned to a reasonable master, and on finding a partner with whom to make plans for another sort of life once they were free.

Mary Bentley, like Elizabeth Williamson and Jean Boyd, was lucky, and her good fortune can be guessed from her conduct record where only one offence is recorded: on 14 August of the year she arrived Mary was charged with 'neglect of duty and disorderly conduct'. The formulaic nature of the charge conceals whatever she had actually done to displease her master sufficiently for him to take the trouble to send her into Hobart Town from his farm in the Sorell district. The magistrate, seemingly less incensed than the master, sentenced Mary to only three days' solitary confinement, and mentioned nothing about starving her on bread and water. Maybe there is a connection between this episode and Mary's relationship to an Englishman from Liverpool named William Peeler who had been in the colony for ten years, serving like her a fourteen-year sentence for robbery (though his was housebreaking). We know that in early December 1838 an application to marry was sent to the muster master on behalf of William, who had never before asked permission to marry anyone, and on 31 December permission was granted. This seems very surprising because Mary Bentley had been in the colony less than a year, and had a charge against her within the last four months, and yet whatever regulations governed the granting of 'indulgences', there was always room for special cases within the endless network of influence.

And by reading for gaps between records, more evidence of special treatment becomes visible. A week or two after the marriage was approved but before it took place, Mary gave birth to a son about whom we know because on 4 March 1840 she registered the death from dropsy of Charles Peeler, aged fourteen months. The birth of Charles explains the delay in his parents' marriage—Mary was probably incarcerated in the Female Factory waiting to give birth when the marriage was approved—but when the baby was five months old, Mary Bentley and William Peeler were married at St David's Church, Hobart Town, under the rites and ceremonies of the Church of England. They said they were aged 23 and 29, though other sources would suggest that Mary was between 25 and 30, and William 33. Where and how did they begin married life? Mary was still in the early stages of her fourteen-year sentence and William as a ticket-of-leave holder was not sufficiently far along to have his wife assigned to him. Did they have an arrangement with their masters allowing them to set up house together with their baby son? When Mary registered the death of Charles, she gave her address as Patrick Street, Hobart Town. Was the baby living there as well? If so, how had the Peelers extracted their son from the convict nursery? Is this another instance of Matron Slee allowing convict parents to give their child a family life? Ironically, if Charles had remained in the nursery and died there, evidence of his existence might have disappeared. His birth was never registered and his death would not have been either, because the Convict Department was not yet complying with the 1838 law Mary herself obeyed as she watched the sad details of her first-born's death entered into the ledger at the Registrar General's office.

Distressing though the loss of their first child must have been for the newly married parents, there was some comfort in knowing that Mary would give birth again in a few months. This time the child was a girl they named Ellen, a child who would have a long life. Where was she born? The certificate registering her death in 1925 says she was born in Launceston, on the north side of the colony, while another story within the family says Bagdad, a village 37 kilometres north of Hobart Town. Was Ellen told she was born in other parts of the colony to cover the shame of her actual birth within the prison walls of the Cascades Female

Factory? In December 1841 when the convicts of Van Diemen's Land were mustered, Mary Bentley was in the convict nursery, Hobart Town. Presumably she was there to breastfeed Ellen.

Within months of that muster, the Peeler family was finally and permanently united. On 21 January 1842 William Peeler's name was published in the *Courier* on a list of persons eligible for certificates of freedom because their sentences had expired. As a free man, William could apply for his convict wife to be assigned to him, and this had happened by the time of the census in January 1843, when the Peelers were living with little Ellen in a community of emancipist householders, several with wives identified as assigned to husbands who were 'mechanics and artificers', labourers who worked in heavily polluting industries along the rivulet within a few minutes' walk of the Cascades Female Factory, that prison Mary had avoided almost entirely except when giving birth. What an occasion it must have been a few months after the census when the Peelers' third child was born, a boy named for the father who this time could cradle the newborn babe in his arms. On 7 June 1843, when baby William was not quite a month old, Mary walked into the office of the Registrar General and entered into the public record the details of his birth.

Two years later, in March 1845 Mary's application for a conditional pardon was approved, a major milestone along the path towards freedom from surveillance. The next month she gave birth to another son, Thomas, and in July 1847 to a second daughter, Jane, whose father is identified on the birth register as 'fellmonger', one whose job it was to prepare skins for tanning. William Peeler was no longer the generic 'labourer' entered on the register when William and Thomas were born, and even though the tanning industry was dirty, smelly work involving corrosive chemicals, the Peelers might have remained in Van Diemen's Land to raise their children, as did many other families in this story. Instead, like Christian McDougall and Michael Wallace, they risked a leap into the unknown. The story of the Peelers' leap and its consequences has recently been uncovered by one of their descendants, George Milford, who had no idea that there were any convicts in his family when as a schoolboy in Victoria he sang:

> There's the Captain as is our Commander;
> There's the bo'sun and all the ship's crew,
> There's the first and the second class passengers,
> Knows what we poor convicts go through.

It was just a song, he remembers, nothing to do with him. But then one day, in answer to his persistent questioning about why and how the Peelers came to be in Victoria so early, a relative laughingly said, 'Oh, they were old lags'—and that set Milford off on decades of research, following family stories in the pursuit of documentary evidence.

From Mary Bentley's great-granddaughter, he heard the stories Mary's son William had told of the family's departure from Van Diemen's Land 75 years earlier. William was only five at the time, but the voyage was so traumatic that he vowed never to set foot in a boat again. And in the Melbourne *Argus* for 22 September 1848, George Milford discovered that William's fears were well-founded. Five months after Mary received an extension to her conditional pardon permitting her to live anywhere outside the United Kingdom of Great Britain and Ireland, the Peelers booked passage on the *John Bull* for themselves and their four children, Ellen aged eight; William five; Thomas three; and Jane one. The *John Bull* was a schooner loaded with 15,000 feet of timber, 6,000 shingles and 140 bags of potatoes when it left Hobart Town on 20 August for a journey that might take 48 to 72 hours with a favourable wind. The Peelers' voyage lasted 32 days. According to the *Argus,* the schooner 'encountered a succession of furious gales, which drove her almost through the Straits from one place of refuge to another', the timber began shifting dangerously across the deck and had to be thrown overboard, and 'two of the crew escaped almost miraculously being victims to the fury of the tempest'. Imagine the prolonged terror of a family with four small children. No wonder the experience was seared into William's memory.

He had other iconic memories, too, of those early days in Victoria. The Peelers lived initially in Melbourne's inner-city suburb of Richmond, perhaps with father William working again as a fellmonger. And then in 1851 came sensational news of gold discovered on what would become the Mount Alexander field centred on Castlemaine, described by historian Tony Dingle as 'over fifteen square miles of what proved to be the richest and most easily worked of all the alluvial diggings'. The goldrush completely transformed the colony of Victoria, which until then had been primarily agricultural, and had been separated from New South Wales for only a matter of months before gold lured the masses to dig up the land. 'In March 1851', writes Dingle, 'there had been just over seventy-seven thousand people in Victoria; by the end of the following year there were almost a hundred and seventy thousand'. The Peelers joined the rush. The two Williams, father and son, quickly headed to the diggings, and the son would remember being sent off by his father 'to find half an ounce of gold each day before he could go off to play'. William the father had joined other 'Vandemonians', as the convict emancipists from Van Diemen's Land were called, and the area they worked became known as Launceston Gully.

Back in Richmond, Mary gave birth in May 1852 to another son, and not long afterwards the family was reunited on the diggings. Mary, who had always lived in towns except when she worked on the farm as an assigned servant, re-fashioned herself as a pioneer mother transforming a miner's tent into a family home. Though the Peelers never struck it rich, the independent way of life on the diggings suited them, and when most of the miners moved on, they stayed put. Privileges coming to William as 'miner's rights' offered the family a toehold on community. A yearly licence fee gave William the right to vote and to build a home in Launceston Gully down what is now called Cat Dam Track. 'Turn to the left and take in the view', writes George Milford of the house site, 'the creek, a tributary of Barkers Creek, a hundred metres down the slope, the sunlight falling on the yellowing grass, the gum trees amidst the diggers' holes'. Memories of William and Mary are inscribed onto the bush landscape of Barkers Creek to the east of Castlemaine in the names of 'Peelers Flat' and 'Peelers Road'. The family settled into the land, and descendants continue to live in the district, caring for Peeler graves in the Harcourt cemetery.

But one grave is in another place. Esther, the last of the Peeler children and the only one born on the diggings, died of dysentery when she was a year old and was buried on 15 February 1856 at Campbell's Creek. Her grieving parents may have found some comfort from religion. Like many of the miners across Victoria in the 1850s, they had listened to the Methodist preachers who travelled the countryside, and it may have been about this time that Mary bought a large Bible for her oldest son, and asked someone to write for her the words, 'Presented to William Peeler by his mother Mary'. Illiterate herself, she made sure that young William had an education, and from the age of nine he walked more than 3 kilometres each way to a grammar school held at night in Castlemaine.

As the children grew into adults, Thomas and John joined their father in mining. The remaining miners of Barkers Creek, convinced that more gold could be extracted from Specimen Gully, urged the Victorian government to invest in a water supply for quartz crushing and sluicing—but urged in vain. The most reliable mining was proving to be slate, quarried at Barkers Creek to roof the terrace houses of prosperous Melbourne. This was every bit as dangerous as mining gold, and in 1883 Thomas died in an accident. 'He was going up a ladder on his way to dinner', reported the Castlemaine correspondent for the Melbourne *Argus*, when about 130 feet from the bottom, he lost his footing and fell 60 feet. Fellow miners (were his father and brother there?) raised the unconscious man to the surface and carried him to a hospital where he died of a fractured skull, 'a very steady and industrious man with a family of seven young children', said the local newspaper.

Mary, grieving for her son and worried about her husband who was now almost 80, may have taken solace in knowing that her eldest son was not a miner. His trade was carpentry and on land adjoining his parents' property the younger William built an unusual house, its front rooms converted from the Bible Christian Chapel he bought and moved after the congregation joined the Wesleyans. The apple and pear trees he planted were the start of a family orchard business which continues today in the Harcourt area, run by a sixth-generation Peeler. When William senior died in 1888, aged 83, Mary moved next door to live with her son, his wife and their large family. A grandchild remembered her as a little old woman, always wearing a shawl, who 'used to look forward to her grandchildren coming home from school and took a kindly interest in their work'.

Mary died on 29 December 1896, 60 years to the month since her arrest for highway robbery on the wintry street in Dalkeith. The young Scottish prostitute had not been 'ripe for transportation' in the Procurator Fiscal's meaning of incorrigible offender, and yet was 'ripe' in the sense of being ready to move, ready to re-fashion herself elsewhere. At the end of her long life, did she ever muse on the irony of punishment as luck? Luck, her descendant George Milford has reminded me, is an important part of her story: 'As luck would have it, her new life lay in the world's richest alluvial goldfield. She had made a home in the wilderness and had five children grow to adulthood. She had 36 living grandchildren, healthy young colonials. (I think that, without exception, all the grandchildren were over six feet in height . . . they would all have towered over their little gran).'

One of them would make the family famous. Walter, the eighth of William's ten children, was nine years old when Mary died. Twenty years later, the name of Corporal Walter Peeler appeared in newspapers across the country under the headline, 'Australian Heroes'. The Adelaide *Advertiser* reported that for valiant service in the trenches of France during World War I, Corporal Peeler of Barkers Creek was awarded a Victoria Cross after he 'rushed a hellhole from which snipers were firing, and accounted for nine Germans', then rushed the gunners twice again, bombed them from their dugout, and 'actually accounted for over 30 enemies. His fearlessness and fine example ensured the success of the attack.' The hero's national significance is recognised by an entry in the *Australian Dictionary of Biography*, but there is no mention of his quintessentially Australian pedigree. The ghosts of his convict grandparents hover unseen.

MARGARET ALEXANDER AND AN ISLAND CALLED HOPE

The last of the *Atwick* convicts to die, as far as I can tell, was Margaret Alexander. Tracing the women after they were no longer recorded in the registers of the Convict Department has been difficult for the usual reasons—because their names are too common to follow with confidence, or because they changed their surnames by marriage, or because like Christian McDougall/Margaret Rae or Ray/Margaret or Mary Wallace, they changed their names to cover their tracks and create new identities. Following post-sentence lives has often depended on the generosity of family and local historians who by working backwards have bridged gaps I was unable to cross. But even if I located death records for all the women transported on the *Atwick*, it seems unlikely that any of Margaret's shipmates remained alive after her death on Hope Island on 9 December 1912.

Margaret's story begins like those of many convict women transported to Australia. On 2 January 1837, she was arrested for theft in her native Stirling, telling the magistrate she was 'sixteen years of age'. The local sheriff's officer said that he had known Margaret 'for about 6 years during which time he has considered her habite & repute a thief and an associate of thieves', and twice he had seen her convicted of theft. Margaret had no education, could not sign her name, and apparently she had been fending for herself from an early age, in spite of living in the same town as her parents and siblings. Her father, she said, was a journeyman baker, and his wages may have been too low to support a wife and five children, of whom Margaret was the fourth. At the time of her arrest, she was living with other young prostitutes who brought clients picked up on the streets below the castle to their landlady's 'house', a room with a separate 'closet' for business. Charged, as so many of the convict women had been, with stealing money from a drunken client's pocketbook, Margaret was tried on 18 April 1837, and even though the *Stirling Journal and Advertiser* reported that her counsel 'addressed the Jury in a very able manner, commenting in pretty severe terms upon the evidence of the witnesses', especially that of the alleged victim, the jury after deliberating for twenty minutes found her guilty, and Lord Moncrieff pronounced a sentence of seven years' transportation. During her first three years in Van Diemen's Land, four different masters charged Margaret with being absent from her work or absconding, and once she was charged with theft. And then her life changed direction because she was assigned to a place which suited her.

Although Margaret had grown up in town, she took to country life when she was sent to work on the farm of Thomas Terry, whose father had emigrated to Van Diemen's Land from Yorkshire, arriving in 1819 with his wife, eleven children, two servants, and a pair of millstones. The father built a mill at New Norfolk, and applied for the land grants which, together with sheer hard work, generated prosperity for the extensive family. Margaret was working for the Terrys in July 1843 when she paid 5 shillings to have her application for a conditional pardon forwarded from the New Norfolk police station, and it was probably through them that she met her future husband, John Broadhurst Boothman, who unlike most husbands of *Atwick* women was born in Van Diemen's Land, and had never been convicted of anything. The Boothmans and the Terrys were socially connected, and John Boothman's sister would soon marry Thomas Terry's brother. When Margaret Alexander married John Broadhurst Boothman, she entered an established network of settler families, but there is no suggestion that she was ostracised because of her convict past. Her husband had his own convict connections.

His father had arrived on the ship which founded Hobart Town in 1804, the *Calcutta*. Transported for embezzlement, John Boothman senior was literate and served his sentence as a clerk in the fledgling colony. By the time his eldest son and namesake was born, he held quite responsible positions in the government, but disastrously for his family he died in 1829 when John junior was eighteen, and the youngest of his five siblings barely four. The family was left totally without income, and until his mother remarried five years later, John probably gave her whatever he could earn. The Boothman family was close and supportive, and the children seem to have been happy with their new stepfather, who for nine years proved a stable provider until his death in July 1843, a few months before Margaret Alexander and John Boothman were married. The will of John's stepfather divided his considerable assets among his wife and her children, bequeathing to John the freehold title for the Pickwick Inn in Liverpool Street. This legacy made John Broadhurst Boothman, identified on the marriage register as farmer aged 32, a man of some property when he and Margaret were married on 16 October 1843 in the elegant new St Matthew's Church of Clarence Plains.

Where Boothman was farming at the time of their marriage and under what circumstances remains unclear, but it looks as if the farm was not his own, because the recently married couple were able to respond immediately when tragedy struck the family of his second sister, Eliza. She was almost the same age as Margaret, and had been married for six years to Alexander Reid, who was farming a property called the 'Meeting Waters' at Great Swanport, on the east coast of the island. On a Wednesday morning early in July 1845, Reid's horse returned without its master, who had been expected home the night before. All day the bush was searched in vain. Finally, on Thursday the body was found amidst wattle scrub in a waterhole where Reid, apparently thrown from his horse, had drowned. The traumatically widowed Eliza, mother to boys aged four and not yet two, must have been very grateful for her brother John and his wife Margaret, who came to help and were still on the property at the time of the census in 1848, though Eliza and her children had gone. The next year the Boothmans left too. Thanks to the insider knowledge of John's younger brother Edward, a clerk in the office of the Surveyor General and Commissioner of Crown Lands, they had found an island where Margaret would spend the rest of her long life.

The story of Hope Island, and of the Boothman family tenure there as farmers for almost 90 years, emerges from the research undertaken by Norm Beechey and Dorothy Baker for their two-volume *History of Dover and Port Esperance*. The island lies near the southern tip of Tasmania in the D'Entrecasteaux Channel at the entrance to Port Esperance, the harbour on which the town of Dover stands. Named perhaps by someone with a wry sense of humour, 65-acre 'Hope' is the largest of three islets, outstripping 'Faith' and 'Charity'. This is a rugged part of the world, and because Hope had the advantage of being one of the few relatively flat pieces of land near the harbour, convicts were sent to clear the island for cultivation during the period of the Dover probation station (1844–47). When the station closed, the island was advertised for annual rental as crown land. The successful tenderer agreed to a yearly rent of £52 7 shillings 6 pence, but before his second year was up, according to Beechey and Baker, 'he had evidently arranged for rental of the island to be transferred to John Broadhurst Boothman', a transfer confirmed in the office where Edward Boothman worked. Lieutenant Governor Denison noticed what looked like 'trafficking in land', and although persuaded that the transaction was legal, was irritated nevertheless. 'I look upon these fraternal copartnerships with great disfavour', he wrote, 'this looks very like a job'.

John Boothman, for his part, was keen to cut a deal, and his correspondence debating terms of occupancy paints a picture of the difficulties he and Margaret faced as they set about transforming a convict outpost into a sustainable farm. To help with the hard manual labour, Boothman hired convict passholders and ticket-of-leave men, paying their wages by mortgaging the Hobart pub inherited from his stepfather. Their first job was to remove large quantities of loose stone from the supposedly cleared sections so that the land could be ploughed and not just dug with a spade. Clearing land would continue for decades to involve what was called 'stoning', and unusually wide stonewall fences soon divided the rocky island into sections. The hired men also helped repair convict outbuildings and added two small rooms to a weatherboard cottage which became the farmhouse. The census of 1851 includes an assigned servant woman, who might have been surprised to learn that her mistress Mrs Boothman had until recently been a convict herself.

The Boothmans were ambitious, and although security of tenancy on Hope Island remained forever an unresolved problem, they invested heavily in their enterprise and worked prodigiously hard. Beginning in January 1855, John Boothman added a pub to their workload. For four years he held the licence of the Port Esperance Bay Hotel, probably nothing more than a taproom attached to the farmhouse. This was the first licensed hotel in the Port Esperance district, and although an island seems an awkward location for locals who were mostly timber-cutters and sawyers, a wholesale liquor licence made boat trips worth the trouble, and a regular clientele developed among boatmen on the trading vessels moving constantly through the D'Entrecasteaux Channel. The hotel seems to have been making money because John Boothman, in partnership with his well-situated brother in the Survey Department, began buying crown land as it came up for sale in the district. After 1858, however, the hotel licence was not renewed, and the Port Esperance Bay Hotel disappeared from the books. New hotels on the mainland diminished the profits of the original monopoly, and Margaret, who may have run the pub while her husband worked the farm, could have decided she'd had enough of rowdy men—especially after she took on responsibility for the orphaned sons of her sister. The arrival in September 1858 of James and Robert Sawers, aged fifteen and thirteen, turned the island into a family home.

No children had been born to the Boothmans, presumably a consequence of Margaret's life as a teenaged prostitute, and the childless couple made a perfect match for boys with no memory of their own parents, who died of fever within three days of each other in March 1846. For twelve years Scottish relatives in Stirling had cared for the orphans, ensuring that they received the education which was to stand them in good stead in a part of the colony where reading and writing were by no means universal skills. Their older siblings, Jessie, then aged seventeen, and John, thirteen, had migrated to Australia five years earlier. I suspect that the Boothmans paid their fares, brought them initially to Hope Island, and then helped them go off to Victoria in the excitement of the goldrush years. Jessie married a widowed Irishman and went with him to New Zealand, where in 1870 she named their first daughter Margaret Boothman Adams, a sure sign of gratitude and affection, even though the aunt and niece could have spent very little time together. And when John Sawers married in Bendigo, the gold town where he would work most of his life as an accountant, he named his first son John Boothman Sawers.

Jessie and John Sawers may have encouraged their younger brothers to make the long voyage from Scotland, assuring them that they would have a real home on Hope Island. The boys were coming to a raw pioneering world, utterly different from the ancient and royal town of Stirling where they were born, and we know that they thrived in this new home because they wrote themselves into historical memory through the pages of 92 diaries. The diaries first came to public view when Norm Beechey and

Dorothy Baker published their history of the area. Intrigued by the diaries, the two researchers then spent years transcribing entries and annotating the text with a view to publication. Unfortunately, Norm Beechey died before the project was completed, and the diaries, in private hands, are no longer accessible. It is through Dorothy Baker's generosity that I have read the transcriptions, and found myself immersed in the day-to-day life of the Boothman farm.

What would turn out to be a lifelong project of record-keeping begins on Monday 18 August 1862, four years after the boys have come to Hope Island. Seventeen-year-old Robert initiates the rigorously systematic routine of writing, almost never missing a day. On the rare occasions when he goes by steamer with his uncle to Hobart Town, his brother James writes the entries. The early diaries are above all a tribute to work. Hope Island was feeding timber-cutters and sawyers who grew few crops of their own, and from the diaries we can guess what they ate. On a typical day, Robert was digging potatoes while his brother ploughed, and Uncle was churning butter after Aunt milked the cows. Robert recorded meticulously, and no doubt proudly, the work they got through each day. On 28 October Uncle repaired the fireplace in the back parlour, while Robert and James spent the morning spreading manure and in the afternoon planted 830 cabbages. Potatoes, allowed to deplete the soil through heavy cropping when the island was a probation station, continued to be important, but planting was diversified into wheat, barley and oats, together with the core vegetables of a British diet: onions, carrots, peas, turnips, and cauliflower. Raspberries and gooseberries grew well, and Margaret made jam in commercial quantities. Mangold, a coarse variety of beet, was grown as fodder for cattle, and tobacco was planted for sheep dip. In addition to the cows, there were chickens and pigs.

Thanks to Robert's diaries, we know that the Boothmans had no trouble finding people to buy the island produce. In 1863 six tons of potatoes were sold at £5 10 shillings per ton, and 264 dozen cabbages brought in £36 9 shillings 6 pence. Settlers bought 215 pounds of butter, and another 70 pounds went to the new store at Dover. From the store they bought staples the farm could not produce—oil, coffee, sugar, salt, flour. Sometimes they indulged their tastes rather than their needs, buying mustard, spices, sardines, mutton, and lollipops. Solitary fishermen stopped by the island to sell barracouta and crayfish. The Sawers brothers show no interest in fishing themselves, but they loved boats and Robert's first diary records progress on the construction of a cutter, christened the *Garibaldi* and launched by moonlight on 3 October in plenty of time to enter the Huon Regatta on New Year's Day. Margaret sewed the seams in the sails.

Even though the Boothmans and their nephews were on an island in a part of the colony unconnected to any town by road, they led remarkably sociable lives. Ships rounding South Cape and coming up the D'Entrecasteaux Channel on their way to Hobart Town could anchor for the night to invite the islanders on board, or to enjoy the Boothmans' hospitality. When passenger steamers began plying the Channel on regularly scheduled trips, anyone from Dover who wanted to board would be picked up mid-Channel, which often meant waiting out on Hope Island until the steamer was in sight. Given the vagaries of weather in this area, the Boothmans undoubtedly sheltered many an intending passenger for the night, perhaps offering a bed in the old taproom. Sometimes the ships brought relatives from the close-knit Boothman family. Other visitors from Hobart Town came ashore when taking the country air on holiday excursions. In 1853 the artist Mary Morton Allport sketched the island when she visited with her lawyer husband on a holiday trip from town. And always the ships brought mail, and gossip, and the books Robert mentions in the diaries, especially English novels and the latest instalment of Dickens. Perhaps he read aloud at night while his illiterate aunt sewed. The young men were undoubtedly devoted to their aunt, though with their Scottish reserve, affection was less likely to be expressed in words than in actions, like helping Margaret plant an ornamental garden with roses, flowers, and an English holly alive 150 years later.

Through page after page, the diaries chart the years of transformation as Port Esperance changes from a rough timber-cutting camp to a community where people had the time and money to do something besides work. Clergymen arrived to hold services in a barn, and to urge the building of churches. Concerts, where Robert might play his flute, and events like 'Penny Readings', moved from occasional happenings to the scheduled features of an active Working Mens Club. During the 1870s, when James begins to keep his own diary, the hard work of farming is set against a busy social life, made possible because other men were hired to help on the farm, especially for seasonal tasks.

In 1874, Robert left the island for a job in a sugar mill near Grafton, New South Wales, but after a year he was back again, 'doing the agreeable' amidst his expanding circle of friends. How Margaret must have enjoyed watching her 'boys' turn into competent farmers and charming young men much in demand. Her husband too was highly regarded. He had been appointed Justice of the Peace in the mid-1860s, and as magistrate on the Dover bench John Boothman spent years immersed in the details of Port Esperance lives while sorting out various legal issues, authorising warrants and licences, approving the movement of prisoners. A clerical visitor to Hope Island described Boothman as 'such a fine benevolent-looking man—quite the English country gentleman'.

A decade later, as John Boothman's health worsened, he made more frequent trips up the Channel to Hobart Town for medical treatment. On 10 May 1882, the entire family gathered around his bedside in town, as Robert wrote in the diary:

> . . . *went up to see Uncle at 10 o'clock, he was asleep, he woke up about 11.30 when I lifted him out of bed and helped him up in a chair while Aunt and Mrs Terry [Boothman's sister Mary Ann] made the bed. Poor Uncle went off quietly in my arms at 11.45.*

John Broadhurst Boothman was 71 years old when he died, and Margaret 63. Forty years and one week had passed since he applied for permission to marry the convict Margaret Alexander. Their marriage as far as I can tell was unfailingly supportive. In finding Hope Island, they discovered a place where they could share day by day the joint enterprise of farming, taking pleasure in their achievements as they stood on the verandah of their substantial house to survey the landscape they had crafted together.

Having no children must have been a blow, but that disappointment was relieved by the arrival of the Sawers orphans, who would never have stayed if they had not felt completely at home, and as Margaret mourned the loss of the man she loved, she could count on the companionship and support of her nephews who were themselves approaching middle age— James would be 40 in a few months. Why they never married remains a mystery. Their diaries, full of social comings and goings, hint at romance but nothing ever eventuates. Both were becoming prominent men, like their uncle, while continuing to work the farm with their aunt. James was the Customs officer for southern ports, and Robert the coroner for the region. As local correspondents for Hobart Town newspapers, they told city readers about life in a region where apple orchards were replacing the sawmills.

Margaret lived another 30 years after her husband's death, and as she grew more frail and left the island less frequently, her nephews, remembered by locals as the 'Scottish gentlemen', kept her in touch with a larger world. It seems symbolically appropriate that in 1911 a small lighthouse was erected on Hope Island, and the Sawers brothers became keepers of the light, refilling it with carbide every few days, a beacon of direction and safe-keeping in an often blustery sea. And it was on this island of safe-keeping, where she had lived for 60 years, that Margaret Alexander Boothman died on 9 December 1912, aged 93. Her body was taken from the island for burial with her husband and his mother in the Queenborough Cemetery of Hobart, which had dropped 'Town' from its name while climbing upward in status to city. Margaret had lived through an historical saga, as the penal settlement of Van Diemen's Land was transformed into the post-transportation colony of Tasmania, and then into a state within the newly federated nation of Australia. And she herself had been transformed from convict transportee to pioneer farming wife to respected pillar of a community. In so many ways, she had prospered. The achievements at the core of her life are visible in the will she signed in the laborious hand of a woman who had learned late to write her name, and probably could write nothing else. The will for an estate valued at probate as £719 (and that does not include the island, leased as crown land) left everything 'unto my nephews James Sawers and Robert Sawers', farmers of Port Esperance, 'to be equally divided between them share and share alike'.

And they did share her legacy, living together in her house until James died in 1922, aged 79. Since neither brother had any experience in cooking or running a household, they invited another member of their complex family to join them, Annie Elizabeth Adams, a step-daughter of their older sister Jessie. Over the years Annie Adams had travelled to the island from New Zealand with some of Jessie's children for extended visits, so she had at least some idea of what she was getting into when as an unmarried woman of 50 she agreed to take on the role of 'host-ess'—or more prosaically and accurately, housekeeper—for her elderly step-uncles. She may have been as set in her ways as they were, and not surprisingly Robert records a tiff in 1916 when James 'kicked up a row at breakfast, was most insulting to Annie & did not show up to dinner or tea'. James took to eating his meals alone in the kitchen, and a few weeks later went off on a trip to Melbourne. Family life seems to have calmed down by the time he returned, and six years later it was Annie who nursed James as he lay dying. Robert writes on 21 October 1922: 'was roused at 3 am by Annie who said Jim was dead'. Without Annie, Robert would have struggled after James died, but she too was sociable and immersed in community life, and the two kept each other company. After she and Robert were both dead, a plaque to their memory was hung in the Dover Town Hall, a mark of esteem from the people among whom they lived. Robert died on 1 February 1935, two months short of his ninetieth birthday. Annie then gave up the lease on Hope Island, and the long tenure of this remarkable family came to an end.

EPILOGUE

If Margaret Alexander had lived one month more, she might have pondered the seventy-fifth anniversary of the January day in 1838 when she arrived in Van Diemen's Land after the long journey from her Scottish home, might have mused on the difference that voyage on the *Atwick* had made to the shape of her life. Lord Moncrieff in sentencing her to transportation had cut her off from the enclosed world of prostitutes and thieves in Stirling, forcing her to travel, and as she travelled she changed until, arriving at Hope Island, she found who she wanted to be. Others were not so lucky.

Within the first three years, twelve *Atwick* prisoners died, eight of them Scottish convicts. Jane Keith died on the voyage, aged 24. Agnes Lees, whose father had said in his petition that she 'laboured under a decease in the head, which there is reason to fear will soon terminate fatally', died on 4 June 1838, aged 21. Mary Ann Webster, convicted of theft in Edinburgh, died in the Cascades Female Factory on 24 January 1839, aged 34. Sarah Rafferty, who had nursed in the hospital ever since entering the Female Factory gates, died there on 17 November 1839, aged 46. Margaret McKenzie, permitted to marry in September 1839, died seven months later in the New Norfolk Hospital, aged 23. Catherine Gates, the 'poor deseased Wretch' belatedly removed from the tollbooth of Dundee, died in the same hospital on 26 September 1840, aged 43. On 31 December 1840 Nancy Lang died, aged 24, while assigned to a settler with a property on the River Derwent at Cove Point. Elizabeth Adams died on 26 January 1841 in the Female Factory at Launceston, aged 29. At the inquest after her death, the Colonial Surgeon said that she had been suffering for some time from dropsy, a disease seldom occurring 'in young persons, except from intemperance', and in his opinion 'her death was accelerated by dissipation previous to her arrival in this Colony'. None of these women who died partway through their sentences had time for the fracture caused by transportation to heal.

Others were hampered not by time but by alcohol. Mary Grant is a classic case, a woman whose life ran in circles, round and round in the same grooves. She had been arrested with several men in Edinburgh at 2 am one morning while busily removing bottles of whisky from a pub where they were drinking earlier that night. Mary, who said she was twenty years old when she reached Van Diemen's Land, was almost as defiant under sentence as Mary Sheriff, though never a part of the Flash Mob. With no intention of serving the settlers, Mary Grant was constantly absconding, and she still did not have a ticket of leave when accused on 27 March 1843 of 'insubordination', code for serious disturbance in the Female Factory. Among the women charged, Mary was the most severely punished. For assaulting Superintendent John Hutchinson with a knife, her sentence of transportation was extended two years, her hair was cut off, and she was sent to the separate working cells. In October 1845, after nearly eight years in the colony, she was issued a ticket of leave, and two years later her certificate of freedom. In February 1850, when she was about 32, her first child was born, Margaret, no father named in the birth register. The next year Mary was arrested but discharged, and about this time she took up with James Woodason, a ticket-of-leave 'lifer' trans-ported on the *Thames*, who was using the surname Wilson. Five children were born to the Wilsons between 1852 and 1858. In 1857, after their fourth child, they married and for some time may have led fairly stable lives.

All that had come unravelled by the time Mary was hauled into the police court for begging in 1869. For the next nine years until her death in the Hobart General Hospital on 29 July 1878, she was an alcoholic vagrant. Ironically, she spent much of her final decade inside the walls of the former Cascades Female Factory, sometimes in the Invalid Depot and sometimes in the Female House of Correction, locked up for being drunk in a public street, idle, disorderly, incapable of taking care of herself, disturbing the peace. Her children must have been humiliated. Certainly they were neglected. Not surprisingly, the third daughter, Ellen, got into trouble with the law when she was in her mid-teens, and in May 1871 an order was made by magistrates to detain her in the Girls' Industrial School for three years. Since her father, whose convict details are entered onto the admissions register, was required to pay 2 shillings 6 pence a week towards her maintenance, he must have been in Hobart, but he wasn't keeping the family together. The story of Mary Grant is a reminder that some convict women never brought a sustainable order into their lives, and inflicted chaos and emotional trauma upon the next generation as well.

Some women seem to have given up on themselves before they even sailed, yielding to transportation as if to fate and living out their lives in an alcoholic stupor. Mary Harper was only 30 on the November night in 1836 when the constable in Stonehaven found her 'lying in a manger, with some wet shirts below her head, and [a] piece of carpet above her, and below the shirts there was a split cod-fish'. She told the magistrate at her precognition that 'her husband left her sometime ago', and if she really did have a child, as she said when arriving in Van Diemen's Land, that connection too was already lost. As an assigned servant, she made no effort at all as she went from master to master, chalking up 31 charges and returning constantly to the Female Factory for yet another bout of punishment. She was often drunk or absent, nothing serious, and she never participated in riots or was violent. One man applied to marry her but nothing came of the application, and after she was free by servitude in 1844 she continued her directionless life, showing up again and again in the police courts for being drunk and disorderly, and hauled off like Mary Grant to dry out as a prisoner in the Female House of Correction or a patient in the Invalid Depot next door, an institution for the old and sick where the 'typical inmate', writes the historian of poverty, Joan Brown, 'was the friendless ex-convict' shunted off to a 'damp and depressing' building barely fit for human habitation. Mary Harper must have had remarkable genes because she survived this rackety way of life for decades and was in her seventies when she died in the New Town Charitable Institution. If she had remained in Scotland, had never been transported, it's hard to see how her life would have been much different.

But for many of the Scottish convicts, the fracture caused by transportation offered an opportunity to break with a thieving way of life pointed invariably towards incarceration. To make something of this opportunity required the genes for good health, an optimistic confidence in one's ability to manage the future, and luck. Unskilled illiterate women in the pioneering conditions of colonial Australia also needed the motivation to do hard work, a motivation they were most likely to find by creating families. Many women like Christian McDougall and Elizabeth Waddell after they were free were employed to do the same sort of hard cleaning work imposed upon them as assigned servants, but they no longer worked as criminals, and that made a world of difference. However difficult the struggle they faced to keep food on the table, they lived with people they cared about and who cared about them. With no background of emotional intimacy and support in their own childhoods, they led different lives, and if they did not rise very far in the world economically, their success in caring for their children was a major, if unsung, triumph. And by staying away from the clutches of the legal system, they had regained control over their daily lives. They were answerable to themselves, to their family and friends, not to the government appointees of the Convict Department and the female factory. They were resilient women who never gave up on themselves. They never allowed the past to overwhelm them, as it might have, and by making the most they could of the present, they took hold of the future.

SCOTTISH CONVICTS ON THE *ATWICK*

NAME	WHERE TRIED	WHEN TRIED
Adams, Elizabeth	Glasgow	4 January 1837
Alexander, Margaret	Stirling	18 April 1837
Armstrong, Mary	Glasgow	29 April 1837
Ashton, Ann	Edinburgh	14 March 1837
Bentley, Mary	Edinburgh	20 February 1837
Bonar, Janet	Glasgow	3 January 1837
Boyd, Jean	Perth	12 April 1837
Boys, Ann	Glasgow	12 September 1836
Brown, Elizabeth	Edinburgh	16 January 1837
Brown, Jean	Glasgow	12 September 1836
Campbell, Mary	Aberdeen	17 April 1837
Chalmers, Mary Ann	Aberdeen	17 April 1837
Chisholm, Catherine	Glasgow	15 September 1836
Christie, Margaret	Aberdeen	28 September 1836
Clark, Mary Ann	Glasgow	13 September 1836
Clark, Sally	Glasgow	3 January 1837
Curle, Helen	Glasgow	14 September 1836
Davidson, Eliza	Edinburgh	22 July 1837
Forbes, Elizabeth McLagan	Edinburgh	5 December 1836
Forsyth, Catherine	Glasgow	26 April 1837
Gates, Catherine	Perth	2 May 1835
Gillon, Margaret	Glasgow	6 January 1837
Gilmour, Agnes	Glasgow	5 January 1837
Gilmour, Christian	Glasgow	5 January 1837
Goldie, Elizabeth	Edinburgh	10 May 1837
Grant, Catherine	Dumfries	1 May 1837
Grant, Mary	Edinburgh	10 May 1837

Green, Margaret	Perth	4 October 1836
Guthrie, Jane	Edinburgh	9 November 1836
Harper, Georgiana	Edinburgh	10 May 1837
Harper, Mary	Aberdeen	17 April 1837
Henderson, Jane	Edinburgh	6 June 1837
Houston, Elizabeth	Edinburgh	14 March 1837
Keith, Jane	Edinburgh	9 November 1836
Kelly, Elizabeth	Edinburgh	9 May 1837
Kirkaldy, Margaret	Perth	12 April 1837
Lang, Nancy	Glasgow	14 September 1836
Lander, Wilhelmina Smith	Edinburgh	12 July 1837
Lees, Agnes	Edinburgh	10 May 1837
Logan, Grace	Glasgow	5 January 1837
Main, Margaret	Aberdeen	28 September 1836
Maitland, Catherine	Glasgow	29 April 1837
Martin, Ann	Edinburgh	9 May 1837
Martin, Catherine	Perth	3 October 1836
McAllister, Mary Ann	Glasgow	14 September 1836
McBrayne, Catherine	Glasgow	5 January 1837
McCallum, Margaret	Perth	12 April 1837
McDairmid, Letitia	Glasgow	29 April 1837
McDonald, Ann	Glasgow	13 September 1836
McDougall, Agnes	Glasgow	29 April 1837
McDougall, Christian	Glasgow	12 September 1836
McKenzie, Margaret	Edinburgh	11 November 1836
McLean, Mary	Glasgow	29 April 1837
McNiven, Margaret	Edinburgh	9 May 1837
McVicar, Mary	Edinburgh	20 February 1837
Mill, Susanna	Perth	4 October 1836
Mitchell, Jess	Glasgow	6 January 1837
Munro, Jean	Glasgow	26 April 1837
Myles, Christian	Edinburgh	16 January 1837
Pennycook, Margaret	Edinburgh	11 November 1836
Rafferty, Sarah	Perth	4 October 1836
Richardson, Margaret	Stirling	3 September 1836
Robertson, Agnes Campbell	Glasgow	28 April 1837
Ross, Margaret	Stirling	3 September 1836
Sheriff, Mary	Edinburgh	13 July 1837
Smith, Jean	Glasgow	26 April 1837

Smith, Mary	Perth	4 October 1836
Spouse, Catherine	Edinburgh	6 February 1837
Stevenson, Sarah	Edinburgh	9 November 1836
Stewart, Sarah	Glasgow	12 September 1836
Sutherland, Ann	Edinburgh	14 March 1837
Tarras, Jean	Aberdeen	28 September 1836
Thomson, Agnes	Edinburgh	20 February 1837
Waddell, Elizabeth	Glasgow	26 April 1837
Webster, Mary Ann	Edinburgh	3 July 1837
Williamson, Elizabeth	Edinburgh	3 July 1837
Wilson, Janet	Edinburgh	15 March 1837
Wilson, Mary	Edinburgh	20 July 1837

ACKNOWLEDGEMENTS

Not long after I came to live in Tasmania in 1997, I became fascinated by the stories of women who arrived here in the nineteenth century as prisoners of the state. While I was making a new home for myself, far from my own childhood on the high plains of the Texas Panhandle and my adolescence in the Great Smoky Mountains of east Tennessee, I pondered these earlier women who travelled across the world under circumstances so different from my own. Who were they? What lives did they leave behind? What lives did they make for themselves in their new island home?

Fortunately for my curiosity, these women were tried and sentenced during the height of the British Empire when global expansion meant amassing archives as well as land. Dedicated bureaucrats in the colony of Van Diemen's Land minutely documented the lives of convicts under sentence, and these surviving records were my starting point in a search for story. I immersed myself in this remarkable archive, its international significance recognised by UNESCO in 2007 when the convict records of Van Diemen's Land were added to the International Memory of the World Register, the equivalent for documents of the World Heritage Register for landscapes and built environment. I am very grateful to the archivists of the Archives Office of Tasmania for the help they gave me, and for their continuing efforts to make the collection digitally available to researchers everywhere.

I am also very fortunate to be working at the University of Tasmania amongst a group of researchers who share my interest in retrieving lives from archival sources. The interdisciplinary research Centre for Colonialism and its Aftermath (CAIA) makes the most of its opportunities to bring scholars from elsewhere in Australia and overseas to seminars and conferences to discuss—and sometimes to debate—the methodology and theory underpinning our individual projects, whatever their archival source. I owe a particular debt of gratitude to my fellow members of the CAIA executive, Anna Johnston, Hamish Maxwell Stewart, and Mitchell Rolls, and to my friend Cassandra Pybus, with whom I share a passion for fossicking in the archives in search of names carrying snippets of story.

My search for the *Atwick* convicts meant weeks spent in the National Archives of Scotland in Edinburgh on research trips made possible by a Discovery Grant from the Australian Research Council. During these trips, I transcribed all the surviving precognitions of the *Atwick* convicts. Back in Hobart, my indefatigable research assistant, Jo Richardson, helped me transcribe the records held in the Archives Office of Tasmania, and Jac Charlesworth designed precisely the database we needed to store material in a form from which I could shape biography. A fellowship at the Humanities Research Centre of the Australian National University gave me valuable time to start writing in an intellectually stimulating environment. Throughout the process, I appreciated the support of Ralph Crane, Head of the School of English, Journalism and European Languages at the University of Tasmania, and of my colleagues in the School.

For many *Atwick* convicts I could find nothing except the documents on public record, but for those who had children and now have descendants, I was sometimes very fortunate indeed. I am immensely grateful for the help of those who have shared their research into family history, and with whom I have had many stimulating conversations by email and in person: Muriel Allison, Craig Anderton, Cliff and Lyn Bennett, Barbara Beveridge, Natalie Cantrell, Leonie Chirgwin, Kevin Clarence, Vic Collis, Cheryl Czarnik, Ann Daniel, Adrienne Dore, Rhonda Engert, Ruth Farrell, Lyn Frost-Fleming, Debi Krych, Steve Landy, Maureen Martin, Lesley McCoull, Carol Merrick, George Milford, Margaret Nichols, Margaret O'Connor, Helen Pampling, Chris Read, Dawn Ridley, Lorraine Roberts, Rhonda Rose, Julie Sawtell, Kevin Shepherd, Pam and Terry

Struthers, Brooke Taylor, Pam Taylor, Gwenda Webb, Melissa White, George Scrimger Whitehouse, Craig Woodhall, and Barbara Wilson. Without the help of these descendants, I would have missed crucial turnings in the lives of their often elusive ancestors.

The most generous contribution of all came from Dorothy Baker, who is not a descendant of Margaret Alexander but an historian who worked with Norm Beechey on important histories of the Port Esperance area. For years they had been transcribing the Sawers diaries, and researching the family's history in Scotland and New Zealand, with a view to publishing an annotated edition. With Norm Beechey's death and the withdrawal of the diaries from access, this long labor of love came to a halt. Dorothy gave me their files, for which I am deeply grateful.

A special thanks goes to the members of the Female Convicts Research Group (Tasmania) who share my passion for telling the stories of convict women. Their critiques of papers I gave to our research seminars always suggested different ways of thinking, and I owe particular debts of gratitude to Alison Alexander, Trudy Cowley, Colette McAlpine, Joyce Purtscher, and Dianne Snowden. Alison also read the entire manuscript, and her comments changed its final shape.

And lastly, I have been very fortunate at Allen & Unwin to have in Elizabeth Weiss a publisher who from our first conversation understood exactly what I wanted to achieve. My thanks go as well to Karen Ward for her meticulous copy-editing, and to Siobhán Cantrill, who as in-house editor has looked after the transformation of the book from manuscript to publication.

A NOTE ON SOURCES

The sources for all material quoted in the text are listed in the Select Bibliography. If the quoted material is from an authored work, the author is mentioned in the text. Most quotations, however, come from government documents, and in particular from the precognitions held by the National Archives of Scotland, Edinburgh, and from the convict and civilian records held by the Archives Office of Tasmania, Hobart. The nature of these records, when not apparent contextually, is indicated in the text.

SELECT BIBLIOGRAPHY

ARCHIVAL AND MANUSCRIPT COLLECTIONS
The National Archives of Scotland
Minutebooks, High Court of Justiciary, JC 8

Precognitions for criminal trials, Lord Advocate's Department, AD 14. The precognitions for women transported on the *Atwick* are listed below. No precognitions have survived for three convicts: Letitia McDairmid, Mary McLean, and Catherine Maitland.

Precognition against Elizabeth Adams, AD 14/37/130

Precognition against Margaret Alexander and Margaret McIntyre, AD14/37/207

Precognition against Mary Armstrong, AD 14/37/283

Precognition against Ann Ashton, AD 14/37/244

Precognition against Thomas Wilson, Mary Bentley and Mary McVicar,
    AD 14/37/393

Precognition against Janet Bonar and Sally Clark or McGregor, AD 14/37/351

Precognition against Jean Boyd or Laird, AD 14/37/108

Precognition against Alexander Fraser and Ann Boys, AD 14/36/236

Precognition against Elizabeth Brown, AD 14/37/382

Precognition against Jean Brown, AD 14/36/213

Precognition against Mary Campbell, AD 14/37/49

Precognition against Mary [Ann] Chalmers or Rennie, AD 14/37/52

Precognition against Margaret McDougall, Agnes Rennie or Munro, and Catherine
    Hall, AD 14/33/6

Precognition against Catherine Chisholm or Hall and Elizabeth McLachlan or
    Scott, AD 14/36/250

Precognition against Margaret Christie or Morrice, AD 14/36/167

Precognition against Mary Ann Clark, AD 14/36/246

Precognition against Helen Curle or Wilson, AD 14/36/233

Precognition against John Julius McDonald and Eliza or Elizabeth Allan or
    Davidson, AD 14/37/464

Precognition against Elizabeth McLagan Forbes, AD 14/36/447

Precognition against Catherine Forsyth, AD 14/37/291

Precognition against Catherine Gates alias McConnacle, alias McMonigal, alias
    McDonald, alias Fraser, AD 14/35/117

Precognition against Margaret Gillon or Reilly alias Mary McCabe, AD 14/37/364

Precognition against Agnes Gilmour or McGilvray, John McKenna or McKinnon,
    and Catherine McBrayne or McKenna or McKinnon, AD 14/37/377

Precognition against Christian Gilmour or McGilvray, AD 14/37/379

Precognition against Elizabeth Goldie and Agnes Lees, AD 14/37/414

Precognition against John Brown or Roney and Catherine Grant, AD 14/37/229

Precognition against Mary Grant, AD 14/37/412

Precognition against Margaret Green or Thomson or Webster, AD 14/36/79

Precognition against Jane Guthrie, AD 14/36/428

Precognition against Martin Thomson and Georgiana Harper, AD 14/37/415

Precognition against Mary Harper or Stewart alias Mary McMullan or Short,
    AD 14/37/55

Precognition against Jane Henderson, AD 14/37/420

Precognition against Elizabeth Houston or Cameron AD 14/37/234

Precognition against Jane Keith, William McConnochie and Mary Chalmers or
    Cowan, AD 14/36/429

Precognition against Ann Martin, Hannah Martin, Margaret McNiven, and
    Elizabeth Kelly, AD 14/37/408

Precognition against Margaret Kirkaldy, AD 14/37/110

Precognition against Wilhelmina Smith Lander or Telford, AD 14/37/442

Precognition against Nancy Lang, AD 14/36/263

Precognition against Grace Logan, AD 14/37/369

Precognition against Margaret Main or Gillies, AD 14/36/162

Precognition against Catherine Martin or Lyall, AD 14/36/99

Precognition against Mary Ann McAllister, AD 14/36/260

Precognition against John McKenna, AD 14/23/25

Precognition against Margaret McCallum or Craig, AD 14/37/105

Precognition against Ann McDonald or Stewart, AD 14/36/244

Precognition against Agnes McDougall, AD 14/37/286

Precognition against Christian McDougall alias Margaret Rae, AD 14/36/212

Precognition against Margaret McKenzie, AD 14/36/418

Precognition against Susanna or Susan Mill and Mary Smith or Douglas,
    AD 14/36/69

Precognition against Jess Mitchell, AD 14/37/360

Precognition against Jean Munro, AD 14/37/277

Precognition against Christian Myles or McGaggan, AD 14/37/385

Precognition against Margaret or Margret Pennycook, AD 14/35/377

Precognition against Margaret Pennycook, AD 14/36/420

Precognition against Sarah Rafferty or Conrey, AD 14/36/98

Precognition against Margaret Richardson, AD 14/36/120

Precognition against Agnes Campbell Robertson, AD 14/35/268

Precognition against Agnes Campbell Robertson, AD 14/37/297

Precognition against Margaret Ross, AD 14/36/122

Precognition against Mary Sheriff, AD 14/37/449

Precognition against Jean Smith, AD 14/37/302

Precognition against Catherine Spouse, AD 14/37/387

Precognition against Sarah Stevenson, AD 14/36/430

Precognition against Sarah Stewart alias Sally Ingram, AD 14/36/211

Precognition against Ann Sutherland, AD 14/37/235

Precognition against Jean Tarras or McDonald, AD 14/36/169

Precognition against Agnes Thomson, AD 14/37/396

Precognition against Elizabeth Waddell or Cunningham, AD 14/37/295

Precognition against Mary Ann Webster, AD 14/37/425

Precognition against Donald McAllan and Elizabeth Williamson, AD 14/37/424

Precognition against Janet Wilson or Smith, AD 14/37/247

Precognition against Mary Wilson, AD 14/37/461

The National Archives of the United Kingdom

Petitions to the Home Office, HO 17

The Archives Office of Tasmania

A. Convict records

Alphabetical register of male convicts, CON 23

Appropriation lists of convicts, CON 27

Appropriation lists of female convicts, MM 33/1/6

Colonial Secretary's Office, general correspondence files, CSO 1–5

Conduct records of female convicts arriving during assignment period, CON 40

Conduct records of male convicts arriving in the assignment period, CON 31

Description list of female convicts, CON 19

Description list of male convicts, CON 18

Journals of surgeons superintendent, Adm 101

Papers relating to the board of inquiry into female prison discipline, 1841–43, CSO 22/1/50

Registers of applications for permission to marry, CON 52

Register of certificates of freedom granted, CON 55

Record of cases heard in petty sessions, LC 247
Record of cases against women heard in petty sessions, LC 251
Register of fees paid in connection with convict deaths, CON 66
Register of convict deaths, CON 63
Supplementary Conduct Registers, CON 32

B. Orphan School records

Register of children admitted and discharged from the infant school, SWD 6
Daily journal of admissions and discharges to Queen's Orphan Schools, SWD 7
Applications for admission to the Queen's Orphan Schools, SWD26
Register of children admitted and discharged from the male and female Orphan
    Schools, SWD 28

C. Other sources

Baptismal records for St Mary's Catholic Church, NS 1052/8
Copies of wills recording granting of probate, AD 960
Death book, General Hospital, Hobart, HSD 145
Female House of Correction, description list of prisoners, 1873–79, CON 105
Householders' census returns, CEN 1
Papers relating to coroners' inquests, SC 195
Passenger lists relating to ships clearances, CUS 36
Register of admissions and discharges, Hobart Gaol, GD 31
Register of baptisms in Tasmania, RGD 32
Register of births in Tasmania, RGD 33
Register of burials in Tasmania, RGD 34
Register of burials at St Andrews Burial Ground, St Andrews Presbyterian Church,
    NS 229/1/64
Register of children at Girls Industrial School, SWD37
Register of deaths in Tasmania, RGD 35
Register of marriages (pre-civilian registration), RGD 36
Register of marriages in Tasmania, RGD 37
Returns of Crews and Passengers on ships departing from Launceston, POL 220
Tasmania Police Gazettes, POL 709

State Library of Tasmania, Hobart

Lempriere, T.J., diary kept at Port Arthur 1837–1838, typescript transcript, Allport
    Library, State Library of Tasmania
Webb, G.M., 'Henry Cox and Elizabeth Waddell and their Family: the first three
    generations', typescript manuscript, State Library of Tasmania, Hobart

Other archival and manuscript sources

Allison, M., Wallace family research files, courtesy of researcher

Baker, D., Unpublished edition of Sawers diaries, together with research files, courtesy of researcher

Milford, G. 'What we Poor Convicts Went Through', family manuscript 1997, revised 2010, courtesy of author

Memorials of conveyancing, Lands Titles Office, Lands Department, Hobart

Registry of births, deaths, and marriages, Department of Justice, Melbourne

NEWSPAPERS

Adelaide *Advertiser*

Melbourne *Argus*

Austral-Asiatic Review

Derby and Chesterfield Reporter

Barbadian

Brisbane Courier

Colonial Times

Cornwall Chronicle

The Courier

The Edinburgh Advertiser

Glasgow Courier

Glasgow Herald

The Hobart Town Courier

Hobart Town Gazette

The Hobarton Mercury

Launceston Examiner

The Mercury

Stirling Journal and Advertiser

The Times

True Colonist

PRINTED SOURCES

Adams, S. and Adams, S., *The Complete Servant* [1825], ed. A. Haly, Southover Press, Lewes, East Sussex, 1989.

Atkinson, A. and Aveling, M., eds, *Australians 1838*, Fairfax, Syme & Weldon, Sydney, 1987.

Bailliere's Victorian Gazetteer, F.F. Bailliere, Melbourne, 1865.

Bateson, C., *The Convict Ships 1787–1868*, Brown, Son & Ferguson, Glasgow, 2nd edn 1969.

Beechey, N. and Baker, D., *A History of Dover and Port Esperance, Tasmania*, 2 vols, the Authors, Dover, 1997, 2000.

Bown, S., *Scurvy: how a surgeon, a mariner and a gentleman solved the greatest medical mystery of the age of sail*, Penguin Books, Melbourne, 2003.

Brown, J.C., *'Poverty is not a Crime': social services in Tasmania 1803–1900*, Tasmanian Historical Research Association, Hobart, 1972.

Boyce, J., *Van Diemen's Land*, Black Inc, Melbourne, 2008.

Burney, I.A., *Bodies of Evidence: medicine and the politics of the English inquest 1830–1926*, Johns Hopkins University Press, Baltimore, 2000.

Carpenter, K., *The History of Scurvy and Vitamin C*, Cambridge University Press, Cambridge, 1986.

Casella, E., *Archaeology of the Ross Female Factory: female incarceration in Van Diemen's Land, Australia*, Queen Victoria Museum and Art Gallery, Launceston, 2002.

Convict Lives: women at Cascades Female Factory, Female Factory Research Group, Hobart, 2009.

Cordwell, S., *Historic New Norfolk: St Matthew's Church burial records*, New Norfolk Council, 1993.

Cowley, T., *Alphabetical Listings by Owner and Occupier of the 1858 Valuation Rolls*, 4 vols, Research Tasmania, Hobart, 2004.

——. 'Ellen Scott', in *Convict Lives: women at Cascades Female Factory*, Female Factory Research Group, Hobart, 2009, pp. 67–68.

Daniels, K., *Convict Women*, Allen & Unwin, Sydney, 1998.

——, 'The Flash Mob: rebellion, rough culture and sexuality in the female factories of Van Diemen's Land', *Australian Feminist Studies*, no. 18, 1993, pp. 133–150.

Dingle, T., *Victorians: Settling*, Fairfax, Syme & Weldon, Melbourne, 1984.

Donnachie, I., 'Scottish Criminals and Transportation to Australia, 1786–1852', *Scottish Economic and Social History*, vol. 4, 1984, pp. 21–38.

——, ' "Utterly Irreclaimable": Scottish convict women and Australia 1787–1852', *Journal of Regional and Local Studies*, vol. 8, no. 2, 1988, pp. 1–16.

Fitzsymonds, E., *Mortmain: a looking-glass for Tasmania*, Sullivan's Cove Press, Hobart, 1977.

Frost, L., 'Eliza Churchill tells . . .' in L. Frost and H. Maxwell-Stewart, eds, *Chain Letters: narrating convict lives*, Melbourne University Press, Carlton 2001, pp. 79–90.

——, *Footsteps and Voices: an historical look into the Cascades Female Factory*, Female Factory Historic Site, Hobart, 2004.

——, ' "Fully Ripe for Transportation": the Scottish convict women sent to Van Diemen's Land', *History Scotland*, vol. 9, no. 4, 2009, pp. 36–40.

——, 'Gifts of Patchwork and Visits to Whitehall: the Ladies' British Society and female convict ships' in S. Thomas, ed, *Victorian traffic: Identity, exchange, performance*, Cambridge Scholars Publishing, Newcastle, UK, 2008, pp. 2–18.

——, '"Wished to get out to our mother": convict transportation as family experience', *Tasmanian Historical Research Association Papers and Proceedings*, vol. 53, no. 3, 2006, pp. 125–137.

[Fry, K. and R.], *Memoir of the Life of Elizabeth Fry*, vol. 1, Charles Gilpin, London, 1847.

Hartwell, R.M., *The Economic Development of Van Diemen's Land, 1820–1850*, Melbourne University Press, Carlton, 1954.

Higman, B.W. *Domestic Service in Australia*, Melbourne University Press, Carlton, 2002.

Instructions for Surgeons-Superintendent on Board Convict Ships proceeding to New South Wales, or Van Diemen's Land; and for the Masters of those Ships, W. Clowes and Sons, London, 1840.

Jackson, R.V., *Daughters of the Poor*, Australian Scholarly Publishing, Melbourne, 2005.

Lempriere, T.J., *The Penal Settlements of Early Van Diemen's Land* [1839], Royal Society of Tasmania, [Launceston], 1954.

Miller, E.M., *Pressmen and Governors: Australian editors and writers in early Tasmania*, Sydney University Press, Sydney, [1952] 1973.

Miller, L.W. *Notes of an Exile to Van Dieman's [sic] Land* [1846], S.R. Publishers Ltd, New York, 1968.

Nash, M., *The Bay Whalers: Tasmania's shore-based whaling industry*, Navarine Publishing, Woden ACT, 2003.

Oxley, D., *Convict Maids: the forced migration of women to Australia*, Cambridge University Press, Melbourne, 1996.

Palk, D., ' "Fit Objects for Mersy": gender, the Bank of England and currency criminals, 1804–1833', *Women's Writing*, vol. 11, no. 2, 2004, pp. 237–257.

——, *Gender, Crime and Judicial Discretion 1780–1830*, The Royal Historical Society: Studies in History New Series, Boydell Press, Woodbridge, Suffolk, 2006.

Pike, D., ed., *Australian Dictionary of Biography*, vols 1 and 2, Melbourne University Press, Carlton, 1966.

Plomley, N.J.B., *Weep in Silence: a history of the Flinders Island Aboriginal settlement, with the Flinders Island journal of George Augustus Robinson 1835–1839*, Blubber Head Press, Hobart, 1987.

Prentis, M.D., *The Scots in Australia*, University of New South Wales Press, Sydney, 2008.

——, 'What do we know about the Scottish convicts?' *Journal of the Royal Australian Historical Society*, vol. 90, no. 1, 2004, 36–52.

Purtscher, J., *Children in Queen's Orphanage, Hobart Town, 1828–1863*, Irene Schaffer, New Town, Tasmania, 1993.

Pybus, C. and Maxwell-Stewart, H., *American Citizens, British Slaves: Yankee political prisoners in an Australian penal colony 1839–1850*, Melbourne University Press, Carlton, 2002.

Reid, K., *Gender, Crime and Empire: convicts, settlers and the state in early colonial Australia*, Manchester University Press, Manchester, 2007.

Reynolds, H., *Fate of a Free People: a radical re-examination of the Tasmanian wars*, Penguin, Melbourne, 1995.

Richards, E., *Debating the Highland Clearances*, Edinburgh University Press, Edinburgh, 2007.

Robson, L.L., *The Convict Settlers of Australia: an enquiry into the origin and character of the convicts transported to New South Wales and Van Diemen's Land 1787–1852*, Melbourne University Press, Carlton, 1965.

Roe, M., *An Imperial Disaster: the wreck of* George the Third, Blubber Head Press, Hobart, 2006.

Schaffer, K., *In the Wake of First Contact: the Eliza Fraser stories*, Cambridge University Press, Cambridge, 1995.

Smith, B., *Australia's Birthstain: the startling legacy of the convict era*, Allen & Unwin, Sydney, 2008.

——, *A Cargo of Women: Susannah Watson and the convicts of the* Princess Royal, 2nd edn, Allen & Unwin, Sydney, 2008.

Staniforth, M., 'Diet, Disease and Death at Sea on the Voyage to Australia 1837–1839', *International Journal of Maritime History*, vol. 8, no. 2, 1996, pp. 119–143.

Tardif, P., *Notorious Strumpets and Dangerous Girls: convict women in Van Diemen's Land 1803–1829*, Angus & Robertson, Sydney, 1990.

Tipping, M., *Convicts Unbound: the story of the* Calcutta *convicts and their settlement in Australia*, Viking O'Neil, South Yarra, Victoria, 1988.

[Wapping History Group] *'Down Wapping': Hobart's vanished Wapping and Old Wharf districts*, Blubber Head Press, Hobart, 1988.

WEBSITES

Ancestry.com indexes and other search materials, http://search.ancestry.com/

Archives Office of Tasmania online name indexes, some linked to records, for arrivals, departures, inquests, wills; Tasmanian convicts and convict applications for permission to marry, <http://www.archives.tas.gov.au/nameindexes>

Female Convicts Research Group (Tasmania),
    <http://www.femaleconvicts.org.au>
The Proceedings of the Old Bailey, London, 1674 to 1913,
    <http://www.oldbaileyonline.org>
'Robert Wettenhall', Immigration Bridge Australia,
    <http://www.immigrationbridge.com.au>
ScotlandsPeople, the official Scottish genealogy resource,
    <http://www.scotlandspeople.gov.uk>

INDEX

Locators in italics refer to picture section